'He is a powerful witness to the interaction between two people in different positions of power, the one political and the other psychological.'
CHRISTOPHER SILVESTER, *Sunday Times*

'Haines precisely dissects the cancer at the heart of an administration that had lost its way even before its unexpected return to office.'
RICHARD STOTT, *Guardian*

'Haines's book is short, crisp and packed with malice. Glimmers of Twilight is no hagiography. Instead, aperçus such as George Brown: "A walking, leering, falling-about disaster who ought never to have been in government"; Richard Crossman: "an arrogant, indiscreet and unprincipled intellectual and a close, unreliable and untrustworthy friend", and more, enliven almost every page.'
EDWINA CURRIE, *The Times*

'Fascinating'
DENNIS KAVANAGH, *Daily Telegraph*

Glimmers of Twilight

Harold Wilson in Decline

Joe Haines

POLITICO'S

First published in Great Britain 2003 in hardback
this updated paperback edition published 2004 by
Politico's Publishing, an imprint of
Methuen Publishing Limited
215 Vauxhall Bridge Road
London SW1V 1EJ

10 9 8 7 6 5 4 3 2 1

A CIP catalogue record for this book is available from the British Library

ISBN 1 84275 092 5

Printed and bound in Great Britain by Cox & Wyman

Life's night begins: Let him never come back to us!
There would be doubt, hesitation and pain,
Forced praise on our part — the glimmer of twilight
Never proud, confident morning again!

The Lost Leader, Robert Browning.

For Albert Murray, Fleet Street printer, MP for Gravesend, peer of the realm, Millwall supporter, loving husband, devoted father and faithful friend.

Contents

Preface

This is in no sense a biography of Harold Wilson, even less so than of Marcia Williams, later Baroness Falkender of West Haddon, his personal and political secretary for more than thirty years. Rather, it is a study of the corrupting effects of power wielded by the unelected and of the growing weakness of a leader of Britain who allowed that power to burgeon until he himself fell under its influence. It is a view from inside the tent of power, one that very, very few are privileged or burdened to hold, and a view substantially different from that of those looking in. Those who want to study in meticulous detail the facts and statistics of Wilson's life will find them amply set out in Ben Pimlott's *Harold Wilson* (HarperCollins) and Philip Ziegler's *Harold Wilson, an authorised biography* (Weidenfeld and Nicolson). Lady Falkender recounted her political life story, a somewhat incomplete and slanted record of her time in Opposition with Wilson and in government at No. 10, in two volumes published in the 1970s by Weidenfeld and Nicolson. If I were to correct or contradict every one of her extraordinary versions of events in which we both took part, this volume would be much longer than it is and would not be what I intended. It is enough to say that fact and fiction have rarely been so thoroughly mixed.

Those students of politics with the stamina to plough through all the books by or about Wilson must make up their own minds about what or who sounds the most convincing, though plausibility is not the prime determinant of truth. Like many such books, the biographies by Pimlott and Ziegler are sometimes as important for what they leave out — for lack of knowledge rather than deliberate intent – as for what they include. Pimlott's is by far the larger book, but appears hurriedly to skate over Wilson's later years compared to the wealth of detail about his earlier ones. Both his and Ziegler's highly professional accounts suffer from the inevitable handicaps which beset all biographers who did not know personally their subjects: they cannot convey the intimate feeling of what life was like, day by day, for those who worked closely with Wilson and observed the relentless political problems which he faced; nor, least of all, can they adequately record the complex relationship between Wilson and Falkender, which was the dominant fact of his private and public life and a crushing burden upon both. Ziegler had a great sense of it, but neither he nor Pimlott was in a position to experience it.

The one biographer who did have an appreciation of the Wilson–Falkender relationship was Andrew Roth, an American journalist and amateur psychologist, who made British politics his work and his passion and brought to them a transatlantic determination to ferret out what, until the latter part of the 20th century, was usually regarded as unpublishable. His acute nose for scandal led him to write *Sir Harold Wilson, Yorkshire Walter Mitty,* which was withdrawn from sale after a writ had been issued by Mary and Harold Wilson. It was a highly entertaining and in many respects accurate account of much of the life behind Downing Street's curtain, but it seriously and actionably defamed Mary Wilson and was withdrawn from publication. The political insights therefore never received the attention they deserved. Roth had the advantage over other biographers of knowing both Wilson and his secretary, if only at the fringe.

In 1977, coincidentally on St Valentine's Day and the fourteenth anniversary of Wilson's election as leader of the Labour party, my book about my seven years as Harold Wilson's press secretary, the *Politics of Power* (Jonathan Cape), was published. As a serialisation in the *Daily Mirror,* it was a sensation, but the reviews were mixed. Much of it seemed incredible to those whose knowledge of politics was derived either from academic theorising or from observations from the Commons Press Gallery. It covered my personal and journalistic history; proposals for the sale of council houses, which preceded Margaret Thatcher's legislation by many years and which Wilson was kind enough to have described as 'historic' before a combination of Labour prejudice and Civil Service obstructionism killed them; my views on a solution to the Irish problem and some sceptical observations about the behaviour of officials at the Treasury and at the Foreign and Commonwealth Office. The latter are, I believe, as relevant today as they were then, but the passage of time has relegated others to the discarded files of history. But, inevitably, it was the last third of the book, dealing with the eternal internal stresses and strains in Wilson's office which flowed from the tantrums, tirades and tyranny of Marcia Williams (she was not created a baroness until 1974, some eighteen years after she became his secretary) which caught the eye and gave the book some notoriety.

Some reviewers said I was jealous of Mrs Williams's position, though I never was. I knew that position was unassailable and jealousy would have been pointless. Others ascribed my motives to bitterness, presumably deriving from that fictional jealousy. But, for all its defects, the destruction of one's social life, the constantly broken sleep and the days off that always turned out to be days on, being Press Secretary to the Prime Minister was and is an unrivalled post for a political journalist and there was no call to be bitter. Critics who thought that then, however, will still think like that and there's nothing I can do about it. Those who instinctively seek base motives – a compelling force in the commentators of today – will always find them, reflecting, perhaps, their own standards rather than those of the people who are the subjects of their criticism.

There were other critics, falling into three main categories: those who thought a Labour party member's first duty was to promote what was good about the party and to conceal what was bad, an approach which not only allowed the bad to flourish at the expense of the good but also overlooked the lucrative crop of memoirs which follows the end of a political era, those who, from a distance, thought that things weren't all they should have been and agreed something should be written, but not undiluted and not yet; and those who had seen and experienced the truth and wondered why I had not said much more. As one civil servant wailed after reading *The Politics of Power* 'Why did you let her off so lightly?' After the passage of a great many years, this book seeks, in large part, to repair that omission.

It is for those good friends and for those who may one day want to write a balanced and objective account of the Wilson era that what follows has been written. It will be impossible to judge Wilson's record and reputation without encompassing Marcia Williams/Falkender's role in its construction and destruction. More than a quarter of a century has passed since Wilson unexpectedly (to the outside world) retired from office and what could not be freely said immediately after his going can be said today. For the sake of continuity and chronology, this book contains something, but not much, of the events previously recorded in *The Politics of Power*. To have recounted the whole truth then might have brought the threat of the Official Secrets Act down upon me, with all the delays that involved, and to have increased the disbelief with which the book was received in some quarters. After all, if things couldn't have been as bad as I said they were, how could they possibly have been twice as bad? In any case, there is a marked reluctance on the part of those in the trade of politics to believe anything that they did not know from their own sources.

But I was gratified to receive many letters of support from people who were close observers of the Wilson years and who had first-hand knowledge of No. 10. One of the FCO's most senior and least-blinkered of diplomats, Crispin Tickell, writing a year after publication, said that 'as far as my knowledge goes, your account with its underlying analysis is substantially correct. Moreover, it needed saying.' Robin (later Sir, eventually Lord) Butler, a private secretary at No. 10 during Sir Edward Heath's premiership and during the second Wilson administration (1974-6) and later Cabinet Secretary for Margaret Thatcher, John Major and Tony Blair, sent the warmest of tributes. I was sure Harold Wilson secretly enjoyed much of my book, though he felt compelled to rebuke me for 'misunderstandings', a judgment softened by his further remark that he hadn't read it. On the whole, his reaction was restrained, though one of the ironies of its publication was that it brought him back into touch with Lady Falkender after a six-week freeze in their relationship – a common occurrence – during which they had not spoken to each other.

My typescript was crawled over by libel lawyers though, interestingly, the only cut of substance was about the serpentine manoeuvrings of civil servants in defence of their departments' or their own positions. Without acquiring government documents kept secret under the thirty-year rule, I might have found it difficult to prove what I wanted to assert. As for other matters, had action been taken in the High Court, a heavy volume of unpublished stories, not all of them known to me at the time, would inevitably have come to light.

I had a great and affectionate, if not uncritical, regard for Wilson, and though the faults in the last years of his leadership multiplied my reservations, the passage of time hasn't diminished it. With hindsight, I believe that the clear deterioration in his mental powers which those close to him noticed in the last year of his premiership presaged the onset of Alzheimer's disease, which eventually destroyed his memory. Without that regard, working for him for seven years and three months – from 1 January 1969 until 6 April 1976 – would have been impossible.

Even if all the holidays from work which he and I took, including Christmas, Easter, summer breaks and his occasional and reluctant retirements to the Isles of Scilly, were aggregated, there would be little more than a few weeks when I was not his 'daily companion, adviser and friend' (Lady Falkender's description of my role) or when we did not speak on the telephone. I would have been obsessively possessive to have wanted more; at times, such as late at night one Christmas Eve when my wife and I had already begun our Yuletide celebrations and I had to interrupt them to find Wilson and put him in contact with the Israeli Foreign Minister, Ygal Allom, calling from his kibbutz near Galilee, less would have been better.

Wilson was easily bored when he had nothing to do and was not able to discuss politics. After a few days in the Isles of Scilly, when the forced pleasure of inaction had worn off and his re-reading of Agatha Christie's mysteries had ended, he would telephone me with his latest thoughts, ask me to consider them and then to call him back. The longer he was away, the longer my return calls became, until he could find an excuse plausible enough for him to return to London and, incidentally, save my telephone bill from rising still further. Politics to him were fun – serious, but fun. Holidays were neither. The joys of Tuscany, the Greek islands or the south of France were not for him. When he was due to make an official visit to Leningrad (now St Petersburg) he asked me where we should go because I had spent a holiday there, and he adopted my suggestions that we should visit the battle-cruiser *Aurora*, anchored in the Neva, and then the Hermitage museum, though his completion of its sights in forty minutes verged on philistinism. He took occasional continental holidays in the late 1940s and early 1950s, but I can't remember his ever enjoying one of the kind which many of his constituents in run-down Huyton took for granted. Even on his Prime Ministerial visits abroad, there was always an urge to get back to Britain. When I was a political reporter on *The Sun* in 1966 and covering a Wilson visit to Moscow while a financial crisis was developing at home, and remembering the Profumo and other, major events which occurred while he was in the Soviet capital, I began my story: 'Something always happens when Harold Wilson is in Moscow, but it happens in London.' The sentence was excised by the editor on the grounds of flippancy, but it was always his underlying worry. He resisted almost every attempt to pay overseas visits while the House of Commons was sitting – a proper attitude cast into disuse by his successors.

Until the last few weeks of my time in Downing Street, it wasn't my intention to write a book; therefore, I never kept a diary. I restricted myself to a few scribbled words, often on a scrap of paper, to record the dates of important or unusual events. Even then, I was not consistent. But as the Wilson administration drew to its final close, several friends and colleagues at No. 10, civil servants included, urged me to disclose at least something of the occasional atmosphere of terror there, along with the main thrust of, and the horrors encountered during, my experiences.

Some such events needed no diary or other notes: they stood out in the memory. There was the European summit in Rome when Lady Falkender telephoned Wilson to demand that he return home at *once* to deal with some real or imagined domestic or political crisis which only she could see. There was a similar demand to return in order to combat a crisis personal to her when he was staying at the British embassy in Paris and holding talks with President Giscard d'Estaing. It was at this time that he had a heart tremor, a 'flutter' as he described it, which began while he was with the President. That incident greatly alarmed me: as he emerged from his talks, his first words were: 'get Joe', meaning Sir Joseph Stone, his personal doctor who always travelled with us and who was greatly concerned at the increasing signs that Wilson's health was failing.

The intemperate demands for Wilson to cancel whatever he was doing were appalling and too frequent; no-one – wife, parent, sibling or secretary – who was wholly balanced should ever behave in such a fashion, but she did, to the distress of Wilson and to the embarrassment of those around him, senior civil servants and advisers, who were powerless to deflect her demands and so did their best to cover them up. One night at that Paris embassy, an official dinner was delayed for forty minutes or more while Wilson argued on the telephone with Lady Falkender. Foreign Office officials desperately sought new reasons to excuse the Prime Minister's late appearance. When he finally arrived, he looked distraught.

The final incentive to write *The Politics of Power* came from my determination not to be associated with what followed Wilson's retirement in April 1976, in particular, the Resignation Honours List. Knowledge of that list convinced me, though little convincing was needed, not to accept Wilson's offer of a peerage or a knighthood. I instantly declined both suggestions. In a Marxist (Groucho) sense, both involved membership of clubs to which I did not wish to belong. I excused myself by saying to him (on a flight to Luxembourg) that a knighthood was a permanent invitation to cocktail parties, which neither my wife nor I enjoyed, and that I wanted to abolish the House of Lords (true), not strengthen it (conceited). It is not given to anyone, least of all a politician, to be perfect, but Wilson was a much misunderstood man. He headed a party which at times was impossible to lead, except as the first lemming. Pol Pot would have better suited some of the factions within it, though others would have suspected even that tyrant's liberalism. Wilson took the burden of criticism, political and personal, while other, lesser, colleagues – guarded by their Reform Club, Fleet Street and dinner party cronies – seemed elegantly to avoid it. Wilson was often hurt and angry by the viciousness of some of the comrades' uncomradely attacks upon him and once said to me: 'I get all the muck while Roy Jenkins and his friends ride by on their white chargers', though 'muck' was not the noun he used. He was not a liar, as superficial editors of broadsheets called him. Nor was George Brown a better man drunk than Wilson was sober, as *The Times* editorialised. Brown was never the better man, whatever the level of his alcohol consumption; in fact, he was a walking, leering, falling-about disaster who ought never to have been in government, let alone deputy leader of his party and Foreign Secretary.

Wilson, when embarrassed by the truth, would sometimes go the long way round before reaching or admitting it. He was a procrastinator more than a prevaricator. If he was also an eternal optimist, there was nothing wrong in that. Good politicians, like good generals, have to be. Politics may be a profession of probable failure even for professional Panglossians, but it is a profession of certain failure for pessimists.

Unlike modern Labour leaders such as Neil Kinnock and Tony Blair, Wilson loved Parliament and never doubted it was the ultimate source of power in a democracy. He spent hours in the Commons listening to back-bench speeches because it was a pleasure, not a chore. Today's leaders rarely stay even to listen to their Cabinet colleagues. Though he might have despised or disliked individual politicians, he hated cynicism about politicians in general. When I told him that a rat had run across my feet in the dining rooms' corridor of the Commons, he asked me what I had done about it. 'Nothing,' I said. 'I didn't know whether to kick it or vote for it.' He was not amused.

I watched Wilson's final two years in office and, in particular, the last few months, with growing dismay and sadness. He was drinking too much brandy. The zest had gone from his living. The Rolls Royce mind, as Derek Mitchell, his first principal private secretary, once described it, was failing and the formerly unquenchable optimistic spirit was dampened, even dying. I have since been told that early in the 1970s – before he became Prime Minister again in 1974 – a specialist had warned him that physical changes were taking place which were likely to affect his mental powers. If so, he never told me nor, I suspect, Lady Falkender. But if it were true, it would explain why he was so determined to resign, for once in his life brooking no interference from her. It would also explain his weary reaction to me in July 1975, after we had argued fiercely about his intended acceptance of a Treasury demand for a compulsory incomes policy. 'Joe,' he said, 'when old problems recur, I reach for old solutions. I have nothing new to offer any more.' His willingness, even eagerness, to retire was noble if he knew his health was failing. Too many politicians have ignored the warning signs and stayed on long beyond their use-by date. The actions he planned to follow that retirement were not noble, however, though I now believe that he had lost the power to resist the pressure for them, which excuses much of what I previously thought to be inexcusable.

The Politics of Power was an incomplete account of my Downing Street years because it was necessary in some matters to put a gloss upon the truth, partly because the whole truth, if there is such a concept, might have put an intolerable burden upon Wilson's successor, Jim Callaghan, who had enough to contend with anyway. But to remain wholly silent would have been to acquiesce in all those things that had happened and which were outside the remit of orderly, proper and acceptable government.

Wilson was told at the retirement dinner given at No. 10 by his Cabinet colleagues on 22 March 1976, that he was leaving office at a time when his reputation had never been higher. Unfortunately, those of us who were privy to the preliminary list of those he intended to honour in his Resignation List and the plans, nominally his, to exploit his premiership, via a TV series, a book and lecture tours, knew that that would be a temporary condition. It was to be an act of self-destruction as fully spectacular as that, say, which ended the footballing careers of sporting icons like George Best, Paul Gascoigne and so many others who squandered the worship which the public was so eager to bestow upon them.

To give the most startling example of the reticence I felt necessary for nearly thirty years: in 1974, I was asked, as set out in Chapter 9, to agree, at least as a passive but supportive and forever silent observer, to the murder of Lady Falkender. Put as bluntly as that, it sounds, and was, horrific. At times since, I have often wondered whether I really heard the proposition aright. It is a comfort, if that is the word, to know that the same suggestion was put to Bernard Donoughue, the Prime Minister's chief policy adviser, and to recall that on the last occasion I heard it, it was put to us together. I believe I was the first to hear of it; what is certain is that both of us rejected it out of hand. It was not, after all, the sort of plot which anyone would commit to paper, even in a personal diary. But reject it we did, and emphatically.

It is fair to ask why, if Lady Falkender's behaviour was so intolerable that it could lead to one of Wilson's closest associates proposing to 'dispose of her,' as he put it, that I and others tolerated it. In my case, there was no single answer, though a life-long love of politics was part of it. But the argument which persuaded was another question: what would have happened had I gone? I don't want to exaggerate a Press Secretary's importance – though since the genre has come out of the shadows in recent years it might be seen to be rather more than the public had generally supposed – but in the circumstances of the 1974-76 government, and especially during the fevered summer months of 1974, my resignation might have done considerable damage to a Prime Minister hanging on to office by his fingernails and also to a Labour party required to win a general election only weeks or, at the most, months away.

I could not have resigned silently. In that summer of rumour and hints of scandal, there would inevitably have been speculation – presented as fact –

about the reasons for my departure, particularly when alternative employment was not available as an excuse. I would have had to give an explanation. In any case, if Lady Falkender's behaviour was intolerable, how could I, by saying nothing, permit it to flourish and strengthen in my absence and inevitably weaken the standing of those who had joined me in resisting her more outrageous demands? The only point in jumping ship would have been the certainty that I would take her with me, and that wasn't likely. If, subsequently, the second election of 1974 had been lost, then, validly or not, I would have been blamed for it. (Bizarrely, since Labour was twenty-three points behind in the opinion polls when I took over from him, I was blamed by my predecessor, Sir Trevor Lloyd-Hughes, for losing the 1970 election because of my propagandist style; logically, I suppose, I should then have been given the credit for winning the October 1974, election, but I wasn't.) Even if that general election had then turned out exactly as it did, I would still have been accused of being responsible for the smallness of the majority. Furthermore, had I resisted all temptation and stayed silent, I could not have guaranteed the silence of others. I cannot speak for them, but I don't believe mine would have been the only resignation. And I have been in journalism long enough to know that if I didn't speak on my own behalf, there would have been no shortage of those willing to speak for me, with or without my agreement.

I came close to leaving more than once and each time discussed the pros and cons with my wife, Irene, Albert Murray and Bernard Donoughue. In the end, I stayed. It wasn't a selfless decision nor a selfish one; I thought I could make a positive contribution towards the government's well being. What would have tipped the balance in favour of leaving would have been a decision by Wilson to continue for a full five-year term, which would have been wrong in every circumstance. The knowledge that he intended to leave by March 1976, or thereabouts, at the latest, thus putting a final date on my employment, kept me there.

Every administration has its scandals and almost every Prime Minister his or her personal weaknesses. It is a fact of life, which iconoclastic television producers, cynical presenters and newspaper columnists never understand, that no man or woman is great or good all the way through, just as very few are totally evil. Disraeli, founder of the modern Conservative party, married for money; Gladstone was a guilt-ridden kerb crawler before the motor car was invented, a masochist who lacerated himself with whips after evenings spent "counselling" prostitutes to give up their sinful ways. Rosebery was probably a homosexual and temperamentally unfit to be Prime Minister; Asquith was tortured by a foolish, indiscreet love for Venetia Stanley, young enough to be his daughter, if not grand-daughter; and Lloyd George was the most corrupt Prime Minister of the twentieth or any other century. He improperly dabbled in Marconi shares and was lucky to get away with it; he flaunted a mistress and he blatantly sold honours for sums huge even in today's debauched currency. Even the century's greatest political hero, Winston Churchill, conducted his financial affairs in a way which today would lead to his being drummed out of office. The Clement Attlees and Alec Douglas-Homes are few and far between. Undoubtedly, some past Prime Ministers were considerably more foolish or less honourable than Wilson.

The lives of all these past Prime Ministers have been crawled over. This book deals with the one administration, the one leader's office, which I knew intimately for most, if not all, of its time. It is more than a snapshot but less than a full history. It is a personal account, from a uniquely privileged viewpoint, of the pressures, motives and influence, not all apparent at the time, which went into the making of decisions by that leader. Where the accepted wisdom is wrong, which it frequently was and is, or misleading about particular events, I have tried to correct it. Where it is only slightly askew, I have tried to straighten it. Sometimes, if there is an insight, even a trivial one, lacking from the public prints, I have tried to give it. As the late Alan Clark, Conservative MP, historian and diarist supreme, once said: 'Trivia is [sic] part of the daily flow and has its own significance.'

This book is not only about Lady Falkender's influence upon Harold

Wilson, but much of concerns that. Its lasting relevance, I hope, for today's and the future's politicians, is as a reminder of how easily the over-mighty may be brought down and of the unchanging impermanence of office. In between the events it describes, much good and hard work was done. The government and party went on, despite the distractions from which its Prime Minister and leader suffered; indeed, the government and party collectively rarely knew of them. The Prime Minister was stressed frequently and disturbed often but not often permanently diverted from what he wanted to do. Various powerless people, innocent people — in a phrase hated by Wilson, 'ordinary people' — suffered emotionally and disappeared from our notice; others found their work and their working hours brutally extended because of the fantasies and furies of one woman. I don't believe that, in today's open politics, such a situation is likely to happen again, but I wouldn't bet on it.

The late Lord Goodman, as I describe, once told me that but for 'that woman' — Lady Falkender — Wilson would have been the greatest of our Prime Ministers. That strikes me as extremely unlikely and I doubt if Goodman himself believed it. He had a weakness for saying what he thought his audience might like to hear. But despite what his opponents in all parties might have said, Wilson was a kind and decent-thinking man and more honest than those who sneered at him as a Boy Scout gone wrong. Goodman's judgment was an excessive might-have-been an improbable alternative history which never happened. But, more than a judgment upon Wilson, it was, in my view, an accurate judgment upon Lady Falkender.

One
In the Beginning

Harold Wilson was elected leader of the Labour party on St Valentine's Day, 14 February 1963, a little over three weeks before his forty-seventh birthday on 11 March and, before the election got under way, an improbable choice. Until the coming of Tony Blair and William Hague, forty-six was almost indecently young for a Leader of Her Majesty's Opposition in the post-war world. The then Mrs Marcia Williams (later Baroness Falkender), his personal and political secretary, almost shared his birthday, though sixteen years his junior. She was born Marcia Matilda Field on 10 March 1932, adding to the numerous political contemporaries of Wilson whose birthdays were clustered around the March-April period. Neither was naturally at home in the social and cocktail circles of London political life, though she was later to make a successful transition to its showbiz fringe. He was Yorkshire, born at Cowersley, near Huddersfield, a Congregationalist and son of a chemist; she was Northamptonshire and the village of Long Buckby, and the daughter of a builder. Both, for reasons which psychologists might be able to explain, were incredibly insecure and this failing in the one fed the failing in the other and became a monster in both.

Soon after his election as leader, Wilson was in South Wales. George Thomas, eventual Speaker of the House of Commons and the most obsequious (and successful) of the flatterers who attached themselves to Wilson, told me that when he congratulated him on a 'wonderful' speech, Wilson turned to him and said: 'George, for the first time in my political life, I no longer have to look over my shoulder.' Thirteen years later, at the end of Wilson's time as Prime Minister, another Welshman, Bill Molloy, who ran Thomas a close second in excessive public loyalty, told him in the Commons: 'You go without any knives in your back.'

Neither Wilson's relieved self-assessment nor Molloy's compliment was true. Sometimes, with good reason, Wilson did have to look over his shoulder. He needed to, to fend off the attacks on him by those ambitious for his crown or from those who never forgave the gods for the death of his predecessor as leader, Hugh Gaitskell. Lady Falkender frequently and sarcastically compared Prime Minister Wilson to Walter Mitty (alternating with 'you silly little man'), but, as party leader Wilson, a comparison with Fred Astaire would have been more apt. He had to be nimble on his feet to survive the pre-conference left-wing plotting, and the all-the-year-round scheming of the clubland cabals, the aspirations of his colleagues and the conspirators of the MPs' tea-room.

But, sadly, he also looked over his shoulder when there was no-one there. He saw the future not through a crystal ball but through a rear-view mirror. He was made that way. He longed to be loved, or admired or respected and he was a kind, considerate and caring man to his staff and those close to him. But in the various phases of his life, his contemporaries don't appear to have reciprocated his warmth. It is often a problem with the gifted. He was no doubt the brightest pupil at his grammar school and the smartest lad in his boy scouts' troop, as well as one of the most successful Oxford students of his generation – a don at twenty-one – and the youngest Cabinet Minister, at thirty-one, in living memory. There is no surer way of arousing hostility. Many people, especially in politics, find it impossible to forgive success.

I knew him – but not well – for some six years or more before I joined him as deputy press secretary and press secretary-in-waiting, but I had been in the Commons Press Gallery since late 1954. I had watched – and marvelled at – his transformation from a debater with the passion and magic of the Speaking Clock to a brilliantly funny, waspish and wounding orator without equal in his party, except, of course, for Aneurin Bevan, who was peerless. Then, suddenly, he began to change again, for a reason which went to the heart of his insecurity. The biting witticisms were greatly reduced – and all because of a cartoon in the *Daily Mail* which likened him to Mort Sahl, an American comedian of renown in the 1950s. Nevertheless, even in his modified mode, he was the greatest entertainment on offer. The Tories hated his success almost as much as Labour's right-wingers did. But the first few years of government changed all that. When I arrived at No. 10, he was still showing the scars of the desperate times he had been through after devaluation in November 1967. Politically, it was the worst thing that ever happened to him. He fought it and he lost. He was no Horatius or Boy David. The financial gnomes he ritually condemned turned out to be invincible Goliaths. His Chancellor of the Exchequer, Jim Callaghan, whose resolution not to devalue was as strong as Wilson's, laid bare his own agony at the collapse of their joint policy and moved, largely unscathed and with dignity, to the Home Office. Wilson stayed where he was and took the blame, not least because he foolishly accepted a suggestion from Richard Crossman, his Minister of Housing, an arrogant, indiscreet and unprincipled intellectual and a close, unreliable and untrustworthy friend, that his devaluation speech should contain the reassurance to the voters that 'the pound in your pocket...has not been devalued'. That phrase has had many attributions of authorship, but Wilson told me it was the suggestion of Crossman, who rightly shared with Richard Nixon the soubriquet of 'Tricky Dicky'. 'Double Crossman' was the most frequent alternative. They were both well-deserved. Yet Wilson treated him, as he treated so many others, with unjustified kindness.

After devaluation, Wilson was nearly forced out of office in December 1967 by a Cabinet crisis over the sale of arms to South Africa. A powerful group of ministers, including the Foreign Secretary, George Brown, and the Defence Minister, Denis Healey, wanted to resume the sales, which Wilson had ended upon coming into office, to help ease the economic crisis which followed devaluation. Wilson was opposed to reversing his policy. In an informal count, he found the Cabinet was split eleven-ten against him. He then neatly and publicly snared – or smeared, as the Foreign Secretary would have it – George Brown as a pro-arms sales supporter by telling an alarmed Commons that a decision would be made after Brown, still deputy leader of the party as well as Foreign Secretary, returned from a visit to Brussels, where his plane was stranded by fog. Wilson wrote afterwards that such an important decision could not be taken in the absence of Brown and that was all he meant by his words, but that was nonsense; it could easily have been taken in Brown's absence if he and the Foreign Secretary were on the same side, and Labour MPs knew it. Brown retaliated by telling journalists that Wilson had been defeated in Cabinet at the meeting held when he returned. Wilson, however, had already inspired the Chief Whip, John Silkin, to organise a powerful back-bench 'revolt' (a hundred-and-forty or so signatures on an Early Day Motion) against renewing arms sales. The rank and file troops – the back-benchers – supported their general, Wilson, against the insurrectionists in the officer class. After Brown had had his fun in the weekend press, Wilson, late on the Sunday night, called an emergency Cabinet meeting for the following morning to reach a final decision. I was a lobby correspondent in those days.

Late that evening, I received a telephone call from a man simply whispering: 'Cabinet tomorrow morning' before the phone was put down. The caller didn't identify himself then or later but I recognised the voice as that of Ted Castle, husband of Barbara, Wilson's closest ally in the Cabinet, and political editor of the *Sun*. Barbara was obsessive about leaks and Ted must have called when she was out of the room. It was obvious that this was a crisis Cabinet, a hackneyed phrase which was, for once, merited, and I wrote the story along those lines. When I phoned the Prime Minister's press secretary, Trevor Lloyd-Hughes, I found he himself had only heard of the meeting a few moments previously. He confirmed the time, and my paper, the old post-*Daily Herald*, pre-Murdoch *Sun*, splashed it the next morning – as did the *Daily Mail*, whose political correspondent was Walter Terry, an occasional visitor to Chequers and Marcia Williams's then lover. But the *Mail* ran the story an edition later than the *Sun*, which gave us a minor triumph. The combined effect of the publicity, with reporters and photographers waiting outside the door of No. 10, and the uprising on the back benches was enough to break the nerve of the weaker Cabinet members. Patrick Gordon Walker, the Education Minister and former Foreign Secretary, was the first to crack, saying that the Cabinet could not put the Prime Minister in the humiliating position of having to announce the reversal of his policy, though that was the line he had supported the week before. At that point, the rest of the Cabinet ran for cover and they decided to continue the ban on arms sales. I believe the story I wrote that Sunday night directly led to the offer of a job at Downing Street a few weeks later, though it was to be nearly a year before I agreed to take it up. Wilson's reputation, however, suffered among his mutinous and defeated Cabinet colleagues. It was all right for them, it seemed, to conspire to overthrow the Prime Minister and/or his policy, but dirty, despicable and unfair for him to respond in kind. The truth, of course, was that he won and they lost. When it came to politicking, they were amateurs compared to him. They also failed to understand the revulsion against South Africa among the parliamentary party – it doesn't take long for ministers to forget their roots. Denis Healey later – much later – handsomely admitted that Wilson was right and he and the other Cabinet rebels were wrong, but the immediate effect of the row was to leave an already isolated Prime Minister even more alone. For months, he was downcast, though his spirits picked up noticeably after his decision, on Friday 15 March 1968 – the Ides of March – finally to act on the latest letter of resignation from Brown, rather than file it with all the others, as usual. As ever, Wilson's most envious and carping critic had played into his hands. Wilson and his new Chancellor, Roy Jenkins, had been faced on the Thursday evening with a sudden and unexpected foreign exchange crisis which required a special meeting of Privy Councillors with the Queen in order to declare the following day a Bank Holiday. Brown, as the second most senior man in the Cabinet, should have been at the meeting, but wasn't. He was to proclaim, loudly and publicly and in the hearing of Tory MPs in the early hours of the next morning, that he and other Cabinet ministers had been deliberately ignored by Wilson. The truth was that he had been drunk earlier in the day and was sleeping it off. He claimed that Wilson made no attempt to get hold of him. I knew that wasn't true because I answered the telephone at the Press Gallery bar that evening and the Downing Street operator asked if Mr Brown was there. When I said he wasn't, she said, in a rare indiscretion, that she had telephoned every bar in the Palace of Westminster in order to try to find him. Eventually, one of Brown's private secretaries told No. 10 not to search any more because it would do no good to succeed. Brown was recovering from a heavy drinking session and was always at his worst during the transition from stupor to sobriety. On this occasion, he compounded his inebriation by arrogance, sending a peremptory message to Wilson calling him to attend an impromptu Cabinet meeting at the House of Commons well past midnight. That was an impossible demand. Cabinets could only be convened by a Prime Minister; if Wilson had surrendered that right he would have been finished. Not for the first time in his life, nor for the last, George Brown had gone too far. Throughout the whole of this dangerous episode, Wilson had the full support of Mrs Williams. Whatever her failings then and later, she was an inflexible opponent of the South African regime (though, contrarily, she admired Rhodesia's Ian Smith). As a consequence of this opposition and fuelled by her paranoiac insecurity and suspicions, she came to believe that Whitehall was infiltrated by South Africa's sympathisers, some of whom were determined to destroy her. As was often the case, there was a germ – a tiny germ – of truth in her suspicions. On a VC10, returning from one of the Prime Minister's foreign visits, I overheard two very senior Foreign Office mandarins speak with astonishing sympathy about the problems South Africa's white government was having with Nelson Mandela supporters. The covert or passive supporters of South Africa, or those who disapproved – but not passionately – of the regime of that country, were not confined to the MCC and England's cricketing counties, nor to the stalwarts of Rugby Union football. Whitehall had more than a few of them.

Two
Press Secretary

Early in 1968, I was asked by Gerald Kaufman, Wilson's political press officer, whether I would be interested in becoming deputy press secretary at No. 10. I wasn't, and I didn't worry when nothing more was said. But towards the end of the year, the press secretary, Trevor (now Sir Trevor) Lloyd-Hughes, asked me if I would join him. I said I wouldn't. Later that evening, as I was writing in the Press Gallery, my telephone rang: it was the Downing Street switchboard operator, asking me to go down to the Prime Minister's room behind the Speaker's chair in the Commons.

He was alone, working at a huge table at which Cabinet meetings were occasionally held. He came straight to the point: 'I understand you don't want to join me,' he said. 'I don't want to be anybody's deputy,' I replied. 'I don't want you to be,' he said warmly. 'Come to No. 10, learn the job and in a couple of months I want you to take over as Press Secretary.' I still hesitated, because I loved my job as a political reporter on the *Sun*. But to cut a long story short, I accepted. When I got home that evening and told my wife, Irene, she protested: 'But you said you wouldn't take the job.' I replied: 'I discovered it is impossible to say No to the Prime Minister', and I began work on 1 January 1969.

I know now that my appointment would not have been possible but for Marcia's enthusiastic approval. When, a little later, I asked Wilson why he had chosen me, he replied with a back-handed compliment: 'Because you get it right about 70 per cent of the time, which is more than anyone else.' If I had been right 100 per cent of the time it would not have mattered if Marcia had disapproved. I must have been her choice, not his, in the first place.

By the time I joined Wilson, he had begun to think about the next election, from a perilous position of twenty-three points behind in the polls. At the time, Marcia seemed an invaluable helpmate, assisted politically by the astute and acute Kaufman, who acted as Wilson's occasional speech-writer. I quickly found out how little the well-informed political reporter actually knew of what went on in government and Whitehall. The first crisis of my experience came when the Foreign and Commonwealth Office – which, like the Treasury, pursued its own policy rather than its masters'– deliberately leaked a highly-secret telegram from our Ambassador in Paris, Sir Christopher Soames, about a meeting he had had with General de Gaulle. Wilson's express instructions, which I conveyed to the Foreign Office's News Department, were that the FCO was not to add anything to the inaccurate stories which had begun to appear in European papers – and those only because the FCO, again against Wilson's wishes, had informed all the other countries of the European Economic Community of the secret discussions – and to confirm nothing. The News Department, diplomats all, blithely ignored the Prime Minister and gave the whole telegram, non-attributably, to its 'trusties,' most of whom showed they couldn't be trusted by making it quite clear next morning that the origin of their stories was the Foreign Office. Perhaps, on reflection, I would have done the same. The defect of non-attribution is that the source is often the most important part of the story.

Wilson let that palpable insubordination pass, however, because he was involved in greater issues: an attempt to change the constitution of the House of Lords – eventually thwarted by a unique alliance between Enoch Powell and Michael Foot – and, more crucially, his and Barbara Castle's attempt to shackle the excesses of the trade unions – an enterprise in which, again, he had Marcia's full support – by bringing in compulsory strike ballots and a twenty-eight day pause before a strike could take place. In the end, that, too, was a failure because of the cowardice of Wilson's Cabinet colleagues; a cowardice which ripened into foul fruit a decade later in the Winter of Discontent and eighteen years of unbroken Tory government. Their lack of courage gave Margaret Thatcher the opportunity to prove herself more of a man than the Labour Cabinet. She took it and unflinchingly destroyed the unions' power to hold Parliament, government and the country to ransom, and many of those who opposed Wilson's reforms then meekly accept today the more punishing Thatcher changes.

Between these serious issues of our future in Europe and union reform came an episode of sheer farce which made me wonder whether I had joined a government or a circus.

The tiny Caribbean island of Anguilla wanted to assert its independence and not be part of the associated states of St Kitts, Nevis and Anguilla. To prove they were serious, they threw out, with menaces, a junior British minister, William Whitlock. Suddenly, I found that we were involved in sending troops (and the Metropolitan Police) to the island to restore order. The No. 10 Press Secretary, Trevor Lloyd-Hughes, and the rest of his department, including me, knew nothing about it until the "invasion" was launched. Indeed, we got more information from the newspapers than the Foreign Office or Wilson's private office. I told Lloyd-Hughes in a memo:

> From the moment the decision to intervene with force was taken, a careful programme to justify the government's decision was essential.
>
> All the elements of a comic opera situation were, inevitably, present – London bobbies, Red Devils and gunboats ranged against improbable hymn-singing revolutionaries whose island paradise sport was to sling lead at pin-striped delegations from Whitehall; or so it was bound to appear in a press which did not know where Anguilla was and already tickled pink by the hurried departure of Mr Whitlock.
>
> . . . We should both have been involved immediately in the presentation of the policy. We were not, and, with hindsight, I would claim that

the damaging hilarity which followed was, in part, a result of our absence.

. . . Any journalist knows information can be obtained from police sources. I, for one, was not aware that the police were involved until I read [the Evening Standard *Political Editor] Bob Carvel's piece on Monday morning . . . The information coming to us from the private office was inadequate – and not for the first time since I have been here. On innumerable occasions you and I have been placed in a position of desperately trying to catch up on leaks which have sometimes gone beyond our own knowledge . . . It does not seem to have been brought home to them that presentation is an integral part of the policy. Our need to know . . . is as important as anyone else's.*

The muddle from Monday onwards makes me despair. While you and I were refusing to give a clue about the operation, the Ministry of Defence were arranging a facility for the press – which we only discovered by sheer chance. Today (Wednesday), I learned that the Foreign Office had a meeting on Monday, at which the Home Office were present, to co-ordinate publicity.

Needless to say, we did not know about it.

The final announcement of the landing was given by the Foreign Office to the press while we were still refusing to admit that a landing had taken place. I don't mind playing Spurius Lartius to your Horatius, provided the Foreign Office does not saw the bridge away while I'm still on it.

There was much more. But from that moment, I determined that when I took over from Lloyd-Hughes (which happened a few weeks later), I would assert, aggressively if need be, the eminence and importance of the Downing Street press office to all concerned, especially the private offices at the Foreign Office and No. 10, so that all private secretaries and others understood that if something was happening, I was to be told, at the worst, immediately after the Prime Minister.

I had the chance later to avenge myself on the FCO News Department. A senior Foreign Office official in charge of disarmament resigned because he disagreed with government policy. The FCO tried to keep it secret, but it leaked to Chapman Pincher of the *Daily Express*. When his story appeared, the deputy head of the News Department, Eleanor Booker, asked me to tell the Lobby that he had retired 'on health grounds'. 'But that's not true,' I said. 'Ye-es, but that's our line,' she replied. 'Tell them yourself,' I said. When, inevitably, the Lobby questioned me, I told them to speak to the Foreign Office, hinting that they shouldn't believe what they might be told. I think the FCO had forgotten that, from the moment of taking over, I had decided that the No. 10 press office would not answer for any other department in Whitehall. I had stopped the frantic ring-around of all ministries which my staff conducted each morning from the moment they arrived right up until the morning Lobby conference. I was at least beginning to grasp the reins, and not before time.

At this period, Mrs Williams was coming into the office less and less often, not surprisingly because, in almost complete secrecy – I didn't know about it until more than a year later – she had given birth to a son by Walter Terry the previous August, was now pregnant by him again and was determined to keep that secret, too.

The relief among civil servants and the political staff at her absence was palpable and their unanimity in rejoicing caused the stirring of my first doubts about her as an asset. Once I became Press Secretary, a few months after arriving as deputy, the civil servants began to confide in me. Of course, I had heard endless stories about her clashes with the permanent staff, including the Garden Room girls – too 'middle class and Tory', a euphemism for 'too pretty' – and about her stormy outbursts. Like most political journalists, I took them with a grain of salt until I found they were all true, and more.

Marcia's upbringing was orthodox, living in a typical English village as a typical, bright, English girl, if with a rebellious streak. She was said to have led a strike of fellow pupils against a headmistress who she believed had treated a classmate unfairly. Whether that was a strike against injustice or a strike against authority – not the same thing – no-one now can know. She grew into a tall and attractive brunette, later a blonde; striking in any company, and with eyes – 'beautiful blue eyes,' according to James Callaghan, who appreciated beauty in a woman and for whom she was briefly a secretary – which bestowed approval or glared hatred more than any thousand words could do. After she left her rural life she was to become, indirectly, one of the most powerful political figures of her generation because of her immense influence over Wilson, a man who was Prime Minister for eight years in all – 1964-70 and 1974-6 – and who won four general elections. She never displayed that influence publicly but she flaunted it in private and it was an abiding fact of his life. She was naturally secretive, known about but hardly known, talked about but seldom talking and that suited Wilson's requirements.

She never made a public speech, before or after she became a member of the House of Lords; she rarely gave an interview and she was never elected to anything, not even a parish council. Her two autobiographical books were bland, designed to rewrite history rather than record it, and, by concealing far more than they told, to deny the myths, the mysteries and the truth about her. Consequently, unless one knew her well, one didn't know her at all. But to borrow Sir John Wheeler Bennett's memorable conclusion about Queen Elizabeth, the Queen Mother, there was arsenic in the centre of the marshmallow. For my first eighteen months with Wilson, I enjoyed the marshmallow until the arsenic spilled out, never to be contained again.

In that the youthful Marcia Williams focused Wilson on the ultimate objective, gave him direction, made him shed his grey image and sharpened his speeches, then she can claim to have moulded the man he became.

Perhaps she saw in him a greater opportunity than he did himself. She became more than his secretary. She was his manager and his political 'wife'. But she also identified a weakness which was not so apparent to others in those days: that he was a man whose private insecurity was huge, as was her own. Perhaps it took one to know one. She fed that weakness. She encouraged him to believe in conspiracies against him because she believed in them herself.

There is some confusion about when Wilson and Marcia Williams first spoke to each other. They had different versions of their meeting. Wilson, to me, dated it in late 1956, when he saw her standing at a bus stop, recognised her as a Transport House employee and offered her a lift. Andrew Roth tells the same story. During that ride, she is said to have confessed to him that she was the authoress of anonymous letters he had been receiving warning of a Transport House plot by Gaitskellites to damage him. I find it hard to believe in the coincidence that he happened to be passing while she happened to be waiting for a bus and that he identified from a moving car a typist from Transport House to whom he had never spoken but who he instantly recognised.

Her version, initially, was different. She said to me that they first met at the notorious dinner given by the Labour party for Nikita Kruschev, General Secretary of the USSR. By that time, when she was working as a secretary for Morgan Phillips, Labour's General Secretary, she had already started to dispatch to Wilson the anonymous letters which, apart from warning him of plots against him in Transport House also detailed weaknesses in the party organisation which he was later to expose in his report on the party's "penny farthing" machine. In her memoirs, she has yet another version, to the effect that the chance of becoming Wilson's secretary was offered to her by a friend of Wilson's, Arthur Skeffington MP, late in 1956.

Her career in politics began in 1955 when she began her job in Phillips's office. The next year was a key one in her life. She took the notes for the record at the Kruschev dinner when the non-abstemious Soviet leader had a stand-up shouting match with George Brown, an even less abstemious rising star of Labour, over the treatment of Soviet dissidents.

Subsequently, though she was entirely innocent of the affair, those notes were leaked to the *Daily Express.* The allegation, which was widespread in Labour circles at the time, but never proved, was that Phillips himself sold the notes to Derek Marks, the paper's political correspondent, for £500 in cash. It was a great story, however the *Express* got it.

But it was a memorable night in other ways, too. She told me that Wilson, who was at the dinner as a member of the Shadow Cabinet, offered her a lift home at the end of it, thus beginning the friendship which changed both their lives.

Yet for some reason, Wilson and Marcia both later denied that they knew each other at that time. But something of significance must have happened that night. Discussions recalling that evening always made Marcia jumpy, so much so that it became a standing joke among a few of us that if I wanted to induce a panic in her, I would simply send her a postcard with the numbers 23456 on it. She would have known that they stood for 23 April 1956, the night of the dinner. But, of course, I never did.

Though he was in the Shadow Cabinet, Wilson's career was on the decline in the mid-1950s. He was an object of derision and suspicion among the right-wing after his 1951 resignation, together with Bevan and a junior minister, John Freeman, from the Attlee government over the cost of re-arming. He was contemptuously and sneeringly dubbed 'Nye Bevan's poodle' by Hugh Dalton, the ex-Chancellor renowned for encouraging promising young men in the Labour party and not always for altruistic political purposes. Nor was he helped when Winston Churchill succeeded Attlee as Prime Minister in October 1951 and took the steps on defence expenditure which Wilson had proposed and whose rejection by Attlee had led to his resignation. He was also distrusted by the left after replacing Bevan in the Shadow Cabinet when the tempestuous Welshman resigned from it in 1954 following a disagreement on foreign policy.

Wilson was never more in need of friends in the two years which followed and, miraculously, in Marcia he found one. Whether by brilliant insight or not, she, by standing with him against his foes, real and imagined, had found the way to Wilson's heart and trust. On his part, to discover an able, attractive and intelligent young woman prepared to risk her own minor career in order to join him in the trenches of back-stabbing party warfare, was to find a jewel beyond price. He repaid her loyalty a thousand-fold and, in October 1956, she became his secretary – more or less for life, as it turned out. It was a relationship without parallel in modern times. Comparisons have been made between Wilson and Williams and Lloyd George and Frances Stevenson, but nearly all historical comparisons are inexact. That Stevenson was the mistress of Lloyd George was an open, though never published, secret and, after the death of his wife, Lloyd George married her. But there is no evidence that she ever fulfilled the political role which Marcia performed for Wilson.

Wilson's working days in early 1969 became increasingly devoured by *In Place of Strife*, the White Paper which contained the proposals to reform the trade unions, but, more and more, part of his evenings was taken up by the necessity to travel to Marcia's home to discuss the political dangers which were gathering. In April 1969, I heard from one of my most reliable former back-bench contacts that a serious plot was developing against the Prime Minister. It was largely inspired by the supporters of Jim Callaghan, who, as a former trade union official, was stubbornly, even blindly, opposed to doing anything which might bring the trade union movement into the 20th century, but it also contained elements who supported Denis Healey. For the first time, it appeared, those who wanted Wilson out were agreeing that the primary objective had to be to get rid of the Prime Minister; who was to succeed him was secondary. That was one of the two scenarios Wilson always feared – the other was that a maverick back-bencher, such as Willie Hamilton, a bad-tempered Englishman, MP for West Fife and an inveterate Wilson-hater, might stand against him and get more than a derisory vote, rather as Sir Anthony Meyer's candidature almost did against Mrs Thatcher nearly two decades later. Wilson had often said to me, even in my early weeks of working for him, that as long as there was more than one Crown Prince, or no Clown Prince, like Hamilton, he was safe. On this occasion, Marcia took charge of coping with the back-bench plotters. Eric Varley, one of Wilson's parliamentary private secretaries but until a few months before Deputy Chief Whip, was summoned back from holiday to deal with the rebels with that mixture of threats, cajolery, flattery and promises with which whips and Prime Ministerial p.p.s's do their work. He was effective and, like most revolts, it fizzled out. Wilson then made a May Day speech in which he declared, in words supplied by Gerald Kaufman: 'I know what's going on. I'm going on.' That ended it. By using my old lobby contacts, I had performed my first real service by supplying the initial information about the situation; Marcia had supplied the political muscle to deal with it. She later retired to the rural Essex home of Lady Plummer, far-left widow of Sir Leslie Plummer, an old Commons colleague of Wilson's, to complete her pregnancy.

Meanwhile, the Cabinet grew more and more afraid of TUC resistance to the mild measures which Mrs Castle and Wilson were proposing. A succession of meetings between Wilson and the union leaders broke down. Len (now Lord) Murray, then Deputy General Secretary of the TUC, whispered to me at one meeting, 'When will the Prime Minister realise that the unions are paper tigers?' I think Wilson always knew it; the trouble was that his Cabinet and his back-benchers didn't.

A final decision on whether to legislate against union recalcitrance had to be made by the Cabinet; it was a sunny June afternoon when Wilson's allies began fearfully to drift away. When Wilson left a meeting with the TUC to tell the Cabinet that they now had to agree whether to go ahead with legislation against the TUC's opposition, they were horrified. According to Wilson, his protégé, Peter Shore, said he didn't realise the Prime Minister was serious about union reform; the Chancellor, Roy Jenkins, when asked for his opinion, said he would go along with the majority, a remark which must have had his courageous mentor, Hugh Gaitskell, spinning in his grave. Wilson dropped heavy hints that he might resign and left the Cabinet room in a fury. I was waiting for him outside. 'I don't mind leading a green Cabinet,' he said bitterly, 'but I'm buggered if I'm going to run a yellow one.' Then his face brightened. Always one to retrieve some consolation from disaster, he said, cheerfully: 'I'll use that.' He had left behind him in the room a Cabinet apprehensive that he would do as he had hinted. In fact, he never ever painted himself into a corner. He always suspected his Cabinet would run scared when it came to it and he had an alternative ready if it did.

At the last meeting between union leaders and Wilson and Castle – going on while the Cabinet waited, trembling, in the Cabinet room – Fred Hayday, leader of one of the larger general unions, pleaded with the Prime Minister not to go ahead with changes in the law and promised to make a 'binding' agreement to achieve voluntarily what Wilson wanted to do by legislation. I scribbled a note – which I still have – to the Prime Minister saying that this might be the way out. Someone else offered a 'solemn' agreement. Shortly afterwards, in his study, Wilson stopped me when I attempted again to raise the question of an escape route, one from which we might salvage something, a Dunkirk or Corunna, at least, rather than a Gallipoli. 'Wait until Barbara is out of the room,' he whispered. After she left, we agreed that if the Cabinet, as expected, turned tail, a 'solemn and binding agreement' would be all that was left, short of total humiliation. Thus I shared in the parentage of the mythical figure immortalised by Bernard Levin as Mr Solomon Binding. It was an undignified episode which set back the government's slow recovery, which appeared to be in the making.

Marcia, no doubt, was in a temper about it all, but the imminent birth of her second son, conceived off Gibraltar on board HMS Fearless the previous October (Walter Terry was among the journalists covering the abortive talks on Rhodesian independence between Wilson and Ian Smith) kept her away from No. 10. But there was little even she could do against a party and a Cabinet united in panic.

The failure of *In Place of Strife* indirectly cost Labour the election of the following year (and Jim Callaghan the election of 1979). The agreement with the unions, encompassing the 'solemn and binding' agreement and the constitutional compromises worked out to save face, was signed on 18 June, ominously Waterloo Day, with Wilson this time playing Napoleon and Vic Feather, the TUC's General Secretary, improbably in the role of the Iron Duke. Iron Boot would have been more appropriate. The agreement, after six months of exhaustive and exhausting debate and negotiation, was to prove not worth the hypocritical ink it was written in. The general public and the newspapers treated it with derision; the Cabinet, with the honourable exceptions of Wilson and Barbara Castle, treated it with relief. They hadn't fought; they had run away to live and lose another day.

The one bright moment of that summer came on 23 July, when the Open University was formally established – it will always remain to Wilson's credit that despite the economic and political difficulties, some of them Oxbridgean elitists, who surrounded the project, he forced it into existence. It is a better and more enduring monument to his life than any other achievement.

There was then a short but sharp difference with Edward Heath and Jeremy Thorpe over a dinner designed to raise funds for the European Movement. Wilson had agreed to speak alongside the other two party leaders until he discovered that the company of the then less-famously known Jeffrey Archer was due to scoop 10 per cent of the proceeds in return for organising the function. Seeing that the dinner was intended to raise £750,000, Wilson decided to pull out rather than help Archer restore his much-battered fortunes with a fee of £75,000. Thorpe agreed with him. In the event, Archer accepted a lower, but still substantial, flat-rate fee and Wilson made his speech. By this time, Marcia had disappeared entirely from our lives. Curiously, nobody had the slightest idea why – gift horses and similar proverbs sprang to mind – though it was generally understood she was ill with "women's problems", an explanation always guaranteed to stop men from inquiring further.

There was a brief meeting at Mildenhall with Richard Nixon in the early days of August when the American President suddenly decided to drop in and see Wilson before he returned to America after a visit to Romania. It was a visit which gave us nothing. After an extremely bumpy flight from Northolt to the USAF base in Suffolk, any attempt I might have made to get favourable publicity for a change for the Prime Minister was wrecked by Ron Ziegler, my opposite number in Nixon's entourage, who clumsily announced over the loudspeakers, to the joy of listening British reporters, the arrival of 'the British Prime Minister, Harold Macmillan.' We could have done without him and without the American heavies who physically manhandled British reporters until I reminded them that they were guests in Britain and not to forget it. For my pains, I was assigned to a group of British civil servants listening to Henry Kissinger expounding on the domino theory as it related to south-east Asia. I'd never heard such implausible theorising in my life and thereafter had little regard for the Secretary of State's reputation as an intellectual.

Wilson then went off to the Scilly Isles, promptly to be confronted by the explosive, in every sense of the word, crisis in Northern Ireland. It was the start of a saga which was to dominate for the next thirty years and about which a whole library will no doubt eventually be written. I wrote substantially on the topic in *The Politics of Power* and nothing much has happened in the following twenty-five years to change my basic views about the long-term future of the island of Ireland. This book, therefore, except in passing, will not be part of the literature of those days, although it will deal with Wilson's visit to the province and Dublin in November 1971, the talks at his Buckinghamshire home with IRA delegates in 1972 and Marcia's lunatic announcement to Wilson in 1975 that she was going to Dublin to meet a representative of the IRA in order to prevent a breakdown in the cease-fire then current.

The situation that August quietened considerably after British troops, cheered by the Catholics, arrived in the North to protect the Nationalist population, and Wilson went back, briefly, to the Scillies. Then we made our way in the first week of September to the annual Trades Union Congress, that year being held in Portsmouth. He was greeted with mock-warmth and real hostility. He said to me before going on to the platform: 'They ain't going to like this.' Nor did they. They wanted him to swallow humble pie; instead, he reminded them why he and Mrs Castle had introduced *In Place of Strife* in the first place and what the TUC had promised him only two-and-a-half months before. His forecast was right – they didn't like it. The atmosphere was more akin to the North Pole than to the south coast. The party conference at Brighton that autumn was destined to be the last before the general election, though the delegates couldn't know that, and it also marked the re-emergence of Marcia. Wilson's speech had been largely prepared in London but we – a small group, including Peter Shore and Tony Benn – met in Wilson's hotel room to discuss and polish it. Marcia was there, sombre and unusually quiet. As the meeting ended, she announced that she was ill and was going back to London, which she did. I was horrified when, on the Monday evening, about sixteen hours before his leader's speech was due the following morning, Wilson told me that he was going to London to see Marcia, whose condition, apparently, had deteriorated. (I still didn't know that she had recently become a mother for the second time.) I told him he could not possibly leave Brighton without the newspapers, radio and television (the word 'media' was not then in vogue) detecting a crisis and that if Marcia was ill now, she would be a lot worse if reporters began to ask why he had abandoned the conference, if only for a few hours, in order to offer sympathy and comfort to his secretary. He had a mandatory round of visits to make that evening to the social functions with which conferences abound. They could not be avoided without rumour and gossip and his absence would be noticed immediately; the first reaction would be that events somewhere in the world, probably Northern Ireland, had become dire. Politically, the truth would have been worse. It was an impossible proposition, typical of many similar stipulations made by Marcia, and he quickly saw it as such. For my part, I was beginning to understand just how demanding their relationship was.

Once back from Brighton, we began to prepare for the next general election, examining, among other material, the TV advertisements for US Presidential candidates; interesting but not relevant to the British experience. The preparations also included a substantial reshuffle in the government, which meant dropping a large number of elderly ministers and bringing in new blood. My outstanding memory of those changes was a personal one. On the Thursday of the Labour conference I had lunch with Richard Marsh, the Minister of Transport and, at forty-one, thought to have a glittering political career before him. Marsh had risen rapidly from being a local union official (he was the branch secretary of my mother's union, NUPE, and she always referred to him as Young Dickie) and Wilson had greatly admired his speeches in Opposition. He was witty, cheeky, irreverent even, about Labour's establishment and Wilson saw him as a future star. But, instead, he marked himself down as a recipient of the black spot when he came into 10 Downing Street late one night to see the Prime Minister. After he had gone, Wilson said to me: 'He is always bringing me problems to solve instead of coping with them himself.' Like so many bright young features of the political firmament, Marsh was better at opposing than proposing, a meteor, not a star. At the lunch, Marsh spoke warmly to me of Wilson – unsurprisingly, none of Wilson's ministers ever spoke less than warmly of him, especially when a reshuffle was in the offing – and of all he owed to him. 'If Harold were to drop me tomorrow,' he said, 'I could have no complaint.' I sat there knowing that on the following Sunday I would be announcing, to general – and, in Marsh's case, a particular – astonishment, that Harold had indeed dropped him. When I did so, Marsh loudly and publicly complained, held a celebratory party to rub in his anger and appeared never to forgive Wilson. In 1981 he was enobled by Mrs Thatcher and became a supporter of her policies, which Wilson would have seen as a vindication of his judgement.

Soon afterwards, on 14 October, George Brown emerged to show his vulgar talent for embarrassment. The Prime Minister had decided to give a dinner in honour of the three American astronauts – Neil Armstrong and colonels Buzz Aldrin and Michael Collins – who had landed on the moon in Apollo Eleven. Wilson made a warm speech and proposed a toast to the three men. Then Brown, who had imbibed a considerable quantity of his own rocket fuel, chose to rise to his feet, glass in hand, and announce: 'I would now like to propose a toast to the real Michael Collins', meaning the IRA leader who was murdered by his own colleagues after doing a deal with Lloyd George to split Ireland into two. At the time, Northern Ireland was seething with menace. Most of the dinner guests were seething at Brown's crass and insulting stupidity. Soon afterwards, I followed Brown and his over-loyal wife, Sophie, down the stairs towards the front door. 'You're drunk,' said Sophie. 'Shut up,' said Brown, ever the prince of courtesy and master of repartee.

We were now moving almost irreversibly towards a general election in the summer of 1970. All our policies and decisions were shaped towards that end, even if the Cabinet remained blithely unaware of its imminence. There is no privilege which a Prime Minister guards more jealously than his right to choose the date for dissolving Parliament and for the election itself, and Wilson had no intention of allowing his colleagues to share in the decision until after he had taken it.

One problem which had to be got out of the way was the 1970 tour of Britain by the South African cricket team. Wilson was determined that it would not take place under any circumstances, partly because he despised the apartheid regime then controlling South Africa and partly because he did not want the inevitable protests and demonstrations interfering with the general election campaign. His intention was to get the MCC – heavily riddled with pro-South Africans and those who bleated: 'keep politics out of sport' – to cancel the tour. His way of doing it was to get Denis Howell, his Sports Minister and a former football referee, to suggest to the BBC's David Coleman that Coleman and Sam Leitch, the producer of *Sportsnight*, should invite Wilson to appear on their programme. They did, and he accepted. The BBC's hierarchy said furiously that the Corporation had been 'conned' by all involved, but because there was a long and recent history of hostility between the Corporation and the Prime Minister – see Chapter 10 – they made no attempt to stop the programme. Wilson ranged widely over various topics of sport, but his principal purpose was to appeal to the cricketing authorities to cancel the tour. Eventually, after further appeals from the Home Secretary, Jim Callaghan, the MCC did call it off. What they never knew was that if they hadn't done so, Wilson and Callaghan would have imposed a ban on the team entering Britain. Wilson said to me: 'I'm not going to have a riot in the streets outside Lord's on polling day, whatever I have to do to stop it.'

The decision to hold the general election in June had been firmly taken more than a fortnight before *Sportsnight* went out. The disastrous opinion polls of the previous autumn – an 11 per cent swing against Labour in five by-elections held in October and a swing of nearly 15 per cent in two more held in December – had to be disregarded. Wilson's reasoning for the early election was simple: he had been elected at the end of March, 1966, and the five-year Parliament had to end by early April, 1971, at the latest. But that was 'the bitter end,' and meant that polling day would be chosen not by the Prime Minister but by the calendar. Alec Douglas-Home had followed that path in 1964 and John Major did so in 1997; both lost. Complicating that option, unfortunately, was the fact that decimal currency, for which Wilson's government was responsible but which Wilson believed to be hugely unpopular, was due to be introduced in February, 1971. To avoid that meant voting had to be in 1970. October had the advantage of cancelling the annual party conferences, a blessing for which all party leaders would have been thankful, but the weather, the steadily darkening nights, an electoral register a year out of date and the fact that it was the favourite bet of most political commentators and politicians were all against that. The clinching argument came in the late winter, when Wilson was told by an informant inside Conservative Central Office (political parties, like newspapers, occasionally have their moles inside a rival's organisation, though in this case the culprit was probably an MP, Captain Henry Kerby, of whom more later) that the Tories were planning to spend two million pounds on a summer advertising campaign in preparation for an October poll. That sum is small change today, but at the time it was enormous, far beyond Labour's ability to match.

Before making an irrevocable decision, Wilson asked the Chancellor, Roy Jenkins, whether he had a view, based on economic circumstances, about the advantages of an early or late 1970 election. Jenkins did not. Wilson tried to persuade him to reduce income tax by 6d. (two and a half pence in today's money) in his Budget due on 14 April, but Jenkins primly refused to dirty his hands and reputation with such an obvious bribe.

The Prime Minister therefore convened a meeting in his study on the night of 13 April, the night before the Budget, to discuss the date of polling day. The only personal advisers there were Marcia, myself and Gerald Kaufman, together with Peter Shore, the only Cabinet minister consulted. With varying degrees of enthusiasm or doubt – Kaufman and Shore strongly favouring June, I reluctantly concurring and Marcia agreeing, 'provided Labour doesn't lose, otherwise we should go on to the bitter end' – we decided, despite Labour's continuing to lag in most of the opinion polls, to go for a general election on 11 June. It was galling when, after defeat, Wilson praised Marcia for being the only 'bitter-ender'. As I have written before on the subject: 'She had backed both horses in the race, in which situation it is easy to be right provided everyone forgets that you were also wrong.'

A lighter, in retrospect, moment – there weren't to be many of them – came on 19 May, the evening after the general election was announced, at another meeting held in Wilson's study. It was the occasion when Gerald Kaufman threw a glass of whisky over me; I was charitable in telling this story in *The Politics of Power* by assuming that Kaufman was unaware that his glass had just been refilled before he flicked it at me. After that book was published, I received a letter from David Candler, who had assisted on the press side in the political office and who had sat quietly in a corner taking a note of our proceedings. The waste of the Prime Minister's whisky came after I commended Marcia for the way in which she had dealt on the telephone with a whining MP. Candler wrote: 'Since . . . you rarely jotted down your words immediately after uttering them, you may like to know for the record what was actually said at the whisky-throwing incident:

JTWH [my initials] (as Marcia comes off phone): On the strength of that, we should make you ambassador to Washington.

Marcia: Oh, I could never do that. I'm not sycophantic enough.

JTWH: Well, you could always take lessons from Gerald.

(GK – who was, incidentally, well aware that his glass was not empty . . . then tosses the contents over JTWH who is seated about six feet away and still looking round at Marcia, smiling).

JTWH to Gerald: You bloody fool. What did you do that for?

HW: Gerald, you're drunk. Go home.

JTWH (angrily taking off jacket): If it wasn't for where we are, I'd hit you for doing that.

GK: I'm not drunk. I'm not drunk.

HW: Gerald, you're drunk. Go home.

GK (jumping up and turning round excitedly): I'm not drunk.

(HW stalks out, Marcia by now helping JTWH brush down jacket and wipes whisky-sodden chair with cloth speedily obtained from adjacent washroom. GK looks crestfallen, still protesting his sobriety. Others present, realising their attendance no longer required, gather up papers and prepare to leave.)

I was in no mood to accept any apologies that evening, but Gerald was handsomely contrite the following day, though he never offered to pay the cost of cleaning my suit. Of more immediate importance on that day was the announcement of a 2.1 increase in the retail price index. Astonishingly, it seemed that the First Secretary and Secretary of State for Employment and Productivity, Barbara Castle, had not been told of it.

After the battering the government, and Wilson in particular, had taken over the previous three years, Wilson had been anxious to protect his back by not appearing to be acting on his own hunches, or those of his kitchen cabinet, in deciding the election date. Better opinion polls, including one after the secret decision had been taken, which put Labour comfortably ahead, gave him his opportunity. As speculation mounted about a May or June election, nothing was done by me or Wilson to dampen it down. Cabinet ministers began to sniff the air of excitement; a paddock of old racehorses fearing the knacker's yard suddenly smelt fresh green grass again. By the time Wilson asked for their opinion on 12 May, Cabinet members were overwhelmingly in favour of an early election. They, no doubt, thought they were taking a collective decision; in fact, all they did was collectively to agree to do what the Prime Minister had already decided to do, and collectively to take the blame, though they didn't know it. Democracy in this instance was a theory, not a fact.

But the ministers did make one crucial, probably fatal, decision about the date: after the Leader of the Commons, Fred Peart, weakly pleaded that he couldn't get essential business through Parliament in time for an election on 11 June (of course, he could have by being rougher and tougher than was his nature), Wilson agreed to defer his suggested date by a week to 18 June – that fateful anniversary of Waterloo again. Tommy Balogh, the former Hungarian economics expert and a friend of Wilson's from the early 1950s, was gloomy about the change. He said that the balance of trade figures for May, to be released on the Monday before polling day would be disastrous because of the purchase of a jumbo jet (in those days, a deficit of £30 million was bad news; today a deficit of ten times that amount is counted a triumph), and so it proved.

An opinion poll published in the *Daily Mail* on 12 June put Labour streets ahead but by 18 June that lead had all evaporated. A deeply gloomy Albert Murray, a junior minister and MP for Gravesend and a close and loyal friend, phoned me on the Monday evening and said there had been a disastrous change on the doorsteps when he had canvassed an hour or two earlier. And so it proved. Edward Heath won with a majority which looked comfortable enough to keep him in power for the next five years. After more than six years in the tied cottage of Downing Street, Wilson's tenancy had ended. Despite the favourable opinion polls close to polling day, the campaign itself had been a disaster. The strategy was largely determined by Marcia. She reasoned that Wilson was more attractive to the voters than his party and, influenced by the films she had seen about the US presidential elections, argued that the campaign should be fought on Wilson's popularity. But the voters were more sophisticated than that and they distrusted 'presidential' elections in Britain. The memories of the years of devaluation, higher taxes, financial crises, tempestuous resignations and caving in to the TUC were not to be wiped out by walkabouts and cheerful waves from local party offices' windows, which Labour's campaign largely seemed to be. Wilson often yearned for 'a doctor's mandate' but the voters were not ready to give it to him.

Though I took part in the discussions on the election date, I was hardly at the heart of the 1970 campaign. I wrote a number of newspaper articles for Wilson – I had been horrified to find that in previous campaigns he had written them himself, by hand; a complete waste of his time, which was his most valuable commodity during an election – and played a small part in the speech-writing. Gerald Kaufman, at that time addicted to prime ministerial speeches without verbs, contributed some drafts before he went off to fight his first campaign in Ardwick, Leslie Lever's old seat in Manchester, but Wilson was mainly his own scriptwriter. One speech I did write (on housing) was hailed by the *Guardian* as being Wilson's sharpest of the campaign up to that point and I began to get the taste for it. My only other contribution, apart from the newspaper articles, was a party political broadcast on radio, which Wilson liked but Marcia didn't but which had to be broadcast because there was no alternative script.

As ever, for a party which purports to shun titles as symbols of privilege, the Dissolution Honours List took up a disproportionate amount of time during the campaign. Leslie Lever, the elder brother of the better-known and more brilliant Harold, had been promised a peerage in return for the generous assistance he gave to Kaufman in obtaining the Ardwick nomination, but he was destined to be unlucky. When the general election was lost, Wilson told Kaufman 'all bets are off,' to the disappointment of Kaufman and, even more so, Lever who had spent weeks introducing Kaufman to the Catholic Mothers of the Poor and similar minority or ethnic groups in order to ensure his success. Lever got his reward in later years, but not then.

George Brown, whose hope of holding his seat at Belper was much more slender than Wilson's fear that he might, began to badger the Prime Minister long before polling day about the peerage which custom said was his due. Wilson had already promised to send Brown to the House of Lords, either in a Resignation Honours List or one for life peers soon afterwards, but Labour's (still) deputy leader didn't trust him. Indeed, the calls from Brown demanding his elevation and the complaints about the delays went on endlessly after the election was over until Wilson at last put him out of his misery and recommended the peerage he craved.

Wilson told me he was going to make Miss Margaret (Peggy) Herbison, a former National Insurance Minister, a life peer in the Dissolution List. I begged him not to try. I may not have known her for as long as Wilson but I knew her better. She was a Scottish socialist of rigid principle and purity and I told the Prime Minister she would reject it, probably with contempt. 'She'll accept it, don't worry,' said Wilson, confidently. She didn't. Wilson asked me to suggest an alternative Scot and I proposed Jimmy Hoy, the retiring MP for Leith. Wilson picked up the phone and called Hoy there and then. He accepted as quickly as Peggy Herbison had refused and spent the last years of his life happily and usefully in the Lords.

In the months before the election, I had been constantly pressed, by telephone and letter, by a former Labour MP to recommend him for a peerage. He was loyal to the party and loyal to Wilson and regularly wrote letters to *The Times* and other newspapers in defence of the government's record. Sadly, he had no chance. When I first mentioned his name to the Prime Minister, Wilson sharply replied that the man was a homosexual, and that was the end of it. Wilson's attitude to homosexuals was curious. He was not homophobic; he just didn't like them. But, basically, he was prepared to tolerate them provided they kept to the practice of 'consenting adults in private' so that their sexual preferences were not publicly known. For a long time he had resisted the Queen's wish to bestow a knighthood upon Noel Coward partly for that reason and partly because the playwright had transferred his domicile abroad in order to escape British taxation, which Wilson famously described as 'taking the Coward's way out'. And it was with great reluctance that, many years later, he gave in to Michael Foot's plea that Tom Driberg, a notoriously promiscuous homosexual and snob whom Wilson deeply despised, should be given a peerage. Although Wilson's last government had at least two homosexuals in it, they would have been instantly dismissed had their private life become public.

It was during the run-up to this 1970 election that I was approached byIan Waller, the *Sunday Telegraph*'s lobby correspondent on behalf of Captain Henry Kerby, a right-wing Tory MP anxious for a title, and clearly not as scrupulous as Miss Herbison. I detailed this episode in *The Politics of Power* and I won't repeat all of it here, but Kerby, who hated most of his fellow Tories, offered to pass Conservative secrets to me in return for a peerage. Later, when I didn't respond, he reduced his ambitions to a knighthood, but Wilson was not to be tempted; nevertheless, Kerby sent to me daily at my home (in envelopes addressed to my wife in her maiden name) everything he received from his party's Central Office. Eventually, he died, without gaining the Honour for which he craved, either from his own party or ours.

By now, I had begun to believe what a former Labour Chief Whip, Bert Bowden, had told me: that in a drawer in his desk he had a list of five hundred names of people – mainly Labour supporters, but including others ready to become so – who were willing to make the supreme sacrifice and accept a peerage for the sake of the party.

Moving out of No. 10 on the Friday after polling day was as grim as everyone said it would be. Wilson arrived back from his constituency of Huyton soon after 7 a.m., having been driven down through the night. I was waiting for him in the front hall. 'Well, Joe,' he said, 'you were always the one who had doubts. Come upstairs, I want to talk to you.' To my amazement, he then showed me the chapter headings of a book on his 1964–70 government which he had drafted in the car on his way back to London and his predicted political oblivion. While we talked – and while someone else ate the breakfast for which I had been longing – he sketched out the immediate future. It was one of those moments when he was at his best. First, he said, there was nothing Labour could do over the next few months. Heath had won with a secure majority; he would make mistakes but mistakes in the early months didn't matter. The people who had voted for him would forgive him – at first. We would have to wait until the turn of the year before we could start competing for the voters' attention again. What he intended to do in the meantime was to write his record of his six years in office, which, he said, would be a handbook for every Labour canvasser when the next general election came along (a claim not to be taken literally; the book weighed 31b 2oz) and the money it would bring would help finance the office. Sir George Weidenfeld's firm would publish it and (Lord) Arnold Goodman would arrange its serialisation. He wanted me to write it from his dictated details of events. On the previous Friday evening, I had told him that I wanted to return to journalism after nearly eighteen months with him but he had asked me to fulfil my original promise to stay two years. Now he repeated his request. Thinking there was little else I would be doing for the next six months – my old newspaper, the *Sun*, had by then been sold to Rupert Murdoch and only its title retained – I agreed.

Unfortunately, things then began to go seriously wrong between Marcia and me. At the moment of defeat, she had been superb. She was calm and controlled and lost her temper only with Joe Kagan for not providing removal vans at the moment she asked for them. She was swift and efficient, and brutally brushed aside a feeble attempt by Ted Heath's assistants to retain their offices in the House of Commons until the following Monday by demanding their immediate evacuation. This would have succeeded, but for two Ministry of Works porters, both black, who were so put out by Labour's defeat that they refused to lift a finger to help remove equipment from the Tory offices. Their emotions and support were commendable but mistaken; we had nowhere else to go.

Three
Opposition

Wilson departed from No. 10 on Friday 19 June 1970, with the boos of the crowd outside ringing in his ears and went off to the ex-Prime Minister's traditional last weekend at Chequers – a visit I, in his place, would have found unbearable, but he loved the old house – and Marcia started to search for a home for him, his old semi-detached in Hampstead Garden Suburb having been sold years before. Apart from anything else, Wilson was nearly broke, leaving office £14,000 – a lot of money in 1970 – less well-off than when he entered it. A temporary house was found for him in Vincent Square, near to the Commons, for eighty guineas a week – which was also a lot of money in 1970 – but before taking up residence, he stayed in a penthouse flat in Arlington House, Westminster, above the fashionable Le Caprice restaurant and owned by a wealthy industrialist of whom, before that time: I had never heard Colonel Desmond Brayley. I was to hear a great deal about him later, especially after Scotland Yard's Fraud Squad displayed an interest in his activities.

An announcement by Wilson that he was going to resume driving his own car was met with consternation by Marcia, who remembered that she had no confidence in his ability behind a wheel when he was driving seven days a week. He hadn't now driven for more than six years and she declared that she would never go in a car driven by him. This problem was, fortunately, solved when an irate Bob Mellish, the Chief Whip, saw his leader, who had been

Prime Minister only a short time earlier, standing in a taxi queue outside Westminster Hall. He immediately went to the Tory Chief Whip, William Whitelaw, and asked that the government should provide Wilson with a car and chauffeur. Whitelaw agreed, obtained Ted Heath's consent, and Wilson was able to settle down again to be a back-seat driver. He asked that he should have his No. 10 driver, Bill Housden, assigned to him, and he was.

But the real shock of losing office was symbolised for me on Wilson's first day back at Westminster as Leader of the Opposition. He told me he was going to call a meeting of his old Cabinet, which would stand in until a Shadow Cabinet was elected. 'Have you got their phone numbers?' he asked. The only numbers I had were of those Cabinet members I sometimes telephoned when I was a Lobby correspondent; I didn't have all of them. With the Downing Street switchboard available, Wilson hadn't had to dial a phone number since 1964. With some help from the Parliamentary Labour party office, we compiled a list and he set about calling each of them.

Trouble in the office began as we started to bed down. There had been minor incidents in the months before which ought to have alerted me more readily to the problem of Marcia, but I was slow to understand their relevance. Until the election was lost, we had never had a cross word. I saw her on one occasion nearly blast into oblivion a poor private secretary, the one charged with keeping the Prime Minister's diary, who had had the temerity to insert an official engagement in place of one already inserted by Marcia. Frankly, I thought he deserved it. In Opposition, however, when we worked so much more closely together, the problem rapidly grew, though open rows between us were few and far between. Indeed, in the hardback edition of her book, *Inside No. 10*, published in 1972, Marcia often commented favourably upon me, though all such praise was rigorously excluded from the paperback version.

The first sign of an unhappy ship came the week after we left Downing Street, when Marcia entered the new Leader of the Opposition's office and quietly began to weep. With impressive dignity, she announced that she was leaving her post after sacrificing any hope of personal happiness by her years of devoted work for Harold Wilson. She was underpaid, she said, at £30 a week (Wilson told me she was getting £80 – neither was telling the truth) The time had come, she went on, to put her family first. At that time, I didn't realise that when she said 'family' she was talking about more than her mother, brother and sister.

As I have recorded elsewhere (*Politics of Power*, 1977) she then rose and said: 'I am now going to the country to start a new life.' Still weeping, she left the office and I, dismayed, asked Wilson what we were to do. 'Pay no attention,' he said, cheerfully, 'I've seen it all a hundred times before. She will be in on Monday as though nothing's happened.' That's exactly what did happen. Resignation was never mentioned by her again, but she did say she intended in future to confine her work to being Wilson's private secretary and asked me to take on the post of office manager.

There was little else to do at that moment – no journalists were ringing seeking our views on anything and I hadn't started on his book – so I agreed. I immediately started to plan the reorganisation (or, more strictly, the organisation, for there was none) of the office. We had nine secretaries, far too many for Opposition and hopelessly beyond the ability of either Wilson or the party to pay for them. But my 'appointment' was part of the fantasy land which I had now begun to inhabit. The next morning I found that Marcia had pasted up a rota of the girls' hours and had laid down precisely what their duties would be, even forbidding them to make tea or coffee in the room in which they worked. That was silly for a start: the nearest cafeteria was more than two hundred yards away; so making tea in the office made sense. Her secretary made tea in her office, but that was another matter: some secretaries were more equal than others. I realised I was no longer office manager, if I ever had been and I was beginning to learn that nothing was for five minutes, let alone for ever.

A few weeks later came the afternoon tea and cake incident, trivial in itself but with far-reaching consequences. To me, it was an irresistible reminder of the evidence about the missing strawberries given to the court martial which destroyed the neurotic Captain Queeg of the *USS Caine*.

One of the secretaries who couldn't stand Marcia's overbearing ways any longer had decided to leave. She bought a cake and defiantly made tea in the office for a small party to which I was invited. Naturally, being the reason for the girl's departure, Marcia wasn't among the guests. The secretary also wanted to say goodbye to Wilson but wasn't prepared to ask Marcia to arrange it. I told her I would take her down to his office so that she could bid him farewell. I did, and he was generous in his thanks to the girl for her services. Marcia's spy in the office promptly told her what I had done. She went berserk, stormed into Wilson's office, denounced me to my face for being sly, crooked, devious, a cheat and a conspirator as well as disloyal – always a shrewd blow when Wilson was the listener – and, finally, of 'treating the girls as equals'. I told her she was absolutely right on the last point.

In any normal office that would have been the end of it. But not in ours. Wilson had just signed a contract with the *Sunday Times* for the serialisation of his book about the 1964–70 Government and I had signed a contract to assist in the writing of it, effectively to be the ghost-writer. (For that, to digress I got £5,000, equal to the annual salary which Wilson had agreed to pay me and which absolved him from paying me at all. Further, he claimed that the three months' pay I received from the civil service in lieu of notice should be regarded as the first three months' pay as his spokesman in opposition, which meant that he didn't have to pay me a penny for the first fifteen months. Either the work I did on the book was for free or the work I did as his press secretary cost him nothing over that period. Lady Falkender's claim in her memoirs that Wilson had annually to undergo fortnightly lecture tours in order to raise enough money to pay my salary and 'other expenses' was heart-rending but totally untrue; my expenses claimed for three-and-a- half years in opposition amounted to £10 and I paid my own telephone and newspaper bills. What's more, when my pay did start to come from office funds, the source of it wasn't a lecture tour.)

Marcia concluded her tirade about the tea and cakes by shouting: 'If you think you are going to write that book, you are mistaken. It's not going to be in your style.'

Had it been in my style, it might have been more readable, even though I say so myself. It would certainly have been a lot shorter. Inevitably, Wilson was to tell me soon afterwards that he (!) had decided that, instead of dictating the book into a tape recorder, he would write it himself, in order to complete it more quickly. This was despite the fact that, as he knew, I had already written much of the first chapter and that I could type much faster than he could write in long hand. In the event, he wrote nearly half a million words, most of it by hand, over the next five months. One Monday morning, he boasted to me that he had completed twelve thousand words the previous day without rising from his desk. Any professional writer would agree that was the path to physical and mental exhaustion, as well as to a poor book, and so it proved.

The speed was illusory, anyway; it took me several months to amend, correct and improve what he had written, not least by cutting out 50,000 words of the speeches he wished to reproduce. This all had to be done secretly, my copies of the amended proofs being handed over privately to Wilson so that he could take them home for approval or not.

Fortunately, the printers were based only a few hundred yards from my home and the proofs were collected by me without their having to go to the office first. I made the changes and Wilson accepted virtually all of them. They didn't make a good book better; they merely made a bad book less unreadable. Marcia, meanwhile, returned her copies of the proofs with 'Rubbish' or 'Nonsense' scrawled across them but never with a sensible suggestion about how any sentence might be reconstructed and improved.

If that wasn't enough to fret about, another of the women to whom Wilson was tirelessly loyal, Barbara Castle, came into his office one afternoon during that summer of 1970 and announced she was going to oppose Roy Jenkins for the deputy leadership of the parliamentary party vacated by George Brown. Wilson snapped: 'No, you are not,' and they rowed about it in front of me.

Finally, Wilson said: 'If you stand against Roy, I'm going to resign.' 'I'm sorry,' said Barbara, in the best John Wayne style, 'you do what you've got to do, but I'm going to do what I've got to do.' 'You won't get ten votes,' said Wilson brutally. She didn't stand and Jenkins became deputy leader. Devotees of alternative histories might ponder what the consequences might have been if she had stood and won.

Wilson wanted Roy Jenkins to know that Marcia had had two children in 1968 and 1969 but, for some reason I didn't fathom, didn't want to tell his deputy himself. He therefore first broke the news to me – it would be trite to say I was astonished, as well as the understatement of the decade – and asked me to tell John (later Lord) Harris, former Director of Publicity for the Labour party, Jenkins's closest aide and confidant, and friend of both Marcia and Walter Terry. Wilson's theory was that if I told Harris in confidence he was bound to tell Jenkins. I told him in confidence – he was stunned, too – but also said he could mention it to Jenkins. It wasn't a matter to play games about or to take chances.

Wilson toiled away at Vincent Square while Ted Heath enjoyed the only honeymoon of his life, and that with the electorate. The only light moment of that dismal summer was when a young lady arrived at Wilson's temporary home and told Mary Wilson that she was her husband's daughter. When Mary told him of the visit, Wilson looked startled. 'What did you do?' he asked her. 'I said I didn't believe her and sent her away,' his wife replied.

'That was very trusting of you,' said Wilson. 'She was black,' said Mary.

Four
By the Left

Dissident factions, partly anti-leadership and wholly anti-policy, immediately sprang up in the parliamentary Labour party and in the party in the country after that summer defeat, and gathered strength during the run-up to, and at, the party conference that autumn. There was, as ever, some talk in the parliamentary party of replacing Wilson, but it was less convincing than it had been in government with no rival thrusting to assume the mantle of opposition leader. Leading a government is exciting; leading an opposition party is boring. The right talked a good fight but no more and the left shirked one because it knew that any replacement for Wilson would be worse. The parties in the constituencies, on the whole, trusted him; they were for keeping him as leader while hoping he might change some of his policies. He was always more popular outside Westminster than within it. But the first stirrings of what was to become the disastrous 1980s for Labour were beginning to be felt and a new disrespect and distaste for the leadership collectively was developing, adding to the unending irritations of the awkward squad who were always against anyone who didn't share their view that Trotsky was the right-hand man of their secular god. The ultimate aim of this element in the Labour party was to achieve power in the party rather than power in government. It preferred to be against rather than for. The parties of the left are a magnet for one-issue zealots and extremists who believe that the world's ills can be cured by protest; acceptance of their existence is part of the task of being a Labour leader. The party began life as a working-class protest movement against endemic poverty, unemployment, bad housing, callous employers and intolerable working conditions in the mines, docks and factories and cotton mills of the Industrial Revolution. It was the creature of the trade unions, formed for a trade union purpose, and in-so-far as it had notions of governmental power in its early days it was trade union syndicalism which appealed, if only briefly, to many of them. The party's constitution was written by the Webbs on the assumption that Labour would remain an opposition party, the smallest of the three main parties in the Commons. (And even smaller in the Lords, where Labour representation was negligible). As the party grew in size, it became a bolthole for protesters, a refuge for those who were against the government – any government – and never wanting to hold the reins of government. Its fiercest consciences were to form the Independent Labour party, which between the wars held power in some local authorities, such as Bermondsey where I was born, and which returned the turbulent 'Red Clydeside' MPs, led by Jimmy Maxton, to frighten middle class England. Even after the Second World War, the ILP was still a force, if a small one, in the Commons and rather more so in the sentimental memories of that era's Old Labour. The movement which grew within the Labour party during the 1960s bore a superficial resemblance to the old ILP, but it lacked its honesty, its personalities and its true idealism. Much of it was a Little England, anti-American creed, especially among those who clung to the belief, against compelling evidence to the contrary, that Stalin's and Kruschev's Soviet Union was a society which set an example for the capitalist world to follow. Clement Attlee had to deal with his out-and-out Soviet admirers in the parliamentary party and did so by expelling several of them. Wilson, who had been to the Soviet Union more than any other Labour leader, had no illusions about the regime there and kept the more supine of his fellow-travellers out of his Government. But the war in Vietnam brought disparate groups to coalesce behind a passionate belief in a rag-bag of policies too incoherent and contradictory to be called a programme, but some of which, or only one of which, were likely to touch a chord somewhere in the hearts of most Labour members. They were anti-NATO, sympathetic towards China, admirers of the Soviet Union, adamant against capitalism – though often themselves living in houses grander than communism provided for those other than its leaders – and, first and foremost, anti-American. I suspect the antagonism towards the USA had as much to do with envy as ideology. They wanted Wilson to denounce the United States and its President for its 'aggression' in South-east Asia, whatever the consequences for the British economy, which might have been dire. They wanted him to stop trying to become part of Europe and to nationalise twenty-five major companies, or two-hundred-and-fifty if that figure seemed more agreeable to their like-minded audiences. They took Aneurin Bevan's striking phrase about 'the commanding heights of the economy' and turned it into a cliché for wholesale nationalisation of almost everything larger than a corner shop, by policies which Bevan himself would have been the first to wither with scorn. They demanded restraint on – or even the complete freezing of – prices, while promoting free collective bargaining for wages, which Wilson was more accurately later to describe as free collective suicide, all backed by euphemistic threats of solidarity action – i.e. strikes. Today, it seems hard to credit the sway such lunacies had over so many party members after the defeat in 1970, but I well remember attending a party meeting during the 1974–76 Government at which a resolution demanding the freezing of all prices at 1970 levels received much sympathy, until I moved the insertion of the words 'and wages'. Later, I chaired a meeting of my local constituency party discussing a resolution to be submitted to the annual conference. The influence of the Militant Tendency was at its height and the resolution was of such inspired insanity as to frighten a party led by Enver Hocha. When a tediously long debate ended, I called for a vote with the words: 'All those in favour of destroying the Labour party.' A forest of hands shot up and I promptly resigned, telling them that I never wanted to sit round the same table with them again. The hard-left cherished the thought of a Fortress Britain, in a world whose boundaries ended at Dover, where scheming never rose above the next resolution for the next meeting of the general management committee, and whose tactics were to harass or shout down any with the temerity to oppose them. They wanted a perennial political Dunkirk, because in their minds Dunkirk was a victory, if only because it got us out of Europe.

Government can be irksome, even unnerving, at times; it means facing up to responsibilities; having to take decisions; having to disappoint; having to choose between what is practical and what is principled; having to be unpopular, even having to tell loonies that they were deserving candidates for removal by men in white coats. But inside the party then, the fact that choices had to be made in the real world was unwanted and unnecessary, not even recognised. Like only spoke to like and thus agreed with like. I remember Tony Benn in the 1980s predicting a great Labour victory at the Crosby by-election because he had received a tremendous reception at a mass meeting in nearby Liverpool. The truth was, however, that a large part of his audience had been effectively bussed in from other parts of Lancashire and didn't have a vote in Crosby. Shirley Williams, Benn's former Cabinet colleague, stood for the new SDP and had the storming success Benn had expected for Labour.

Wilson, both as Prime Minister and as opposition leader managed to keep control of his left-wing, but it wasn't easy and it formed a large part of the stress which is normal for Prime Ministers. Once he had gone, Jim Callaghan was sabotaged by the rising tide of militancy and the Militant Tendency, the most successful of the Trotskyist movements which sought to infiltrate the party. Callaghan had neither Wilson's skill nor experience in out-manoeuvring the left and his leadership saw Militant moving inexorably towards the high tide of its success. But even in Wilson's time, no one ever answered awkward questions like David Owen's: if one member one vote was right for South Africans, why wasn't it right for the Labour party?

The trade union block vote at party conferences never did represent the number of trade unionists who paid the political levy but instead the number which union leaders decided best suited their own ambitions for power.

Absurdly, they bought their votes by increasing their levy payments, in some cases above the total number of members they had and far more than those who paid the political levy, the supposed basis for deciding the size of the vote. Constituency parties, though much less powerful, were no more accurately represented because each was judged to have a minimum thousand members and voted that number accordingly. That would have given Labour over six-hundred-and-thirty-thousand members, or about three times its real strength, and fifty per cent more than Tony Blair was able to achieve at the height of his popularity. The fact was that many local parties didn't have enough members to fill a mini-bus. After the 1966 election victory, the National Executive of the Labour party grew ambitious beyond its station and its capabilities. MPs whose quality – or, in Tom Driberg's case, patriotism also – was too low for them to be considered for even a junior ministerial post, won positions on the NEC which gave them the illusion of power. No one paid much heed, say, to Driberg, Frank Allaun, Renee Short or even Ian Mikardo when they made speeches in the Commons. Indeed, the sight of one of them rising to speak was the signal for a mass exodus to the tea-room, but as members of the Executive, they had power in the land – even if it were only Never-Never Land. As a result, two policies began to emerge which, if adopted, would have put Labour out of power for ever, not just the 18 years of Mrs Thatcher and John Major: the wholesale nationalisation of the twenty-five major companies (in Tony Crosland's wounding words, so that Marks and Spencer's could be brought up to the level of the Co-op) and abandonment of attempts to enter Europe. Wilson could and did deal with the first. His attitude was that the NEC and the party conference could advise on policy but not decide it. He would listen to them, but listening was all he ever promised, and then with only half an ear. A man whose career in opposition began on the left was so outflanked by the new left that he took on the aura of a right-winger. In that role, he rejected everything he didn't agree with, whatever the party conference or the NEC might have decided.

However much the left huffed and puffed, Wilson had one threat before which they always blanched. If they pushed him too hard, he would resign and whoever succeeded him would be of the genuine right, whether it was Jim Callaghan, Roy Jenkins, Tony Crosland or Denis Healey, the Four Horsemen of the Apocalypse so far as the left was concerned. It was a card he used sparingly, but he used it more than once. As he said brutally to one of his old friends on the left: 'You've nowhere else to go but me.'

Wilson was the left's candidate for the leadership in 1963. Only Fred Lee (irreverently known as 'Flea') of Hugh Gaitskell's Shadow Cabinet voted for him in the leadership election. The left's disillusion set in after the seamen's strike, starting six weeks after the landslide election victory of March 1966, caused a State of Emergency and wrecked the economy. Wilson famously denounced the strike leaders as 'this tightly-knit group of politically-motivated men,' declaring that he had 'a good reason' for saying it. The 'good reason' came from the fact that he had ordered that secret meetings of the strike committee held in a North London flat should be bugged by the security services. The transcripts of this eavesdropping convinced him he was facing a political strike, not an industrial one. As he wrote later: 'The moderate members of the seamen's executive were virtually terrorised by a small, professional group of Communists or near-Communists who planned their tactics with outside help. From various sources we began to receive undeniable evidence of what was going on.' Those sources were the security services.

The strike led to the contempt which Wilson ever afterwards had for the then opposition leader, Edward Heath. He saw the Tory leader privately, together with MI5 officers, and gave him the facts as he had them. But Heath then attacked Wilson in the Commons for not giving the public enough information. Wilson complained after that Heath 'exploited my weakness' – the fact that he couldn't publicly disclose his sources.

The left was always high on spite, and its hard-core never forgave Wilson for his handling of that strike. Opposing him became a matter of left-wing and union ideology. Year after year at the party conferences, Wilson was defeated on one major issue or another. He coped by ignoring the votes. And although he had promised, on becoming Prime Minister, that no Member of Parliament would have his or her telephone bugged, he continued the bugging and surveillance of others. I was with him in his study at No. 10 when Jim Callaghan reported that Alex Kitson, the Transport and General Workers' Union representative on the NEC, had been followed by the security services after leaving Transport House at the end of an NEC meeting. Kitson had gone straight to the headquarters of the British Communist party at King Street, near Charing Cross station, London. The inference drawn was that he had passed on details of the proceedings to the CP, though seeing that the NEC was never trusted with matters which were secret and that, anyway, the proceedings were always leaked in full to journalists by one or other members, it hardly seemed worthwhile Kitson telling King Street. I'm surprised they didn't meet somewhere else. The CP's headquarters had been bugged since 1947, on the orders of the Attlee government and they knew it. One of the minor embarrassments I had to deal with came in 1969 when workmen rebuilding the King Street offices found the original listening device planted behind the panelling. By 1969, however, surveillance was much more sophisticated and less detectable.

Wilson's attitude to the security services was ambivalent. He used them, but he didn't trust them (and, as Peter Wright's book of memoirs, *Spycatcher*, made clear, some of the crazier members of the security services didn't trust him, either). When he came back into office in 1974, he was presented with a report from MI5 saying that Mrs Judith Hart, who he was about to appoint to his Cabinet, was secretly in touch with the British Communist party. MI5 had listened in to her telephone conversations with Bert Ramelson, industrial organiser of the CP and one of its most prominent and hard-line leaders. These calls had taken place during the last months of the Heath government. The ban on tapping the telephones of MPs related only to their own instruments, not to the telephones of those whom they might be calling. Wilson told Mrs Hart that he could not, in the circumstances, include her in his administration. She was furious and protested her innocence so vigorously that Wilson asked to see copies of the transcripts of the calls. Once he had read them, he rejected MI5's accusations. The calls Mrs Hart had made to Ramelson were in pursuit of a task given to her by the National Executive (of which Wilson was a member) to monitor events in Chile where the Marxist president, Salvador Allende, had been murdered in a right-wing coup. Like it or not, outside of the British Government, the Communist party was the best-informed about events in Chile and Mrs Hart had sensibly kept in touch through Ramelson. A curious story grew up after this episode that Judith Hart had been confused with a Mrs Tudor Hart (no relation) who was treated with suspicion by MI5, but, in fact, it was Judith Hart who was targeted.

Mrs Hart was at least as loyal as any other left-wing member of the Wilson government, though he had to discipline her later in 1974 when she and two other ministers, Joan Lestor and Tony Benn, all voted for an NEC resolution criticising government policy over the Simonstown naval base in South Africa. That was yet another example of playing to the party gallery by dissociating from the government of which they were part and whose ministerial salaries they drew. Wilson was at his most astute with them: previous slaps on the wrist for breaking ranks had been largely ignored by rebellious ministers. This time, Wilson asked each of the three to give him an unqualified assurance that they accepted the principle of collective government responsibility, adding; 'I should have to regard your failure to give me such an assurance, or any subsequent breach of it, as a decision on your part that you did not wish to continue as a member of this administration. I should, of course, much regret such a decision, but I shall accept it.' The assurances were given and the rebels conformed thereafter.

Europe was, for the last ten years of Wilson's leadership, a running sore in the party, a fate he shared with every Labour and Conservative leader during and after his tenure of office.

Wilson himself, in his book *Final Term* – a curiously forgetful record of his last government – said of his struggles over Europe: 'In all my thirteen years as Leader of the party, I had no more difficult task than keeping the party together on this issue.' That part was certainly the truth. Europe cut across the boundaries of left and right yet united them about his leadership: both anti and pro-marketers distrusted him, but didn't want him to go. Even two of the left's most prominent flag-wavers, Eric Heffer and Tony Benn, had once been in favour of Britain in Europe, though when the trumpet of dissent sounded the retreat from Continental entanglements they retreated. Throughout the years of opposition (1970–4) Wilson contained the left by hinting that they might get what he had no intention of giving them, which was a pledge to withdraw from the EEC. But the right was more difficult because it preferred to believe those hints rather than the assurances he gave to them. For example, he privately assured Harold Lever, a passionate advocate of European entry, that whatever he might have to say and do in order to keep the party together, he would, in the end, do 'the right thing' on Europe. Lever believed him for a long time before he, wrongly, lost faith. He accompanied Wilson – though many of his pro-European friends didn't – in a Commons vote that was basically anti-European but excused himself by telling journalists afterwards that he had vomited in the lobbies. Asked to comment, I responded by saying, off the record, that he must have been the original sick man of Europe, a remark which was promptly reported back to him. Lever laughed uproariously, unlike Roy Hattersley who, when I told a journalist that the MP was part of the 'Reform Club mafia' constantly critical of Wilson's leadership, went to Wilson to complain. Wilson told him to get a sense of humour. Press secretaries had their problems with egos in my day, too.

But while the right had been poised more than once to topple Wilson in government, in opposition it hesitated. It was the left which, first in opposition then in government, sought to organise what could have been the most devastating coups against Wilson's leadership, naively believing that they could cage him while keeping him as leader. They clearly had never heard of the young lady of Riga who went for a ride on a tiger. He defeated the first attempt – at the party conference in October 1973 – to overthrow his long-term policy of staying within the EEC by his usual process of out-manoeuvring his opponents. The TUC, not for the first time, had thrown a spanner in the works a month earlier, by carrying a resolution at its annual Congress committing the trade union movement to withdrawing from Europe. (It had also carried a resolution committing Britain to stay in Europe. There was no image the unions hated more than that of Mr Facing Both Ways, and none which they deserved more.)

The unions' clumsy intervention encouraged the anti-marketeers on the Labour National Executive. When it met on the Friday before the annual conference, Wilson totted up the votes and found a majority in favour of pulling out. I thought he was too pessimistic, but there was undoubtedly a crisis. 'You had better go and see your girl friends,' said Wilson to me, 'and tell them that I'm going to resign if I lose this vote.' Any woman MP whom I admitted to knowing, Wilson invariably described as my 'girl friend.' In this case, he meant Judith Hart and Joan Lestor, both of whom I had known before they became MPs. I wandered around the conference hotel until I saw Judith Hart having a drink and I joined her. 'You look down,' said Judith. 'Harold's going to resign,' I said. She was shocked and asked why. I explained that the resignation was conditional: he would go only if he lost the Common Market vote, which he thought was likely. After making sure Judith had panicked, I left her and went in search of Joan Lestor, found her and repeated the ploy. Joan didn't panic. She was resentful. So far as she was concerned, Harold was blackmailing the left in order to get the vote he wanted. I didn't disagree, but nevertheless insisted that if his bluff was called he would go. Wilson was to describe that time as 'a weekend of button-holing, cajoling and fierce argument.' Judith had previously supported Wilson's stance but he feared she might backslide. She didn't. Joan Lestor changed her vote and so did Barbara Castle, whom Wilson saw but didn't describe as his girl friend and the anti - marketeers were defeated by fourteen votes to eleven. It was another 'damned close-run thing'.

But the row and the plotting were not over. The next attempt to overthrow the policy of staying in Europe was even more serious because by then Labour was in government again and it came after completion of the renegotiations of Britain's terms of entry into the EEC. On Saturday 26 April 1975, six weeks before polling day in the referendum on Britain's continued membership, Labour held a special conference at the Sobell Centre in Islington, London. The conference voted overwhelmingly – 3,274,000 to 1,986,000 – against staying in the EEC. That decision didn't particularly worry Wilson; he had ignored conference decisions before and he afterwards dismissed the conference as a non-event, forgotten by the following week. But that was the judgment of hindsight. It wasn't the truth at the time.

Before the conference broke up, Mrs Mary Wilson, sitting behind and above the platform, saw what she thought was a round robin being circulated among some members of the National Executive. That night, we were leaving for a ten-day Commonwealth conference in Jamaica. It was obvious that while the cat was away, the mice were planning to have a ball. Wilson soon found out what was afoot. At the instigation of Ian Mikardo, a silver-haired, black-browed, pot-bellied conspirator of the old (Tammany Hall) school, with a serpentine mind, a shuffling gait and clothes which looked scruffy even when new, the NEC was to be asked at an emergency meeting the following Thursday, halfway through the Commonwealth conference, to commit the party officially to all-out support for a No vote in the referendum. We were virtually on the way to the airport before discovering what Mikardo and the other plotters were up to. Wilson scorched the telephone line from Jamaica in an attempt to prevent such a vote. Had it been carried, Wilson would have found it difficult, if not impossible, to stay as party leader. There is a limit to the extent which any party leader can defy his party when it is against him.

We arrived at Kingston, Jamaica, on the Sunday after the Sobell Centre conference. Wilson spent much of the first two days there trying to thwart Mikardo. When he and Jim Callaghan and the rest of the UK delegation went to a reception given by the Queen on the royal yacht *Britannia*, I was left behind to man the phones to London and to keep talking to Ron Hayward, the party's General Secretary, about how to stop Mikardo. Hayward, however, was another committed anti-marketeer and I wasn't sure which hand he was playing. In the end, it was Wilson who devised the killing blow. When persuasion failed, he phoned the Israeli ambassador in London, reminded him of all that he had done and was doing for the Israeli cause (including, at that time, negotiating the emigration from the Soviet Union of two Jewish ballet stars, the Panovs), and asked him to tell Mikardo to stop his mischief.

Shortly before the NEC meeting was due, on the Thursday, Mikardo withdrew his resolution. That is why Wilson could later say it was a non-event; Mikardo, MP for the heavily-Jewish constituency of Tower Hamlets, Bethnal Green and Bow, and whose devotion to Israel was absolute, had listened to the Israeli ambassador after turning a deaf ear to his own Prime Minister. What his furtive allies thought of the withdrawal of the motion, we never heard. Perhaps Mikardo never told them of the reason why. In any case, no one was going to admit what had been afoot. But the counter-manoeuvre was typically Wilsonian: he always had one more club in his golf bag than his opponents knew. He was mockingly grateful, too, to his wife, Mary, to Marcia and to me for the parts we played in overcoming Mikardo's shabby conspiracy while he was out of the country – because we were all, each of us, privately anti-marketeers.

Less successful was his attempt while in Jamaica publicly to put down Tony Benn without leaving his fingerprints on the story. Wilson had spent too much of his time squashing 'initiatives' from Benn in his role as Industry Minister and had decided to move him to the Department of Energy. But first, he wanted to test the water by floating a story (the one and only time in his life, he was to write virtuously later, that he ever did such a thing) that Benn was to change ministries. He asked me to fix a meeting with Harry (later Sir Harry) Boyne, a former colleague of mine on the *Glasgow Herald* and then the political editor of the *Daily Telegraph*. Wilson made it a condition of giving Boyne the story that it should appear to be sourced at Westminster,

London, not Kingston, Jamaica, and with a *Telegraph* by-line reading: 'By our Political Staff', the customary credit given to Boyne's deputy, David Harris. I told Wilson the scheme would never work: Boyne's writing style was too distinctive and Harris, a truthful man, would never be able convincingly to claim the story was his. But Wilson was fascinated by his ingenuity and insisted on going ahead. Sure enough, when the story appeared in London, every political journalist knew at once that Boyne in Jamaica had written it and who his source must have been. I don't doubt Tony Benn knew it, too.

The departure of Benn from Industry to Energy was scheduled for when the Common Market referendum was safely out of the way. When it happened, Benn didn't see that he was being treated kindly. He always believed in the ulterior motive. I doubt if it ever occurred to him that he was not up to, or not right for, the job he had been doing. But instead of standing firm on his own behalf, he decided to fight against Wilson – by his own decision, what MI5 had wanted him to do a year earlier – dropping Judith Hart, the Minister for Overseas Development, from the Cabinet. Benn enlisted Michael Foot and Barbara Castle in support of her. This led to the ugliest-ever confrontation between Wilson and his long-time friends on the left. Bernard Donoughue and I stood for nearly an hour with our ears close to the door of Wilson's room at the Commons, listening to Castle and Foot berating the Prime Minister. 'Judith's blood is all over the floor,' bawled Foot at one point. The implied threat, never made explicit, was that if Mrs Hart were dropped then Foot, Castle and Benn would resign. But in the end they backed down – it is rare, in British history, for one minister to sacrifice his political life for another's – and Mrs Hart refused the Ministry of Transport post, outside the Cabinet, which Wilson had offered her. The row over the reshuffle went on for days and there was a sub-plot when the Chief Whip, Bob Mellish, was offered the Transport job and refused it. He violently objected to being dropped from the Whips' Office and resigned. It was left to Lady Falkender and myself to smooth him down, while an official dinner and reception was taking place at Downing Street. Wilson had a quick word with him and wrote out a press notice in his own hand: 'After a discussion with the Prime Minister, the Chief Whip, Mr R.J. Mellish, has withdrawn his proposed resignation and will carry on.'

On the main changes, however, the Left had once again shot themselves in the feet. It had been Wilson's intention to sack the extreme right-winger and Education Secretary, Reg Prentice, from his government at the same time as he moved Benn slightly downwards. It needed doing and would have been a neat balancing act. Prentice, an east London MP, had the public face of a solid, dependable man. In reality, he was highly strung with a touch of hysteria, difficult to reason with, criticised the policies of other ministers and was not an effective one himself.

But there was talk of Roy Jenkins resigning if Prentice was sacked and Wilson said to me: 'I can't fight on two fronts at once', and kept Prentice in the Cabinet in Mrs Hart's old job. So the only effect of the Left's attempts to keep one they cherished from being demoted was to ensure that one they hated was saved. Prentice later left the Labour party and eventually became a minister in Mrs Thatcher's government, proving that Wilson's instincts about him were right.

When Wilson finally left office, the left discovered that the threat the more realistic of them had always feared was to be translated into fact. James Callaghan, whose left-leanings, such as they were, had disappeared decades before, was elected leader and, thus, Prime Minister. The fact that he seemed the best man for the job didn't make his coming easier to bear, especially as his first move was to end Barbara Castle's ministerial career for good. The left's ability to snatch disaster from the jaws of defeat was never more brightly illuminated, though they had to wait several more years before they could turn disaster into catastrophe by triumphantly organising the election of Michael Foot, the most unsuitable leader of the Labour party since George Lansbury, even if the most literate.

Five
The Irrevocable Split

A little over eighteen months after the election defeat came the worst of several appalling episodes in the Wilson–Williams saga. It was almost too dreadful to comprehend and it marked the beginning of a permanent split between us, Wilson's two closest assistants. The rift, so far as I was concerned, was irreparable, irrevocable and unforgivable. I worked with her when I had to and even tried, though not over-zealously, to restore civility to our relationship from time to time. I spent days and weeks defending her over the Wigan slag heaps affair in 1974, but I did it because the Prime Minister wanted me to and because I was trying to protect him from the fallout, not out of any regard for her or her family.

Greed, jealousy and uncontrolled rages had for some time been eating into her previously acute political perception. But what she did on 12 January 1972, demonstrated how startling that change was.

As in the case of so many of the explosions which originated in Marcia's home in Wyndham Mews, the cause was tiny and appeared to be innocuous. I first heard of it on the evening of that day. After leaving his Leader of the Opposition's office to visit his home in nearby Lord North Street, an agitated Wilson returned and asked to have a private word with me. He was strained and sounded embarrassed. Earlier in the day, in the late morning, I followed my usual practice of pinning a few sentences about Wilson's engagements for the day on to the Lobby correspondents' notice board in the corridor of the Commons Press Gallery. It contained a minor item for newspaper gossip columns: that Wilson had taken his wife to his favourite eating house, the L'Epicure restaurant in Old Compton Street, Soho, to celebrate her birthday. Like most routine announcements I put out, the news was hardly worth a mention. But the fact of it had consequences which were huge. Had the details of what followed been published either Marcia's career or Wilson's, or both, might not have survived.

For a man inured to Marcia's ways, Wilson had made an astonishing basic – though probably deliberate – mistake. He had failed to tell her that he was taking Mary to lunch. Only the unknowing and naive might have wondered why he needed to tell his secretary, anyway. But the fact was that if he moved a muscle in public without her prior approval and knowledge and being entered by her in his diary, a scene was likely to result. That included going anywhere with his wife. On this particular day, one of the secretaries who had seen my notice for the reporters – she was known to me, though not, unfortunately, to Wilson, to be Marcia's informant in the office – repaired Wilson's omission and phoned Marcia at Wyndham Mews from where, since December 1971, she habitually worked. Marcia was incandescent and promptly took her revenge. Wilson was not allowed to go to any public engagement unless she, The Keeper of The Diary, was consulted in advance. (Her efficiency in this was intermittent. One year, she entered the Labour conference in Wilson's diary for the week after it actually was. On another occasion, in opposition, she phoned the German ambassador to say Wilson was on his way to the embassy to fulfil a luncheon engagement. Ever courteous, the ambassador made room at his table, leaving the French ambassador to wonder why the Labour leader hadn't shown up at his).

The eruption which followed the L'Epicure celebration was on a different scale from any other. According to Wilson's description of it to me, when Mary returned to Lord North Street afterwards, Marcia phoned her and said: 'I want to see you.'

Incredibly, instead of telling Marcia to call upon her, Mary Wilson went to Marcia's home. Perhaps Marcia had said she couldn't leave her young children at home, a plea which Mary would have understood and accepted. When his wife arrived at Wyndham Mews, Wilson told me, she was abruptly informed by Marcia: 'I have only one thing to say to you. I went to bed with your husband six times in 1956 and it wasn't satisfactory.'

What Mary's reply, if any, was, Wilson didn't say. But her phone call was enough to send him flying over to Lord North Street to hear her story, which he then repeated to me.

From the start, Wilson denied the allegation to his wife and to me, though he must have telephoned Marcia in between the two denials, because he was later to tell me the action, such as it was, he had taken in retaliation. At the time, I found his rejection of Marcia's story convincing. It had force and apparent sincerity. He said that Mary believed him rather than Marcia and, on the whole, so did I. Looking back over the years, however, his final words to me that evening seem today to be more significant than they did at the time. Like the legendary newspaper proprietor who, told by his editor that the world was on fire, said: 'Put something cheerful on the front page', Wilson was always an optimist. At the end of our conversation he said, his face brightening: 'Well, she has dropped her atomic bomb at last. She can't hurt me any more.'

It was a remark I later thought about and tried to give an alternative sense to the obvious. Atomic bombs are not like high explosives, one big bang, that's it, and if you're still alive you stay alive. He knew that it wasn't just the explosion which mattered; if the scene became public, it would be the fall-out which would do the damage. Had the allegation at any time appeared in print, or even been gossiped about in the bars of the Palace of Westminster, and, even more, if Wilson's bizarre 'punishment' of Marcia for her outburst had become known, his career might have ended there and then. In those post-Profumo, pre-Clinton days, press, public and party opinions were less tolerant and, almost certainly, he would never have been Prime Minister again.

There were a number of incidents, equally unbelievable and disproportionate to the supposed offence, over the years when I worked with both

Wilson and Marcia, but none so violent and cruel as the one of which he told me that evening, nor over such a trivial cause.

When I asked Wilson what he was going to do, he replied that he had already acted: he had banned her from coming into the office for six weeks. That, as he knew, was a totally inadequate, even laughable, response. As I pointed out to him, she had decided the previous month that she wasn't coming into the office, anyway. But it was no joking matter, nor one for me to score points. The offence should have led to her instant dismissal. Anything less tended to support those who said that she had a hold over him. After sacking her on the spot, he should have told her to do her damnedest; if she had done so, he should have accepted the consequences. I have never believed she would have done anything – she usually collapsed when her bluff was called – but if she had, the public might even have been sympathetic, though still denying him their votes.

The irony of this seminal incident was that for the next few weeks Wilson began to shine again in Parliament and even *The Times* said he was back to his old form. But it didn't last. She went; he advanced. She came back; he went back.

There was one other major distraction during those opposition years, a consequence of that behaviour which was largely hidden from me and others during the 1964 and 1966 governments. Wilson had a faithful principal private secretary, Michael Halls, who worked for him when he was President of the Board of Trade and a member of Clement Attlee's Cabinet. Halls was not an intellectual, but he was incredibly hardworking – indeed, too hard-working for his own good – and he was privy to the most of the turmoil and tantrums which peppered the Wilson and Marcia relationship.

Halls died suddenly in April 1970, and we attended his interment at a bleak south London cemetery, chilled to the marrow in a driving snowstorm. Wilson was deeply shocked by his loss. Halls's wife, Marjorie, was naturally grief-stricken, but she was in no doubt who was to blame and she eventually decided to apportion it publicly.

For those, and there were a number, who believe that the stories about Marcia Williams were coloured, exaggerated or even invented, Mrs Halls is a striking independent witness, showing that what I and others later experienced she and her husband had been burdened with long before I went to work at Downing Street.

In March 1973 Mrs Halls issued a writ against the Civil Service Department asking for damages of £50,000, an action which sent Marcia into a panic and a rage when she heard of it. She knew that it was directed against her, a fact which became clear in Mrs Halls's statement of claim, dated a year later. In it, Mrs Halls claimed under the Fatal Accidents Acts 1846-1959 'in respect of [the death of] her husband Arthur Norman [his given Christian names] Halls on 3rd day of April, 1970, such death having been occasioned by the negligence and/or breach of duty of the Defendants their servants or agents.'

She continued:

> Early in 1966, my husband was called to No. 10 Downing Street to be interviewed for the post of Principal Private Secretary to Mr Wilson. My husband did not want to take the job. Mr Wilson, however, persuaded him to do so . . .
>
> Mr Wilson wanted the office at No. 10 reorganised. After some very hard work, my husband achieved this and all was running smoothly until Mr Wilson, in 1968, told my husband and me that Mrs Williams, his Political Private Secretary, whose office was also in No. 10, was pregnant; from then on, her private circumstances impinged upon Mr Wilson and my husband. My husband and I were told by Mr Wilson to keep the matter secret. However, my husband informed the then head of the Civil Service, as was his duty on security grounds.
>
> Mr Wilson informed my husband and me, early in 1969, that he and the head of the Civil Service had decided that my husband would shortly take up a new appointment implementing the Fulton Report [on the future of the Civil Service].

Mr Wilson informed my husband and me in the spring of 1969 that Mrs Williams was again pregnant and that he was very worried. The dislocation caused thereby affected Mr Wilson and imposed considerable extra strain upon my husband.

Although my husband was exhausted by the circumstances prevailing, he was not relieved and the appointment he had been promised was given to someone else . . .

He was called upon continually to placate Mrs Williams in order that Mr Wilson could do his own work. My husband was, therefore, having to stay later and later every evening at the office and to work at the weekends to get his normal work done. The head of the Civil Service was kept aware of all these circumstances.

Messrs [Edward] Youde [Foreign Affairs private secretary] and [Roger] Dawes [a junior private secretary], vital members of my husband's team of four, were posted away in December 1969. [Youde was suffering from angina.] This greatly increased the burden upon my husband, who was almost dead on his feet with tiredness.

Mr Wilson visited Canada and USA in January 1970. He knew my husband was too tired to go but insisted he could not do without him.

Shortly after their return, Mrs Williams was arranging to move house. She embroiled Mr Wilson in every detail, such as getting the telephone and television installed. Again, Mr Wilson called my husband away from his proper work to deal with these domestic details in a highly explosive atmosphere.

In March, 1970, my husband took to his bed with influenza, but because of the pressure of work was away from the office for only two days.

On one occasion, Mrs Williams even telephoned me and threatened to cause Mr Wilson's downfall if my husband did not get her telephone put right.

At about the same time, my husband told me that he felt they would give him a heart attack.

My husband had already told the head of the Civil Service that he could not continue to carry the burden.

He was looking forward to the Easter holiday to get some rest. He said he must arrange a meeting between Mr Wilson and the head of the Civil Service prior to Easter to clear some important matters. This meeting took place on Maundy Thursday 26 March. When my husband came home that evening, he said that the stress and strain were quite intolerable. Mr Wilson and Mrs Williams had consumed so much of his time that he had not been able to complete his own work and that he would now have to go into the office over the holiday to do so. He told me that Mrs Williams and Mr Wilson were in the midst of a quarrel when he left. When we had gone to bed, Mr Wilson telephoned and said, 'She has gone off at last, screaming her bloody head off.'

The rest of her story was tragic. On 28 March, Michael Halls's doctor diagnosed fluid on the lungs and gave him medicine which he said might cause indigestion. On Easter Day, Michael worked at No. 10. The next day, the predicted indigestion occurred. On 1 April he went to hospital for a chest X-ray. He dealt with several telephone calls from No. 10 but later that afternoon took to his bed with severe chest pains. He went to hospital again the following day, where a consultant said he had had a slight heart attack but had a 90 per cent chance of a full recovery. The next day he was dead.

Mrs Halls's statement went on:

The consultant . . . and my husband's doctor were deeply shocked that my husband should have died. They, however, had no idea of the conditions under which my husband had been working; as, of course, he could not tell them . . . They were not fully aware of his total exhaustion and that he was in a condition when a mild heart attack could develop into a killer, hence the inaccuracy of their prognosis.

Mrs Hall's statement concluded:

> *The reasons my husband continued working in his enfeebled state,*
> *despite my pleading, during the final months were as follows:*
>
> *1. By this time he had found out that the then Head of the Civil*
> *Service had opposed his appointment [to be Wilson's principal private*
> *secretary] in 1966.*
>
> *2. The news of his appointment had started press attacks upon my*
> *husband which appeared to have been instigated within the civil Service.*
> *He had appealed to the head of the service to have this stopped, but*
> *without success.*
>
> *3. At the time of his appointment, it was general gossip in Whitehall*
> *that now Mr Wilson had got my husband to No. 10 against the wishes*
> *of the Civil Service, they would break him.*
>
> *4. My husband and I discussed the position in March, 1970. He said*
> *that he had done so much to build up the 'show' and now with his*
> *weakened team and the behaviour of Mr Wilson and Mrs Williams, it*
> *was in danger of going to pieces. Therefore his own reputation was at*
> *stake and he could not afford to give up at that stage, moreover,*
>
> *5. The situation had been aggravated by a rift between the head of the*
> *Civil Service and Mr Wilson. They had not had a meeting for some*
> *time. This made conditions extremely difficult for my husband as a go-*
> *between. It was therefore essential to bring about the Maundy Thursday*
> *meeting.*

Mrs Halls said she considered the failure to transfer her husband from 10 Downing Street was the 'direct cause' of his death. She sought compensation of £50,000 which, invested at reasonable rates, would bring her an income of £2,500 a year, miserably inadequate in view of the subsequent years of inflation, but on the whole it was a modest request. The matter never came to court. It was settled privately by the Civil Service Department. The burdens placed upon Michael Halls during his years at No. 10 were enormous, well beyond what is one of the most onerous tasks in government. Mrs Halls was right about that. But he was also a workaholic who demanded to know everything that was going on. For example, late one Saturday evening, after the first editions of the Sunday papers were on the streets, I phoned Wilson at Chequers. The Downing Street operator said she would phone me back. At about 11.30, I phoned again, irritated, and asked why I hadn't been put through. 'I haven't been able to find Michael Halls,' she said. 'I don't want to speak to him,' I replied, 'I want the Prime Minister.' 'We have instructions from Mr Halls not to put your calls through until we have first connected him,' she said. It appeared that for several months, every call I made to the Prime Minister had been listened to by Halls without the knowledge of Harold Wilson or myself. He was placing an unnecessary extra load on his own shoulders; I ensured that it was lifted immediately so far I was concerned.

After Halls's death, no civil servant was privy to Marcia's secrets or those of her family, perhaps because he trusted no one as much or, more likely, because no senior civil servant invited such confidences. All Halls's successors were well aware of what had happened to him. Wilson confided more in me while in opposition and with Dr Bernard Donoughue as well when Labour returned to power in 1974, but always in a nervous, tentative fashion, as if fearing she was listening behind the door.

More painful to me and to Bernard Donoughue was the death in 1980 of our dear friend, Albert Murray. His doctor told his wife that the stroke which killed him might well have been related to stress he endured five years before – when he was Wilson's office manager and subject almost daily to complaints from Marcia.

Six

Bizarre and Ridiculous

Opposition, especially for the party which is officially Her Majesty's Opposition, is a chore. The public accord it responsibility even when they have denied it power. It is expected to propose alternative policies to the government's, even when those policies have been found wanting by the voters. It is expected to stand by its principles and thus remain unelectable; if it commits a U-turn on those principles in order to become more popular it becomes, temporarily at least, more unpopular with voters who regard with cynicism all changes of opinions other than their own. Even if the voters sometimes have to pay for their mistakes, they never have to admit them; political parties are expected to do both. Nowhere is the demand for new policies stronger than among those who swore by and fought for the old policies at the most recent election, something William Hague discovered on assuming the leadership of the Conservative party after the general election debacle of 1997. The problem is that being Leader of Her Majesty's Opposition in the immediate months after a defeat is like swimming with lead weights on the feet. Either the leader stays afloat, just, and hopes to reach shallow water before the next general election or he disappears to the financially rewarding oblivion of his memoirs. Wilson's tactics of ignoring party conference decisions, National Executive Committee opinions and party resolutions worked, but only up to a point. No party leader can forever be against his party and survive. He has to bend with the wind and Wilson bent.

The first task in opposition in 1970 was to complete his book on his Government. The money it would bring was desperately needed. The terms of the contract for its serialisation gave Wilson in the region of £240,000. According to his driver, Bill Housden, a chunk of that money was paid to Marcia. (It's a curious fact that all politicians believe walls have ears but forget that their drivers have them, too.) No doubt there was more money in royalties from Weidenfeld and Nicolson and Michael Joseph, his publishers, and from limited overseas sales. Wilson bought 5 Lord North Street, a few hundred yards from the Commons, for about £20,000 and a house in Buckinghamshire, a few miles from Marcia's country home, where he installed his housekeeper, Mrs Pollard, and where he spent many weekends, but most of his money went on paying the costs of his office. He worked hard to promote the sale of his book, even flying to a publisher's party for him in Germany at the home of a wealthy industrialist, Dr Konrad Henkel. It was a magnificent house, whose floodlighting could be seen from miles away. The journey there, however, was less than luxurious. Sir George Weidenfeld's office asked me to pick up our tickets for the flight at Heathrow airport, a request I was too slow to suspect. When I collected them I found they were economy class. Neither Wilson nor I was particularly inconvenienced by that, though I thought a former Prime Minister deserved better treatment from his publishers. I felt it rather more strongly when, in the air, the curtains to the first-class compartment parted and Sir George emerged to talk to us. Wilson was amused; I wasn't.

We did travel first-class to New York, however, to promote the book and for Wilson to appear on David Frost's early evening show. Later that evening, we went to Frost's sumptuous hotel suite for dinner with his delicious girl-friend of those days, Diahann Carroll, and a few others including the editor of *New York* magazine, Steve Smith, and his wife, Jean, one of John F. Kennedy's sisters. Just before we sat down to eat, the telephone rang: Rose Kennedy, mother of the late President and of Jean and many others and then in her eighties, just happened to be at the hotel next door and wondered, could she come in for a drink with us? She was, of course, enthusiastically invited to stay for dinner by Frost and she appeared a few minutes later wearing a stunning Dior dress. I couldn't help thinking that she knew exactly what she would be doing that night. She was a remarkable lady. When the talk got round to politics, she spoke dispassionately, almost disinterestedly, about the assassinations of her sons, John and Robert, and then said that she hoped and expected her younger son, Edward, would run for President in 1980. When someone tentatively mentioned the murders of the president and his brother, she almost brushed the thought aside of a third killing. Teddy, she said, had to take the risk. In the event, Chappaquiddick put an end to that dream or nightmare.

Wilson had to balance the duty to his publishers with his greater duty to the party and public and decided he would go to Northern and Southern Ireland to investigate the possibility of finding a peace settlement – a chimera which was to dog succeeding prime ministers for the next twenty years and more. I have fully detailed our meetings with Irish leaders in both parts of the island of Ireland elsewhere (*The Politics of Power*) and those meetings are just a small part of the crowded history of the ancient troubles which were renewed in 1969. It is ironic to look back now, though, and remember that Wilson promised a united Ireland fifteen years after an IRA ceasefire. Had he been taken up on this and the other points in a fifteen-point proposal, the fifteen years would have been up in 1986, though whether the Ulster Unionists would have peacefully settled down to rule by Dublin is another question. But armies, Irish Republican or otherwise, do not stop fighting or give up their arms except in unconditional surrender following over-whelming defeat. The failure to realise that torpedoed every attempt thereafter to bring a permanent, genuine and just peace.

In March, 1972 we heard through a Labour member of the Dail, Dr John O'Connell, that the IRA wanted to see Wilson and we met three of its leaders, including the IRA's Chief of Staff, David O'Connell, and Joe Cahill, the convicted murderer of a policeman. Later in the year – on 18 July – three

IRA representatives, including Cahill, flew by private plane to England and we met them at Wilson's home in Buckinghamshire. Both meetings produced nothing at all; indeed, the second was far worse than the first and we hardly proceeded beyond a lengthy lecture by an Irish lawyer, Miles Shevlin, on the iniquities of the British in 1610. The IRA could not get it into their heads that Wilson was not an emissary of the Heath government and was not able to negotiate with them on its behalf. The meeting received little publicity, not least because an event of much greater immediacy was taking place in London that evening. Edward Heath's effective deputy, Reginald Maudling, resigned as Home Secretary because of his past dubious business connections, especially with the crooked businessman John Poulson. Had he not resigned he would have been sacked. Wilson was quick to hear all about it: Maudling, not unusually, had been at a party when he was called to No.10 to see the Prime Minister. Another of the party guests offered him a lift to Downing Street. He was Wilson's and Marcia's friend, Eric Miller, whose own crooked dealing was to have a more tragic result some years later, when he blew his brains out rather than face criminal charges for fraud.

For much of the ensuing eighteen months, the boredom of opposition continued to alternate with its frustrations. Europe continued to divide the party and Wilson continued to tack with each new breeze, while never losing sight of his objective. The industrial scene grew no easier as Heath first stood up to the unions and then backed down and Labour looked less and less like a party soon to be in government again.

In Wilson's office, the Marcia–Mary storm subsided never to be mentioned again and Marcia resumed her remote control of our daily working lives, though her brother, Tony, who became office manager for a while, would stand no nonsense from her. He left after getting married in June 1973, and was succeeded by a man, Ken Peay, who managed the office brilliantly for the short time he was allowed to remain.

At the time of Tony's going, we endured another event which was so unreal that the average fiction writer would have rejected it. Though Tony and her sister, Peggy, were extremely close to her, Marcia's overbearing personality could dominate her family, too. Late on the evening of Tony's wedding, an agitated Wilson phoned me at home with a factual tale which only P. G. Wodehouse would have dared to invent. That afternoon, in or near Leeds, Tony had married the secretary of Joe Kagan, businessman, manufacturer of the Gannex raincoat, contributor to Wilson's office funds (and Marcia's) and another crook in the Miller and Brayley mode, though less attractive than either of them. It was not a marriage of which Marcia approved.

Compelled by sibling loyalty to attend the nuptials, Marcia and her children flew to Leeds with the Wilsons in a private plane. According to Bill Housden, Marcia, allegedly further upset because her sons had not been chosen to be page-boys for the ceremony, had walked into the reception, glared at the presents on display and said to her brother: 'You've done well. You're getting nothing from me.' At which point she left, went to Leeds airport and instructed the pilot to take her back to London. Housden's story became confused after that, but it appeared that when landing in London she walked through the wrong door in attempting to leave the airport and was challenged by immigration officers who demanded to see her passport. Quite reasonably, seeing that she had only been to Leeds and back, she didn't have it with her. The immigration officers then asked her if anyone could vouch for her. 'Harold Wilson,' she replied and identified herself as his secretary.

Unfortunately, the Wilsons by then were on their way back to London by train, Marcia having appropriated the aircraft in which they were supposed to return. She had to wait at the airport until they got home and he could guarantee that she was who she said she was. Wilson's call to me was to alert me to what he feared would be the consequences of what happened next. He and Marcia – particularly Marcia – had long suspected that police from the West Central station were conducting a vendetta against then both. It was all part of her unchanging paranoia about officialdom and authority. It seemed that while she was confined at the airport, her brother – who had been staying with her at Wyndham Mews –

had returned in order to pick up his passport, air tickets and money for his honeymoon. They were missing.

Wilson said that Tony, convinced that his sister had stolen them in order to spoil his honeymoon, had phoned the police. They arrived just seconds after Marcia returned from the airport and before Tony was able to ask where the missing documents were. High farce then became low farce.

The police banged on the door and galloped in when Marcia opened it. She demanded to know whether they had a warrant to enter her house. They said they hadn't. She then insisted that they go out again, ring the bell and ask properly if they could enter. Chastened, they did as they were told. She then admitted them and asked what it was that they wanted. They said they had a complaint that Marcia had stolen the passport, money and air tickets. At that point, Wilson continued, she went to a drawer and took them out, saying that her brother had left them on open view and she had put them away for safety. The police then left and Marcia phoned Wilson and told him the story; he, in turn, phoned me. Certain that the first action of the police would be to inform the Sunday papers, especially the *News of the World*, Wilson asked me to stall any newspaper inquiries until he and I could concoct a plausible story to cover the night's events. Not for the first time, he was deeply embarrassed.

I waited until well after midnight. There were no calls. The police didn't leak the story that night, nor at any other time. Perhaps they felt that nobody would believe it. Or it could simply have been that Wilson was wrong about them and there wasn't a vendetta after all.

The arrival of Ken Peay in the office promised much. He was a former Labour party employee who had left Transport House to make his fortune, did so and then offered to work for Wilson for nothing, always an attractive proposition in an organisation strapped for cash. He brought considerable order and discipline to our routine. Indeed, he was a god send; excellent, competent, clear and focused on the job and doing it better than it had ever been done before, which was no doubt the reason why he had been such a personal success in business. He was an efficient problem-finder and a ruthless solution-seeker.

Inevitably, he perceived that our particular problem was Marcia. He proposed what to him was the logical solution: sack her. Unfortunately, he had not even begun to grasp the tangled truth which he was proposing to untangle at a stroke, as it were. He thought he was cutting the Gordian knot; in fact, he was fashioning the hangman's. The inevitable corollary of his proposed solution was that if it wasn't accepted he would go. It wasn't and he went. His one mistake was to believe that Wilson would share his analysis of the problem (which he probably did) and accept his answer (which he never could).

Albert Murray then succeeded him, another breath of fresh air in the office although of an entirely different kind. A smile was never far from his lips and a joke never far from his mind. Albert was a cheerful Cockney and before he entered Parliament as MP for Gravesend had been a Fleet Street printer. We had been good friends for years and I feared his association with me might count against his chances of getting the job when I first proposed him. I need not have worried. Marcia proclaimed: 'I like Albert'. Wilson heaved a sigh of relief, convinced himself that Albert was Marcia's choice and told me of his appointment. Albert's trouble was that he, too, was efficient. He quickly discovered the awful truth about the office, without any assistance from me. He and I shared with Bob Mellish a lifelong devotion to Millwall Football Club – indeed, Albert died there – so much so that Wilson was to complain, half jokingly, that he was surrounded by Millwall supporters. Our visits to The Den, Millwall's infamous ground, in rain, snow and ice when the results weren't much better than the weather, taught us what it was like to be loyal to an organisation which was wheel-less and broken-backed. It was an attitude that Marcia didn't understand – that some people could work for a cause and that material advantage was not the first priority.

But, eventually – after about a month – Albert, too, had to make his protest against the bewildering instructions, counter-instructions and fantasies which emerged from Wyndham Mews. Marcia always blew hot and cold with Albert – as with most people she regarded as significant – so that he never knew where he was with her. He had joined an exclusive club. But as she withdrew more and more from attendance at the office, so the winds blew colder and she began to persecute him.

Two examples suffice. At 10 o'clock one evening, after Wilson had become Prime Minister again, Albert's loyal wife, Anne, also a Labour activist, phoned me in distress. Albert had arrived home, clearly upset, and had gone straight to bed. She soon found out what was wrong: in revenge for yet another imagined slight, Marcia had stopped the payment on time of that month's wages for the staff. Albert and Anne had just moved into a new house at Gravesend. The mortgage had to be paid and they were living on slender financial margins. Not to get paid was a minor disaster. I immediately phoned Wilson, in a temper myself, and told him what Marcia had done. 'I don't believe it,' he said. 'She wouldn't do such a thing.' 'She would and she has,' I retorted. He repeated his belief in her innocence and then gave the game away: 'Tell Albert to see me first thing in the morning,' he said, 'and I'll give him my personal cheque.' A few days later, the wages were paid and Wilson blamed the accountants. But we both knew the truth.

On another occasion, I was in Marcia's office – sometimes it was necessary to display that we got on well, if only on the surface – when Albert came in. Marcia immediately offered him a gin and Albert immediately accepted. Soon afterwards, she pressed a second gin upon him. Later that evening, Wilson called me to his study. He was worried about Albert, he said. Marcia had complained to him that Albert was drinking too much. I told him what had happened that afternoon and that was the end of it.

In the spring and summer of 1973, the orderly political world which Wilson had known all his adult life was blown apart by the Arab oil crisis. The price of Arab oil was quadrupled and restrictions placed upon its export; the more friendly a country was towards Israel, the greater the restrictions – in Britain's case, a modest 15 per cent cut in supplies. It was a crisis which not only lost Britain the battle against inflation but one which was quickly to destroy the Heath government. Few commentators understood just how much politicians of all parties, as well as economists, were shaken by the increases in the cost of living which followed the oil price rise. Since the war, the rises in the retail price index had been modest; indeed, the index often fell in the summer months. An annual average rate of five per cent was a crisis level. Suddenly, the index began to shoot up alarmingly and five per cent became an impossible dream. The miners, whose industry had been run down while cheap oil imports were increased, believed that their value to the nation had returned with a vengeance and that coal had become an amazingly economic fuel, after all. If huge profits were to be made by the oil producers, the miners wanted their share, too. That summer, their annual conference had committed the National Union of Mineworkers to demanding a thirty-five per cent wage increase, totally impossible under Heath's incomes policy. But he couldn't afford a miners' strike, either. The Arabs had put the miners in an impregnable position for the last time in their history: Heath needed coal to save oil. A reduction in the supply of either was bad enough; a reduction in both was a crisis peculiar to Britain. The union committed to smash the pay policy had now been handed the weapon with which to do it. The Tory government tried by every device possible to increase the National Coal Board's offer to the miners, stretching it way beyond the pay limit of seven per cent to over sixteen per cent – but it was still below half of what the miners were demanding.

The mining muscle was quickly flexed. Firstly, the NUM banned overtime, beginning on 12 November – a move which immediately cut coal production by forty per cent. The government retaliated by introducing a State of Emergency and Heath announced he would not give way to the miners' threats. Heating and lighting restrictions were introduced. By December, TV was ending at 10 p.m. each night. The train drivers' union helped the miners by also banning overtime, the so-called secondary action later to be outlawed by Mrs Margaret Thatcher. Coal deliveries were severely restricted and street lighting, during the longest nights of the winter, was halved. In the run-up to Christmas, the three-day week was announced to begin on 1 January.

Though Heath was reluctant to concede it, the only solution was either to give in to the miners without an election or to give in after an election; after more than one delay in accepting advice from his more aggressive or fearful colleagues, Heath finally decided, on 1 February 1974 to call the nation to vote on 28 February, effectively running on the theme of 'Who Governs Britain?' It was only the latest in a series of catastrophic mistakes. Firstly, he had already made such concessions to the miners that it was inevitable they would ask for more. Secondly, he had introduced the three-day week. Thirdly, he had a sufficient majority to make an election unnecessary and he should have said so from the beginning. As long as an election was thought possible, the miners' hand was strengthened, not weakened. People who sat huddled in blankets for warmth, illuminated only by flickering candlelight, denied their radio and television programmes and afraid to go out into streets darker than at any time since the wartime blackout, had a ready response to the crisis: whoever it was governing Britain, it clearly wasn't the government.

We had heard early in January that some of Heath's most senior ministers, especially Lord Carrington (Energy) and Jim Prior (Employment) were pressing for an early election. We expected it to take place on 31 January, when the electoral register was fifteen months old and therefore of least use to the Labour party, whose local organisations were vastly inferior to those of the Tories. But Heath delayed giving in to his hawks and the time for calling a January election passed. Marcia and I, temporarily reconciled for political purposes, exchanged notes about our disappointment.

The election, however, was inevitable. Too many ministers wanted one and readily confided their desires to journalists. Their frustrations were only temporary. The pressure on Heath grew daily until his reluctance to go to the country – the outcome of which showed that his political antennae were better than theirs – was finally overcome. His announcement of a general election two weeks after a new register was due to come into force was gratu-itously helpful to Labour.

What Heath's advisers knew, and we didn't, was that the Treasury had prepared estimates of future inflation – surging beyond the twenty per cent already in the offing – which spelled certain defeat for the Conservative government if it held on for a few more months and which were to prevent the incoming Labour government from doing anything but try to cope, day by day, with a crisis whose nature no administration in modern times had ever had to face.

Wilson's small group of advisers – Marcia, myself, Bernard Donoughue, who was temporarily recruited from the London School of Economics, and Albert Murray – discussed with him how the election was to be fought. The outlook was seemingly bleak, if not black, for Labour. The last platform on which it had ever wanted to fight was one which could be portrayed as the legitimate elected government against militant unelected strikers, particularly when it was obvious that the miners were about to turn their overtime ban into a full-scale strike. Indeed, they countered the 'Who Governs Britain?' election with an announcement of their own on 4 February that the all-out strike would begin at midnight on 9 February.

At the start of the campaign, Wilson was physically unwell – not only was he suffering from the after-effects of influenza but, on that first afternoon, Alf Richman, a journalist semi-permanently seconded from the *Daily Mirror* to Wilson's political office, had zealously closed the door of Wilson's car before Harold had put his foot safely inside it. Richman was an invaluable, if chronically clumsy, fixer of anything political. But only narrowly did we avoid beginning the battle with a broken-legged leader rather than a badly bruised one.

The imminence of a desperate political fight stimulated Wilson mentally. Some, especially in the Tory party, had forgotten or under-estimated his political skills; if he had declined from the man of 1964, he was still the outstanding politician of his day. His strategy was clear: the only hope of winning was to change the single-item agenda set by Heath and adopted by the newspapers, even the *Observer* which was normally sympathetic to Labour. The voters had to be persuaded that Heath was going to the country not to increase his authority but to safeguard his majority before the nemesis of inflation appeared to wipe it out if only by the attrition of by-elections.

Wilson calculated that the best Labour could do on the union issue was to fight a draw – though ultimately, we did slightly better than that – and said he would nominate Jim Callaghan to be the party's champion in that respect, 'seeing that he is such a friend of the unions'. Callaghan accepted the challenge and was a success, aided by a late surge of sympathy for the miners. On the second issue, the terms of entry into the EEC which Heath had negotiated, Wilson was convinced the Labour pledge to renegotiate them would prevail with the voters. He was offering something better or, at least, no worse. But he didn't expect the EEC to win the decisive votes: they would come, if they came at all, from the rise in the cost of living, which grew more and more ominous almost every day and was to show a twenty per cent increase over the previous year when published mid-way through the campaign. That was an issue every household understood and it was an issue he would handle himself. None of his colleagues in the Shadow Cabinet dissented; few of them had much idea what to do and even fewer had any hopes about the outcome. Wilson also, crucially, abandoned the disastrous policy of walkabouts which had helped lose the 1970 election, as well as the one-man band approach which had won him the 1964 and 1966 elections. If it was a crisis then he was going to look like a man for a crisis; no longer the whizz-kid of 1964 but avuncular, a family doctor ready to chase the quacks from Whitehall. But he was also a team leader, not the team. As he never tired of saying, though many grew tired of hearing, he was no longer going to play centre-forward; 1974 was going to see him as a deep-lying centre-half, surrounded by an expert and experienced Shadow Cabinet on which he and the country could rely. It may have been simplistic, but it struck a chord because it made sense. He could parade a team – Callaghan, Jenkins, Healey, Williams, Crosland, etc – all of whom had been tested in office and been comparatively successful, which was more than could be said for Heath's current crop of Ministers.

There were two more matters, one secret to all but our small group, and the other unknown to any but Marcia and Wilson, which were to play an important part in our personal campaign. The first added excitement because it had a genuine air of mystery, and the other frightened the daylights out of us.

When I got home after midnight on the day of the election being announced, there was an urgent message for me to telephone a London number, whatever time I came in. I spoke to Andrew Alexander, a brilliant, sardonic journalist who was closer to Enoch Powell politically than anyone. Powell had announced that day that he regarded the election as 'fraudulent' and said he would not be contesting it. Alexander, cautiously, went farther. Because Labour had promised a referendum on the terms of entry to the EEC – to which he was irrevocably opposed – Powell intended to make a few speeches on the EEC issue, supporting Labour's stance and he wanted to co-ordinate his speeches on Europe with those of Wilson, by which he meant that he would speak out and Wilson would follow his lead. We had a different view: Wilson would speak and Powell would follow him. In the end, we compromised. Each would inform the other of when he was making a speech on the subject and, by happy chance, they more or less co-incided.

I told Wilson, Marcia and Bernard the next day about my conversation. Wilson was excited but apprehensive; Marcia astonished. It was immediately agreed by them that only I should have any contact with Alexander. I had no doubt why: Powell was still a hate figure in the Labour party because of his notorious 'rivers of blood' speech on immigration. If, by accident or design, the news of the contacts between the two camps leaked out, Wilson could claim it was all an unauthorised private enterprise on my part and nothing to do with him. This isn't fanciful: he did the same on two later occasions – once when I met a representative of the IRA in London and again when we received a stolen – and thus advance – copy of the Tory manifesto for 1974's second election, entitled, *Putting Britain First*. In each case, the Prime Minister officially was not to know about it. I was to be holding the parcel if the music stopped (and I still have it). Albert Murray, as will be seen, was put in a similar position just before the second general election of 1974, when a strike was threatened at the *Daily Mail*. Had No. 10's role in it been discovered, Albert would have borne the blame.

Wilson and Marcia's reaction to my news about Alexander's phone call made strange the statements by them both years afterwards that the Wilson-Powell arrangement came about when the two men stood side by side in the stalls of the men's lavatory in the House of Commons and after Powell had told Wilson his only speeches would be on Europe. According to Wilson at the time, the two men spoke in guarded and general terms, with Powell expressing a preference for a Labour victory should an election be called. Pimlott's biography of Wilson says that Powell says there were several meetings of this kind. That seems unlikely, requiring, as it would, co-ordinated bladders and, in any case, such meetings, by the nature of things, would have been necessarily brief and dependent upon no other MP following the call of nature at the same time. I also find it hard to believe that Powell would have offered his co-operation while he was still a Conservative MP, before Heath had announced the general election and before he himself had announced he was not standing. Whatever may have been thought about him by others, Powell had a rigorous honour code and treating with the conventional enemy at such a time would seem to have been outside it. What's more, if he and Wilson had discussed co-operation in detail, Wilson had never mentioned it and if his surprise was feigned, it was a superb piece of acting. I suspect the truth was that after the election was announced, Powell decided to harden a general sympathy into semi-concrete action.

A farcical element crept into the drama whenever Alexander phoned me at Wilson's office at Transport House. Marcia, who invariably took all calls, would announce, excitedly: 'It's Joe's friend. Everybody out.' Everybody included her and Wilson. They could have both sworn hand on heart, had it been necessary, that neither had first-hand knowledge of what Alexander and I were talking about.

Powell didn't win the election for Labour. What he did do was to weaken the already fragile Heathian strategy of 'Who Governs Britain?', the strategy which he had denounced as an opportunistic fraud. But if Labour was to win, it was essential that we switched the campaign to our topics, not

Powell's single one. We did not start well. On the first day of the campaign, Wilson, goaded by Marcia, decided to write his own speeches. The first one took him five hours to draft and dictate. It was rambling and unfocused and completed so late that there was no handout available to the press, radio and TV, which negated the whole purpose of the speech. The press he did get was bad.

Marcia – who could be quick to change a tactic when things were going wrong – Bernard and I soon decided that Wilson did not have the time and energy to waste each day on a repetition of that dreary process. We agreed that I would take Wilson's main themes and make a master speech on some five or six different subjects. Each evening, we would change one section of the speech to make it the most newsworthy and that would be given as a handout to the press and broadcast reporters. The rest would not be circulated. I only went a few times with Wilson on the road, including to Cardiff, where I snatched a few moments with Alexander in the gloom of a hotel lobby, while Wilson desperately engaged Jim Callaghan in conversation so that he wouldn't notice what was going on. Alexander, briefly, had been allocated by his newspaper the task of following Wilson around the country, though he was abruptly taken off that responsibility after a week or so. After that, I stayed at Transport House and rarely left it except to sleep. Albert Murray replaced me as Wilson's companion on the campaign trail.

After I had completed the following day's 'new' speech, Marcia would place the completed draft on Wilson's pillow at his home in Lord North Street. However late or tired he might be when he arrived back home, he had his bedtime reading. It worked well. He brightened up, threw off the final effects of his 'flu and Labour's campaign began to strengthen. Soon, we had begun to get other issues talked about. At the beginning of the campaign, our private polls showed that the issue which the public had at the forefront of their minds was the miners' strike. At the end, the cost of living was first, with the miners way down the list. That change in voter priorities was what determined the result.

Marcia's reluctance to let me have control of the speeches, however, never stopped. I was doing them all, including the radio and TV party politicals. She was willing to let me write the unglamorous radio broadcasts but – deriving from her increasing obsession with show business – wanted a glamorous professional scriptwriter for the TV ones. Without consulting me or anyone else – except, perhaps, Wilson, though he never admitted it – she recruited the playwright and Labour sympathiser, John (now Sir John) Mortimer, to write the party politicals for TV. It was an absurd idea, only slightly less ridiculous than a proposal by Callaghan's office to ask Jeffrey Bernard, the Soho writer, gossip and bar-fixture, to write the Prime Minister's speeches for the 1979 election. Mortimer's brilliance didn't transfer to political speech-writing, not least because he could not possibly know the intricacies of Labour politics, nor Wilson's style, nor what Wilson had said in the past. His draft would have suited a play about a political Rumpole of the Bailey, but not real life. Wilson wouldn't look at it himself but asked my opinion. I tried to be as objective as possible – indeed, had Mortimer been able to produce what was needed, I would have been more than grateful – but I had to say it wouldn't do. A second draft was no better. Wilson then asked me to resume writing the broadcasts. Valuable time, not least Mortimer's, had been wasted in pursuit of an intermittent vendetta; while we were trying to win an election Marcia was trying to score points. Lady Falkender was later to claim that Wilson wrote his own TV scripts. A dozen people knew better.

The campaign was a struggle. The personal disputes were never far below the surface. I gradually formed an alliance with Bernard Donoughue to join the one I had with Albert Murray. I'm sure Marcia felt isolated, especially as I threw a former lover of hers, John Scofield Allen out of the office – actually the office of Ron Hayward, the party's General Secretary – when he tried to raid the drinks cupboard in his eternal quest for free alcohol. But we were all working a fifteen-hour day, which Marcia cheerfully admitted she could only do with a plentiful hoard of tranquillisers, and our camp was optimistic. Though the polls showed we were not doing so well overall, we were succeeding remarkably well in some of the marginal seats and we had had an unexpected bonus from Ted Heath, of all people, in our fight to expose the fraudulence of 'Who Governs Britain?'

Having decided to campaign against the miners' pay demands, Heath then announced that he was turning the issue over to the Pay Board and would accept the findings, whatever they were, of the Board's inquiry into the claim. As that inquiry was bound to suggest a figure higher than the government had been prepared to go – because inquiries always did and always do – that made calling the election pointless. The Board then, in the middle of the campaign, held a briefing for the press at which a Labour-leaning member of the Board said that, compared with other industries, the miners were not doing so well as had been imagined and were well down a league table of wages.

The BBC, which had accepted Heath's theme from the beginning and wouldn't be shaken from it, for the first time was, inadvertently, helpful to us and their *Nine O'Clock News* that evening presented the Pay Board's calculations as a crucial mistake by the government. One of the journalists at the briefing had telephoned me as soon as he had left the meeting. Only Marcia and I were in the room. I phoned Wilson at his home in Lord North Street just before he went on a west and north London speaking tour. We agreed that I would draft an insert into his speech and Marcia would arrange for him to get it. That involved her putting the fear of God into a poor caretaker at the school where Wilson was due to make his second speech of the evening, threatening almost to disembowel him unless he got to Wilson before he spoke and ensured that he telephoned the office. It worked. Wilson spoke off-the-cuff at his first meeting and got it slightly wrong, but that didn't matter. At the second meeting, he spoke from our script. He was seen on the TV news denouncing the government for needlessly causing the misery of a strike and the consequent blackout. Suddenly, the election agenda was not about the bloody-mindedness of the miners but the incompetence of the government. We had nobbled the Heathian horse. That episode convinced me thereafter that the fewer in a campaign team, the better it would be, though the lesson hasn't been learned by our current political leaders. Heath, with a much larger team, knew nothing about the Pay Board briefing until an old friend of mine, Gordon Greig, of the *Daily Mail*, broke it to him at 11.30 that night – too late for TV, which, because of the lighting restrictions, was going off the air early. His staff at No. 10 did try to alert him, but he had only one civil servant with him, one of the Garden Room secretaries, who, at the vital moment, was travelling between one speech centre and the next. Heath might well have felt in later life that had he had a mobile phone in his car in time for the 1974 election, victory could have been his.

Then the unnamed fear which grips every party at every general election – that somewhere lurking in the undergrowth was an unknown monster with the power to devour us – emerged to put everything into the melting pot again, or so it seemed.

A *Guardian* reporter, Gareth Parry, called to see me at Transport House about a story his paper had received, to the effect that Harold Wilson was involved in land speculation in the Wigan area, not all that far from his constituency at Huyton. I told him that there could not be any truth in the story; he accepted my word and left. When I told Wilson about my conversation with Parry, he reacted over-sharply and, unnecessarily I thought, telephoned Alastair Hetherington, the then editor of the *Guardian,* to deny it in person. Hetherington accepted what Wilson said and his paper did not use the story. Although I was well aware that such a story could have been extremely damaging just before polling day, I did not then wonder sufficiently why Wilson had taken it upon himself to repeat what I had already done.

The next evening, a *Daily Mail* reporter came to Transport House asking to see Marcia on 'a personal matter.' My first, unjustified, thought was that the paper was intending to write about her two sons, whose existence was then known to only a comparative few, including, of course, their father, the *Daily Mail's* political editor. I asked the reporter what it was all about. He said it concerned land deals in the Wigan area, involving Marcia Williams and Harold Wilson. I repeated to him what I had said to Parry: any accusation of a Wilson involvement was false. He said his paper had documents concerning the deal. I said they must be fakes, as indeed they were so far as they involved Wilson.

We were lucky that nothing appeared in the press before polling day, but it was the beginning of an affair which never completely stopped reverberating during the two years of Wilson's last premiership. As I wrote in 1976: 'It first diverted our attention in the last vital days before the vote; it later irremediably damaged our relationships with the press; it occupied the time and energies of those people around Harold Wilson who ought to have been his companions and advisers in the early weeks back at Downing Street. It was wholly destructive and to my mind Marcia was never the same person again.'

At the outset of this affair I was given a categorical assurance by Wilson that nothing improper or illegal had occurred, nor had it, technically. Marcia's brother, Tony Field, a trained geologist, when office manager, had frequently mentioned to me the land he held at Ince-in-Makerfield, near Wigan, which he had possessed since 1967, long before Wilson announced a Labour policy for the nationalisation of land. What he didn't tell me was that his two sisters also had an interest in the site. Marcia's financial involvement meant, inevitably, Wilson's political involvement.

As long as her brother appeared to be the only owner, it was a commercial development. When it became known she was involved, it became a political development. The newspaper interest was not revived before polling day, perhaps because Labour were thought to be inevitable losers, but it was to lie in wait for us.

Meanwhile, the last of Heath's misbegotten chickens was about to come home to roost. The three weeks of campaigning had been in almost unbroken sunshine. On the evening of the day itself, after a tour of the polling stations at Huyton, I started to ring round Labour's regional agents. The one in the West Midlands was ecstatic. 'You're going to win,' he cried. 'The three-day week here was Monday, Tuesday and Wednesday. Nobody's working today. The council house turnout has been almost 100 per cent [he exaggerated] and all the men laid off have voted already.'

Wilson, Albert Murray, Alf Richman and I went out for a further tour of the polling stations in Huyton. When we visited party headquarters, Richman managed to upset the chairman of the Huyton party by snatching a cup of tea from his grasp on the grounds that he needed it more, thus justifying the ban on his appearance in the constituency which Wilson's agent, Arthur Smith, had operated for nearly ten years, and then returned to our base at the Adelphi Hotel, Liverpool. In the foyer, the group of political reporters assigned to follow our trail stood around waiting to interview the inevitable loser while their more senior colleagues attached to Ted Heath in London enjoyed having the real story to write. Not one of the journalists said a word to us as we made our way up to Wilson's suite. They felt sorry for us; we, on the other hand, had no sympathy for them.

In that general election, ITN was pioneering exit polls, in which voters were asked how they had voted, not how they intended to. Its ten o'clock bulletin reporting the first of these polls showed that Labour were the likely winners. Moments later, a bewildered journalist from the group in the foyer knocked timidly at the door of Wilson's suite and asked if Wilson wanted to say anything. The answer was that he didn't. Then the local manager of British Rail turned up, offering to lay on a special coach, with press conference facilities, to take us back to London. The answer to him, too, was thanks but no thanks; we had already arranged to fly back in Eric Miller's private plane. As the railman left, several silent and physically imposing men began to take up posts in the corridor outside the suite to ward off further visitors. The Special Branch had been watching television, too.

Wilson went to his constituency to hear of his own massive triumph there and then we switched hotels to the Golden Eagle in Kirkby before flying back in the early hours. Victory was still not certain. Labour had become the largest party in the Commons but did not have a majority. As the afternoon wore on, it became clear that Heath was not going to give up his office without a further fight. Bernard Donoughue had kept in close touch with one of the most prominent members of the Liberal team. Word began to spread that Heath was offering a deal to the Liberals which was unacceptable to Donoughue's friend but tempting to the Liberal leader, Jeremy Thorpe. All day, we sat in Wilson's upstairs drawing room waiting for the calls from Downing Street and Buckingham Palace which never came. At 7.30 pm, Robert Armstrong, Heath's civil service principal private secretary, telephoned to say that he was going out to dinner and would not be returning to Downing Street that night. The message was unmistakable. Nothing was going to happen which would warrant Wilson taking his best suit out of the wardrobe.

Wilson took it all calmly. During the hours of waiting, he had told Marcia, Bernard, Albert, me and Terry Lancaster, the political editor of the *Daily Mirror*, that he intended to serve no more than two years as Prime Minister and would retire on his sixtieth birthday in 1976. Meanwhile, he told us what he intended to do if Heath offered a Cabinet post to Jeremy Thorpe in order to keep his own job as Prime Minister. He was not going to take any chances, he said. If Heath decided to cheat the voters, then George Thomas, a former junior minister at the Home Office and future Speaker of the Commons, would come forward and expose Thorpe's affair with Norman Scott, an eccentric homosexual who claimed to have had the affair in the 1960s and was obsessed with Thorpe's alleged retention of his National Insurance cards. What's more, Wilson added, his deputy, Ted Short (later Lord Glenamara), who also knew of the affair through his time as a minister, would do the same. That would have made impossible the rumoured post of Home Secretary for Thorpe; Heath had already parted with one Home Secretary, Reginald Maudling, because of his connection with John Poulson. Lady Bracknell had a phrase which could be adapted to suit a Prime Minister who lost two Home Secretaries. Wilson was certain that Heath knew nothing of the Thorpe-Scott friendship, though Heath subsequently made it clear he had been informed by the Cabinet Secretary (Sir Burke Trend) that there were allegations of homosexuality against Thorpe.

In the meantime, Wilson announced his grand strategy for putting pressure upon Heath to resign: he would go to the country for the weekend and say and do nothing except to be photographed playing with Paddy, his huge and clumsy Labrador. He told me to go home – for the first time in three weeks – and not to answer the phone, novel behaviour for a press secretary, even by my standards, and to wait calmly for the inevitable. In the event, that came on the Monday evening, 4 March, when Heath at last resigned and the need to play the Thorpe card was for the time being, avoided. Subsequently, soon after becoming Prime Minister again, Wilson asked Barbara Castle, his new Secretary of State for Social Security, to let him have details of Scott's National Insurance record for possible future use: i.e., if the Heath-Thorpe coalition proposition were to be revived in another closely-fought general election that October, he would have the Scott card ready to play. Mrs Castle was uncomfortable about the Prime Minister's request, and he told her, sharply, to 'get Jack Straw' to do it. Later, I asked Wilson if he had got what he wanted and he said he had. I didn't ask how Mrs Castle got the records or from whom and Wilson didn't say. In October 2002, however, Straw, by then in the Cabinet himself as Tony Blair's Foreign Secretary, confirmed that he and a civil servant (Mrs Castle's private secretary, Norman Warner) had seen the NI records and had written a report on them for the Prime Minister.

But on that Monday evening, all that was in the future. The long-awaited call came for Mr Wilson to see the Queen, and our team – Marcia, Bernard, Albert and I – all went off with him to the Palace. For the journey back, I usurped Robert Armstrong's place in the official car and we returned in triumph to 10 Downing Street. It was the last time we were all tolerably happy together.

Seven
Back in Power

Once we got back to Downing Street, and after a few brief words on the doorstep, Wilson disappeared into the maw of the waiting civil servants while I set about shaping my office in the way I wanted. I first telephoned Janet Hewlett-Davies, an old friend and long-time civil service senior press officer, asking her to abandon the Home Office where she was working and to report to No. 10 the next morning. I also recruited Jean Denham, the most popular press officer ever to work for the Labour party, to come in and lend some political wisdom to an office where it was notably lacking. I instantly had in place two calm, hard-working, intelligent and efficient women who, effectively, ran the press office and left me free for other things. Both had the considerable advantage of knowing the Prime Minister well and being liked by him. What's more, neither stood in awe of him, which meant that both could press him for a straight answer when he might not have wanted to give one.

The next morning, I reduced the overall staff level of the office by five, and then added another after being asked by Robert Armstrong not to remove any more, for the sake of civil service morale. I understood his point and took it seriously, but I had to demonstrate, as had not been done during Wilson's first term at No. 10, who was in charge of the press office. I therefore removed the most senior man still left in post. Armstrong was hurt and later nominated that civil servant to be secretary to the Royal Commission on the Press which Wilson was setting up. Neither Wilson nor I were told. When I discovered the proposal, I regarded it as an affront to the Press Secretary's position and to the

Prime Minister; it was an assertion of power which could not be tolerated, however well intentioned. At my request, Wilson vetoed the appointment. Curiously, there was none of the furore which occurred more than 20 years later when Alastair Campbell, Tony Blair's press secretary, took less drastic steps to change the government's press office personnel and to assert his position.

Wilson worked immediately to get the miners back to work, largely on the basis of the Pay Board's recommendations, which Heath could have had without resorting to a general election. The strike moved peacefully, if expensively, towards it close, though Wilson's face was a picture late one evening when a sudden hitch occurred and he needed his Energy Minister, Eric Varley, urgently, only to be told that he was at the Royal Opera House, Covent Garden, with another of his ministers, Gerald Kaufman. The idea that any minister, let alone the Energy Minister, could take an evening off at such a desperate time, bemused rather than angered Wilson; he disliked frivolity among his ministers and frivolity especially included the Royal Opera House. Varley's sin was compounded in Wilson's eyes because he had not left his seat ticket numbers with his office. If he had, Wilson would have called him out in mid-aria, if necessary, however much it might have upset other opera buffs.

For a while after the election, Wilson seemed to recover his old zeal for playing the political game, but it didn't last for long. Great causes, however, still captured his full attention. At one point, so shocked was he by the mass slaughter – thousands, every week – taking place in Idi Amin's Uganda that he consulted me about the desirability of having Amin assassinated. We were both life-long opponents of capital punishment, but there was a strong case for making an exception in the case of Amin. It was a rare opportunity to save thousands of lives by eliminating one man, and a lot cheaper than subsequent attempts to disarm tyrants in Bosnia, the Sudan and Kosovo.

The Foreign and Commonwealth Office, however, didn't see it like that and the few officials who were asked to consider the idea were almost frightened out of their diplomatic straitjackets. Diplomacy is like cricket used to be: a way of life. If once the ball was tampered with, anarchy would reign. Assassination, in their view, was cheating; the ultimate in foul play. If you start killing heads of state, they asked, where do you stop? Suppose there is retaliation? Their argument was impeccable, except that it would also have applied to Adolf Hitler, whose assassination was periodically proposed and ultimately planned by the British towards the end of the 1939-45 war. Inevitably, the FCO won the argument because of their ability to manufacture trump cards at will. When Wilson pressed for a firm answer to his suggestion, he was simply told: 'We don't have anyone to do that kind of thing,' and he was forced to drop the subject. That answer, however, did not accord with the revelations of a former M15 officer in 1998 who claimed that under the British Conservative government a few years earlier, proposals were considered for the assassination of Colonel Gadaffi of Libya (where, ironically, Amin took shelter after being evicted from Uganda). It was left to the Israelis, for whom playing the game is no substitute for direct action, to punish Amin by raiding Entebbe airport in Uganda to free their citizens being held hostage there. The dictator's prestige never recovered from that humiliation and his rule didn't long survive it.

It only took a few weeks for the slag heaps to emerge again to interfere with the serious business of government. This time, they looked more like mountains, and involved a letter on which Wilson's signature had been crudely forged by Ronald Milhench, a former arms dealer and business associate of Tony Field and, by extension, of Marcia and her sister, Peggy. At Milhench's subsequent trial, he was described as 'a man whose vanity and ambition far outreach his intelligence and financial resources', but before that came about, the Field family's close ties with Wilson had once again damaged his reputation. On 18 March 1974, two weeks after Wilson became Prime Minister again, the *Daily Mail* published a lengthy article about Milhench and his offer (for which he did not have the resources to meet) to pay £950,000 for the Field-owned land at Ince-in-Makerfield. Whether through political indigestion or not, the rest of Fleet Street paid little attention to the story. My office took a couple of calls about it, one from the London *Evening News* and another from the *Birmingham Mail* and that was all until 3 April, more than a fortnight later.

Chapman Pincher, a right-wing journalist who was unremittingly hostile to Wilson, wrote a story in the *Daily Express* about another of Tony Field's associates, a man named Harper. The *Daily Mail,* in that mysterious way newspapers have, learned what the *Express* was doing and ran a more sensational story, one they had had since February: that Wilson's signature had been forged and appended to a letter, similarly forged by Milhench, which appeared to show Wilson deeply involved in the sale of the land. Milhench, whose wife had died in a drowning accident on the eve of polling day, had tried to sell this story to the *Mail* for £25,000 in the run-up to the vote. The letter was written on Harold Wilson's notepaper – stolen by Milhench when he called on Tony Field at the Leader of the Opposition's office at the Commons – but the newspaper knew it was a forgery from the beginning, otherwise they would have printed it. However, fraudulent though it was, it was the spark that produced the explosion. Over the next few weeks, more than six thousand column inches were devoted to the slag heaps story in national newspapers, no doubt on the basis that there was no smoke without fire. Wilson and Marcia issued several writs for libel, including writs by Wilson against the *Mail* and the *Express.* As far as I know, no financial settlement was ever made.

Bernard Donoughue, Albert Murray and I made several visits, at the Prime Minister's request, to Marcia's home at Wyndham Mews, while it was besieged by journalists and photographers. Their behaviour, including tossing a coin to see who should next knock at the door, encouraging local children to do so, and peering through the windows so that the curtains had to remain drawn, was disgraceful by any standard. Our antagonism towards Marcia temporarily took second place to our outrage at the way the press were behaving towards her. It was a sorry episode; we were excessive in our reaction to the excesses of others, though I never regretted walking out of a

Lobby meeting where a half-drunk Lobby correspondent – the same one who had tried to enlist my support for a peerage for Captain Kerby – went too far in his insulting insinuations about Marcia.

But it was all a dreadful distraction from our main task. The country was in crisis, with fears of inflation rising to banana republic levels and presided over by a Prime Minister and Cabinet which lacked a majority in Parliament. Every working hour ought to have been devoted to helping the Prime Minister in every way possible to master that situation. Instead of that, day after day, we were stuck with coping with the troubles afflicting his personal secretary and her family.

Throughout, Marcia was in a distraught state, unable to think properly. The Prime Minister was in a state of continuing agitation and facing a House of Commons where hysteria was never far from the surface throughout 1974. As Prime Minister, Wilson could not be questioned in the Commons about events which occurred when he was Leader of the Opposition. He had nothing to do with the land deals affair, he did not know of the existence of Ronald Milhench until the story of the forged letter came out and he had done nothing of which he should be ashamed. But he still felt compelled to defend Marcia, and drafted a rambling statement to be made to the Commons to which Bernard Donoughue and I responded with a joint minute: 'To issue the statement in its present form, whether in the House or any other way, invites disaster. You would inevitably involve yourself in the transactions …which were not your concern.'

Wilson modified his statement but insisted on keeping in it the phrase to which we had taken particular exception: that the land at Wigan concerned 'reclamation' rather than 'speculation,' which brought the laughter we had predicted and did nothing to stop the day-by-day press coverage.

The culmination of that coverage for Marcia came when the editor of the *Daily Express,* to which Walter Terry had switched his employment, discovered that his political editor was the father of Marcia's two children. He must have been the last journalist in Fleet Street to know. He thought it such a wonderful story that he decided to lead the paper with it on a Saturday morning. Terry tipped off Marcia, who, in turn, told Wilson, who dispatched Bernard Donoughue and me to Marcia's home as unwilling comforters and roped in Lord Goodman to stop the story being published. Lord Goodman rarely dealt with editors. He went to the top and spoke to proprietors and his tactic on this evening was to try to speak to Sir Max Aitken, the then owner of the *Express,* who, unfortunately, seemed to be between islands in the Bahamas, where he was holidaying with his mistress. Only after being unable to get Aitken, did Goodman lower his sights and try to influence the editor. Whether it was his persuasion or whether it occurred to the editor that what he was intending was hardly the way to treat the most senior of his reporters, the story didn't run, after all. Yet another afternoon and evening had been spent by us trying to prevent Marcia's private affairs from becoming public at a time when the whole country was beset by infinitely more serious problems.

Finally, Marcia drafted an excruciatingly self-pitying statement for the *Daily Mirror* and Wilson asked me, once again, to go to Wyndham Mews and 'see if it's all right.' It wasn't all right and when Marcia and I got on to other matters, I slipped the statement into my pocket, made my excuses and left for Downing Street, hoping she would forget it. By the time I got back she had telephoned the Prime Minister to complain that I had stolen her statement to stop it being printed, which was more or less true and what Wilson wanted. I said that I had taken it away to strengthen it, which I was then obliged to do by virtually rewriting the whole of it. So impressed was the *Guardian* with the outcome that it declared, with that innate ability to grasp the wrong end of the stick which has survived the departure of several editors, that Mrs Williams (as she still was, though not for much longer), was the only one to emerge from the affair with dignity but advised the Prime Minister to sack his Press Secretary.

There was to be a final scene over the slag heaps. The first thirty-four acres of ninety-five had been sold before Milhench was exposed as a fraud and a considerable amount of money was involved. At times, £12,000, £10,000 and £8,500 an acre were sums mentioned. In 1975, Marcia made one of her occasional visits to the office in a state alternating between rage and panic. She had been billed, she said, for £20,000 capital gains tax by the Inland Revenue, who were threatening to send her to prison unless she paid up by the following Monday, which she couldn't because she didn't have the money. I sat and watched while Lord Goodman, who had been summoned to solve her problem, listened to her tirade against the taxman and the Treasury. It was the same old story: they were conspiring against her; there was a 'plot' to destroy her. The scenario was unreal and untrue, but, as ever, Lord Goodman was expected to soothe her, pooh-pooh her fears and promise to straighten it out. The improbable threat of imprisonment was the justification for calling him in, but Wilson's accountants could have settled the matter more speedily.

What was real, and what was certainly true, was that Wilson, engaged day and night in trying to cope with an economic, industrial, and financial crisis such as Britain had not known in peace-time – a Prime Minister who had won more general elections than any man since Gladstone and to whom the country had once again given its trust – was being worn down by the increasingly demanding and hysterical calls upon his time and emotions by a woman of no elected position who, publicly, never claimed to be more than his personal and political secretary.

From the moment he assumed office on 4 March 1974, a second election that year was inevitable. The date of 10 October was chosen almost straight away. Wilson exhorted his ministers to concentrate their policies, their speeches, their every action, on winning a clear majority for the election when it came. Yet, week in and week out, he himself was being distracted, his eyes forced away from the main target, his time taken up with the personal trivia which Marcia believed to be of overwhelming importance.

One lesson in politics which I learned while with Wilson is that it is not true that things cannot get worse. They can, they do, and they did. In a technical sense, it was Wilson, as Prime Minister, who decided that the best way to get back at the press for its treatment of Marcia was to 'recommend' that she be made a baroness. Such recommendations are invariably accepted by the Queen, however reluctant she may be, as she appeared to be on this occasion. But though it was Wilson's proposal in the formal sense, he was merely endorsing Marcia's demands. When he announced the peerage to us, the thump of our hearts hitting our boots must have been heard in Outer Mongolia.

Until the very last minute, Bernard Donoughue, Albert Murray and I tried to stop the honour being gazetted. It was not out of personal dislike for Marcia – if we had operated on that basis, more than one Honours List would have been a lot thinner – but because we knew the damage it would do to him. As he had told us that he intended to give up the premiership by March 1976, we believed that he should have waited until his Resignation Honours List, the traditional opportunity for outgoing Prime Ministers to reward long-serving staff. Wilson's principal private secretary, Robert (later Lord) Armstrong, agreed with us. Encouraged by the absolutely certain knowledge that the Queen, when asked to give final approval to Marcia's elevation, had raised an eyebrow and said: 'If the Prime Minister should wish to change his mind about this he can, of course, do so at any time,' we went to see him in one final, desperate attempt to stop it. Armstrong, whose only motive was to safeguard the reputation of the Prime Minister's office, went with us, but as he knew we were going to argue the case on political grounds, stayed outside the door of the Prime Minister's study, though willing to come in and support if we called.

I told Wilson that the party would be dismayed, particularly when we were encouraging the idea that there might be a mid-summer election (that was an unconvincing hoax, helpfully published by the *Mirror*, to mislead the Tories; we never varied from the October date). I concluded, thinking of the countless hours we had wasted over the land deals affair, 'What is more, I do not see how any longer I can protect her.' The Prime Minister had been agitatedly walking to and fro while we talked. But at that point, he spun round and sharply demanded to know what I meant by that. I told him that we – Bernard and I, especially – had always sought to shield Marcia from publicity on the grounds that she was a private person. What he was proposing to do was to make her a public person, a member of one of the Houses of Parliament, with the right to participate in legislation. By making her a public figure, he was making her a legitimate person of public interest. We could no longer complain if the press commented upon her power and influence upon him.

The Prime Minister countered that, in fact, she intended to surrender her influence to the three of us in return for the peerage. She was likely to leave his service altogether and take up an executive position with Weidenfeld and Nicolson, his and her publishers, and even to become the latest in the series of George Weidenfeld's wives. I don't think any of us believed that for a moment, and no doubt Weidenfeld would have been taken aback by it, but short of calling the Prime Minister a liar to his face, which is and ought to be impossible for advisers, we could do nothing. Whatever his developing failings, Wilson hadn't lost any of his skill in checkmating those who opposed him. That evening, with a straight if unsmiling face, I announced the peerage to disbelieving Lobby correspondents.

Marcia's version of the nomination was that it was Wilson's intention to wait until the Resignation Honours List before creating her a peeress; if that was true, she could have said 'No', a stance not unfamiliar to her. Though I might still have doubted its merit, I would have had no public quarrel with that. Commoners have been elevated to the peerage on more flimsy grounds than working for the Prime Minister for twenty years. But to do it immediately after the land deals affair was insulting to the voters, to the Labour party and to Parliament. It was also extremely crass. Marcia described the honour as 'a very generous acknowledgement of his support for me.' It would have been truer to say that I saw it as yet another occasion on which he gave way to her demands, and those demands were fuelled by her constant need to be well regarded. If she could not have that regard in fact, then she would ensure it by title. It was she who wanted the peerage, there and then.

There had to be a sadistic side to the peerage; there always was. In this case, it was her insistence that Wilson, having written the formal offer letter to her, should draft her letter of acceptance. In effect, he would be writing to himself. When he meekly complied, she scrawled 'rubbish' diagonally across it and told him to do it again. Once again, it was an exercise in the power to humiliate.

If Marcia glowed in her new status, even though it did not carry the respect for which she craved – the office typists put up a notice, which I fondly retain, saying: 'Mrs Falkender still wishes to be known as Mrs Williams' – our relationship with her grew more distant. And I was faced with the unpleasant fact that, a few weeks before, I had vehemently denied a story by the political editor of the *News of the World,* Noyes Thomas, that Marcia was to be appointed minister in charge of the Civil Service and sit in the House of Lords. I had spoken to Wilson about the story before reacting to it. He told me it was absolutely untrue. The first half certainly was – we would have had the first-ever all-out strike by Whitehall's bowler hats if it had been correct – and that was the main thrust of the story. At the time we spoke, I think the second half was untrue, too, but it might have put the idea into her head. However, Thomas was popular among his fellow political reporters and there was no chance that my version of events would be believed.

A further twist to the story came when I was attending a meeting of a committee discussing events in Northern Ireland. A private secretary whispered into my ear that Marcia had chosen the title of Baroness Falkender, but I thought he said 'Faulkner'. At the time, Brian Faulkner was the leader of the Ulster Unionists and hated by the nationalists in the province. For one brief, horrified moment I thought what the reaction to her choice might be, until the name was repeated to me.

Ironically, Marcia had at last achieved a position of public importance through the gift of the Queen, whose courtiers she despised. At a farewell dinner to Robert Armstrong in April 1975, she was placed, by someone with a mischievous or naive mind, next to Sir Martin Charteris, the Queen's private secretary. 'I suppose you realise,' she said to him, in a variation upon the usually superficial dinner-time conversation, 'I loathe all you stand for?'

When she was awarded the CBE by Wilson in 1970, she refused to go to the Palace to collect it, saying she was unwelcome to the senior staff there. She then complained when the honour arrived at her home 'in a brown paper parcel'. I think her resentment on that occasion, however, had more to do with the fact that I had refused the honour which she had accepted, and that she saw my action as a criticism of her rather than of the system.

Wilson told me more than once that she was convinced that the courtiers at the Palace made certain she was not invited to functions there because they knew she was of royal blood, even though it was on the wrong side of the blanket. He said there was an affair between either her grandmother or great-grandmother – I was never sure which – and Edward VII. If it was her great-grandmother then it would have been when Edward was Prince of Wales. If it were her grandmother, then conception would have taken place after Queen Victoria's death, when the Prince had become King – if there was any truth in the story at all. In 1974, the *Daily Mail* unearthed Marcia's mother's birth certificate, which showed she was born on 8 March 1902, when Edward had been King for fourteen months. Her Christian names were given as Dorothy Matilda Falkender. No name was given for her father. According to Wilson, an aide of the prince, said to be a Captain Falkender, had agreed to admit to the parentage of the Prince of Wales's/Edward's child to avoid a scandal – thus, the choice of name for her title. If the story seems fanciful, if not a fantasy, it may, again, have the germ of truth.

When the Queen and Prince Philip came, in March 1976, to a dinner at No. 10 to honour Wilson after he had announced his retirement, Marcia at last came face to face with her monarch. Her curtsey was, as everyone agreed at the time, superbly executed. Later that evening, the Prime Minister's new private secretary, Kenneth Stowe, who knew little first-hand of Marcia, reported to us (Donoughue, me and the other private secretaries) that the Queen had said to her Prime Minister: 'If you wish me to speak to Lady Falkender, I will, of course, do so.' There was only one possible course of action or inaction the Prime Minister could take and he took it. He did nothing.

The award of the peerage continued to plague us. Marcia was soon invited to a reception at the House of Lords and gladly accepted. Nevertheless, she was neurotically nervous at appearing anywhere in public without an escort and it was hardly the occasion for her hairdresser, a frequent companion, to accompany her. She, therefore, decided to go to the very top for one and demanded that Harold Wilson should go with her.

Wilson and I were working on a speech in his spacious office off the corridor behind the Speaker's chair at the House of Commons when she suddenly burst in and told him he had to escort her to the function, a couple of hundred yards down the corridor.

'I'm too busy,' he pleaded.

The familiar darkening of the face began, always the prelude to a storm. 'Don't tell me that,' she said. 'You have got to come.'

He rose wearily, said: 'Joe, you come as well', and we walked on either side of her. Wilson hated receptions and cocktail parties and he was genuinely busy – prime ministers sometimes are. After a few minutes there, and seeing Marcia engaged in conversation with a small group of peers, he turned to me and whispered: 'Come on, let's go.'

A few minutes after we had returned to his office – when I had left him for a moment with Albert Murray – a furious Marcia crashed in and, according to a shocked Albert, who described the scene to me immediately afterwards, shouted: 'You little c***. What do you think you are doing? You come back with me at once.' This time, Wilson put his foot down and refused and she blew out again. (Marcia never actually glided or walked or stepped into a room – she always came and went in a blaze of sparks, like a plane landing with its under-carriage up. On these occasions, when Wilson was the target, contempt was her weapon. She spoke to him in terms which would make a slave master blush.)

As ever, the purpose was to humiliate him and she didn't care if there was a witness. Indeed, a witness was important. But to me, the use of such language was beyond comprehension. My upbringing wasn't all that sheltered but until I met Marcia I never heard a woman swear like that, though nowadays it is commonplace. At that time, many men when spoken to in those terms would be sorely tempted to thump the speaker. It was comforting on this occasion to think Wilson was merely ignoring her, but her language, like the whole issue of her peerage, from conception to publication, was yet another an essay in the assertion of her power.

Throughout 1974 and 1975, the atmosphere of hysteria continued unabated. An army exercise involving tanks around Heathrow airport was seen by Marcia as the start of a military coup against the Labour Government and she, for a moment, half-persuaded Wilson there was something in it. For another imagined slight, she demanded the sacking of one of the Prime Minister's private secretaries, Robin Butler (later, to be knighted, appointed cabinet secretary, and ennobled) while claiming in her second book of Downing Street memoirs that it was Bernard Donoughue and I who had wanted Butler, Robert Armstrong and the other private secretaries to be fired. The truth was that Bernard Donoughue and I had taken Butler's side so strongly against her – a fact which he has publicly acknowledged – that Wilson kept him in place, removing a threat to his subsequent career.

Meanwhile, on a serious level, the economic situation grew worse. The union snouts in the trough – in the notorious phrase of the railwaymen's leader, Sid Weighell – grew more numerous by the hour. The civil service won a pay rise of thity-three per cent which the Donoughue Policy Unit only managed to delay by a fortnight. John Silkin, one of the Cabinet members who voted for it, told me much later that he regarded that decision as the worst mistake of the 1974-6 government.

Running it close was the decision to rescue British Leyland from collapsing under the weight of its own incompetence. Wilson was told that eight-hundred-and-fifty-thousand jobs, mainly in the Midlands, would go if BL closed its gates. That was unacceptable, if true, but it was a big 'if.' The crisis there occupied ministerial minds for weeks and it turned the newly-proposed

National Enterprise Board from a body supposed to provide healthy new industries into an intensive care unit for unhealthy old industries. The tales of horror which came from BL were almost unbelievable. One was that BL had no idea what, if any, profit it was making on the Mini; at first, it was said that a loss was made on each one sold. Later, a more optimistic account suggested that £1 profit was made on each car.

Between them, the substantial cost of reaching a peaceful settlement with the miners, the civil servants' pay award and the BL rescue, put the government in an impossible financial position from which it never recovered. The alternative to giving way, however, was to stand firm and no-one would contemplate for a moment a continuation of the miners' strike, a strike by civil servants and hundreds of thousands of jobs lost in Midlands marginals. The art of politics is to save the ship from going down or, if that is not possible, to avoid going down with it; and this was a ship which was foundering fast.

These were the serious crises. The more newsworthy but less important ones continued to occupy a disproportionate part of our time. It isn't true that there is no smoke without fire; otherwise a significant part of each day's journalistic output would never be printed. Allegations that Ted Short, Labour's deputy leader and Leader of the House of Commons and a man of rigorous honesty, was holding a secret bank account in Switzerland, distracted us, though, once again, the basis of the story was a forgery, though a carefully conceived one sufficient to deceive the *Daily Mail*. At the same time, Arthur Lewis, an east London MP and a man as perennially angry as he was obtuse, was busily circulating rumours about the dubious bookmaking connections of the chief whip, Bob Mellish, a south-east London MP. When Lewis detailed his allegations to me in an unsigned letter (I easily recognised his idiosyncratic spelling and typing from signed letters he had sent to me in the past) I wrote back, 'Dear Arthur, Thank you for your anonymous letter . . .' He never replied. Both Short and Mellish sought my advice on how to handle their problems, in Short's case about further unfounded rumours, this time concerning the political activities of his wife. I told them not to reply to inquiries but merely greet them with a blank stare or a telephone put down. Short, however, said: 'No comment' when questioned about his wife which enabled a newspaper to begin a report next day: 'Mr Edward Short last night refused to comment . . .' Mellish was much more robust. His answer to a journalist's inquiry began, 'Print that, old son' [or words to that effect] 'and I'll take your editor for £50,000.' That was more effective than my solution and not a word appeared about him.

Wilson was properly furious about the unfounded attempts to smear his colleagues, especially Short, and he drafted in his own hand an Early Day Motion for a backbencher to put on the Commons Order Paper to refute another slur on him. It read: 'That this House dissociates itself from political and press hounding of the Leader of the House arising from an expense payment of £250 from a then highly regarded local government leader; demands early action to provide a compulsory public register of financial interests of hon. Members of this House, and of journalists enjoying special facilities within the Palace of Westminster, and further calls upon those hon. Members and newspaper proprietors who have shown their politically sensitive interest in these questions to devote equal energy and time to inquiring about the sources of funds for the purchase of yachts.' The 'then highly-regarded local government leader' was T. Dan Smith, once the powerful boss of Newcastle City Council and later jailed for fraud. The motion was classic Wilsonism: he was defending a colleague unjustly accused; he was demanding a register of MPs, because he thought it would embarrass the Tories, and for journalists because he knew many of them had substantial freelance incomes derived from their Westminster privileges (and, because, in any case, he hated them); and he was airing his long-held suspicions that Ted Heath had been privately subsidised to pursue his hobby of yachting. To cap it all, the piece of paper on which it was written had a note to him on its back from a member of my staff saying: It is being said upstairs [the Press Gallery] that the evening papers today will be naming

Walter Terry.' In its way, those two sides of the paper encompassed nearly all our problems at that time.

Meanwhile, as October grew nearer, the coming election took up more and more of our time. All ministers had been told to provide upbeat proposals for the future which might capture the voters' support. All did so with some skill, but a White Paper on the future of British industry, drawn up by Tony Benn and, principally, his deputy, Eric Heffer, was so disastrously vague and, where it wasn't vague, threatening, that Wilson tore it up and dictated the headings of it himself. Heffer and Benn were the main believers in the theory that what the British voter wanted in 1974 was state control of industry and a hefty dose of nationalisation. Heffer was certain that if he was allowed to speak to the voters, they would flock to us in their millions, a theory unsupported by anyone outside the closed minds of the left and which caused an explosive clash between us.

A significant part of most days in the press office was taken up in considering requests from ministers to appear on radio or television, the decisions on which had been delegated to me by the Prime Minister. My instinctive reaction in that period to most of these requests was to refuse them; I thought the public had had enough of politicians for the time being and we wanted to save our ammunition for the general election. It was also the case that most ministers were not as smart as they thought they were when confronted by a microphone or a camera's lens. But one particular refusal caused a stormy outburst from Heffer. He wanted to appear on BBC TV to debate the middle-classes with a Tory MP, John Gorst, who was chairman of the Middle-class Alliance. I'm sure that if a Tory press secretary had asked whether the Duke of Buccleuch was a suitable candidate to discuss the working classes, he would take the same attitude as I did that day. Gorst would have made political mincemeat of Heffer and I told my press office junior who had received the request to refuse it. He came to my room a few minutes later, deeply troubled, saying that Heffer had threatened to report him to the Prime Minister. I had the call transferred to me and immediately told Heffer not to bully my staff. He apologised but said he was going to insist on taking part in the broadcast. I said he could not. He then said he would come to No. 10 and demand to see the Prime Minister. I told him that if he did, I would instruct the policeman on the door to refuse to admit him. If by chance there should be a press photographer outside to watch the door being shut in his face, how would that look? He dropped his protest.

As a former pro-marketeer, Heffer had to go farther than most on the left to reiterate his credentials as an anti-marketeer. Wilson had, remarkably, granted his ministers the freedom to campaign on public platforms for a No vote in the run-up to the referendum on whether Britain should remain in the EEC, despite the fact that official government policy was to vote Yes. But he drew the line at ministerial anti-Government speeches in the House of Commons, even if they spoke from the backbenches. Heffer, alone among anti-marketeer ministers, felt compelled to cross that line to eliminate any doubts which might still exist among suspicious colleagues about his sincerity. He was warned, through the whips, that if he went ahead with the speech, he would be sacked and Wilson asked me to compose a letter of dismissal which I could take to the Commons and personally deliver to Heffer if he made the threatened speech. I took a seat in the Press Gallery where I could face Heffer though looking down upon him. He saw me and he knew why I was there, but he was not to be put off. As soon as he had finished his speech, I dashed downstairs to the Commons Lobby to wait for him as he left the Chamber and give him the news that henceforth he could deliver any speech he liked from the backbenches because it was to there he was returning.

But though I took little more than a minute, he was too quick for me, moving at great speed for so burly a man. He left the Palace of Westminster as soon as his speech ended, a rare act of discourtesy even for him, because the convention of the House is that a speaker remains to hear at least part of the speech of the MP who follows him. Civil servants searched for Heffer but he couldn't be found. Wilson decided that I should announce his sacking at 10 p.m. by releasing the terms of the letter I had drafted. In the end, Bill Housden took it to Heffer's flat and put it under the door. The next day, Heffer had the brazen cheek to accuse Wilson of discourtesy in announcing his dismissal to the press before telling him of it. It was as convincing as Bernard Manning complaining that someone had been rude to him.

More seriously, trouble was building up on another front (Marcia was later to describe it as 'a small cloud on the horizon' but it was a lot bigger than that). Sir Desmond Brayley, industrialist and ex-army friend of George Wigg (they both rose, I believe, from a sergeant's stripes to full colonel, as did another of Wigg's mysterious pals, Lord Goodman) had been made a peer when Wilson formed his Government in March and was appointed Army Minister in the House of Lords. Fortunately, no wars broke out while he was in office.

Brayley was a cheerful but, politically, incredibly ignorant man. He had been friendly to Wilson after the 1970 defeat, when he had loaned him his penthouse flat at Arlington House, Westminster, above the Le Caprice restaurant. He was also a generous supplier of a particular brand of large cigar, shaped like a submarine without a conning tower, of which Wilson was especially fond. His main, perhaps only, talent was for making money. That was the admirable side of his character to those for whom that ability mattered more than any other. Less admirable was a tendency to confuse the money of the company he chaired, Canning Town Glassworks, with his own, a failing he shared with Eric Miller, chairman of Peachey Properties, to whom I will come later. Brayley was inarticulate, an embarrassment to his Upper House colleagues and unfit for a ministerial post. After a few months in office, a deputation of Labour peers, led by the Lord Chancellor, Lord Elwyn-Jones, called on Wilson and asked that Brayley be dropped from the administration. Reluctantly, Wilson agreed.

He told me the deputation said it was unfortunate Brayley couldn't write his own speeches, but, even worse, that he couldn't read those written for him by his department.

There was no doubt that Brayley had to go and the traditional reshuffle immediately after the general election seemed to be the right time. But the intention to sack him for incompetence was overtaken by more sinister events. Just as the date for the second election of 1974 was being announced, the rigorously honest Peter Shore, Secretary of State for Trade, told Wilson that he intended to order an inquiry into Brayley's past handling of his company's affairs. That was bad enough but the *Daily Mail* was worse, giving details of Brayley's alleged fraudulent mishandling of his company's money. Labour has always been sensitive to accusations about financial malpractice (as the Tories are about sexual ones and the Liberals are about both). As soon as I read the paper's story, I went to Wilson's study and urged him to dismiss Brayley that day. He agreed there was no alternative. But the hurt which sacking anyone usually caused him led him to delay the dismissal for several hours. If an event could be sad and hilarious at the same time, this was it.

Wilson's first intention had been to tell Brayley the bad news immediately that morning but he needed the fortification of a lunch and a brandy or two before he could bring himself to do it, and Brayley was told to come to No. 10 in the afternoon. I had a chance to speak to him before his formal meeting with Wilson began and he told me a miserable tale about his terrible night. The telephone had never stopped ringing in his penthouse as other newspapers tried to follow up the *Mail*'s story, he said. Incredibly, the Minister for the Army, a rich man, had, in the end, climbed over the back wall at Arlington House and, shunning five-star hotels, spent the night in the anonymity of a doss-house in Kennington, on the south bank of the Thames – on the whole, a better story for the tabloid press than the one which had caused it. He was clearly distressed by his experience. 'Why didn't you take the phone off the hook?' I asked him. He looked at me in wide-eyed astonishment. The thought hadn't occurred to him.

There were five of us, including Wilson, in the Prime Minister's study that afternoon. Brayley was flanked by his solicitor and Robert Armstrong, there in his role as principal private secretary. I sat close to the Prime Minister. Wilson hated this part of his job and on this occasion he was at his worst. In a rambling opening, he assured Brayley of his trust in him and said that the real target of the press was himself, and that they were attacking him through his Minister for the Army. His flattering, if implausible, words were totally misunderstood by Brayley, who thought he was being given a vote of confidence and he thanked the Prime Minister for what he had said. There was an awkward silence. Brayley beamed, but those of us who knew what was happening all sat there dismayed until Wilson began again. This time he was more direct and at last a dim light began to glow in Brayley's hitherto unlit mind. When Wilson finally stopped, Brayley asked: 'What do you want me to do, Prime Minister? Do you want me to resign?'

The fish wasn't going to escape the hook again. At once, Armstrong slipped a piece of paper from a folder placed upon his lap and slid it in front of Brayley. 'What is it?' asked Brayley. 'Your letter of resignation,' replied Armstrong. Guided by his solicitor, the bewildered Brayley signed. Armstrong then took another piece of paper from the folder and put it before Wilson, who signed it. 'What is that?' asked the solicitor. 'The Prime Minister's acceptance of Lord Brayley's resignation,' said Armstrong, in the highest tradition of a civil service mandarin's efficiency.

'What happens now?' asked the solicitor. I told him that I would release the news at six o'clock. He asked about press calls and I replied that I would refer them all to him, as Lord Brayley was no longer a member of the government. It all went astonishingly well and the Brayley scandal became more or less a one-day wonder; it had no significance for the general election.

But, immediately, another problem sprang up. On 20 September, the day the general election was announced, Chapman Pincher, the biggest journalistic name on the *Daily Express,* wrote a story about Marjorie Halls's claim for compensation from the Civil Service Department for the death of her husband. Pincher's hostility to Harold Wilson was of long standing and it was reciprocated, especially after a vicious exchange of letters between Pincher and Martin Gilbert, the historian, who objected violently to Pincher's attacks on Wilson at a private lunch party. None of this stopped Marcia, after Wilson's death, from suggesting to Pincher that the two of them should write a book about the infiltration of the Labour party by the left, based on Wilson's private papers which she possessed. Nothing came of the project and Pincher returned his share of a substantial advance paid by a publisher.

Pincher did not write all that he might have done about Marjorie Halls's claim, but it was enough to send Marcia into a frenzy. At the very start of the election campaign, that story caused us to be diverted yet again from real issues down the path to the imaginary. We never found our way back. There are many ways to start fighting a general election campaign but to do it by a generalised attack on the press is not one of them. Wilson's response to Pincher was to kick off the campaign by writing his own speech for delivery at Portsmouth on 20 September. He knew I wouldn't willingly write such nonsense but by that time, to put it mildly, he had got out of the habit of composing his own scripts. The speech he prepared was a rant against 'the cohorts of journalists' who were scouring the country with a mandate to find any story 'true or fabricated' for use against the Labour party. He claimed that he had information that money was being offered to those who had worked with Tony Field in return for information about his business activities. It was the first I had heard of it and I never did hear of it again. I believe what the Prime Minister was attacking was a garbled version of Milhench's request to the *Daily Mail* for £25,000 for the fraudulent letter bearing Wilson's forged signature. One of our problems was that everyone in and about our circle believed, erroneously, he or she was an expert on the press. The less they knew, the more expert they were convinced they were, and they advised the Prime Minister, a willing listener, accordingly, usually by circulating rumours among themselves which grew in the retelling. Part of my job was to squash them.

There was much else besides the 'cohorts' passage. When the speech came to me for a final polish, I struck out every hostile reference to the press. When Wilson saw what was left, he called me to his study. 'Joe,' he said, 'you've taken out too much,' and, despite every argument I could think of, the 'cohorts' were put back to ramble through the undergrowth. He got the predictable press for it.

Press matters went from bad to worse throughout the campaign. Once again, rumours of a dastardly Fleet Street plot to destroy Wilson on the eve of polling day began to circulate within our circle, mainly settling on Wilson's income tax. Wilson had for weeks been worrying about the disappearance of his tax returns from his home in Lord North Street. He had left them on his desk, he said, and they had disappeared. I never had any doubt as to where they had gone. Wilson sometimes had a simple method of dealing with his affairs. He would put the personal letters he received in a pile on his desk, along with other unsorted papers. When the pile grew too big, he would skim through them and then throw unwanted ones into the wastepaper basket. I hadn't any doubt that his missing tax papers had suffered that fate.

But that was too simple an explanation for him. Then Bob Carvel told me there were rumours in Fleet Street that a Tory journalist working for the *Daily Mirror* was going to explode a story about Wilson's income tax. Terry Lancaster didn't believe it for a moment. In fact, anyone wanting a scandal to be published would have chosen a Tory paper. It then became apparent that people close to Marcia, principally Peter Lovell-Davies, a publicist, who believed the tax plot story, were making inquiries in Fleet Street about this hypothetical scoop. When I reported the Carvel conversation to Wilson, he and Marcia took it as confirmation that something sinister was afoot. In fact, what Carvel had heard, somewhat embellished, was the story which began with Lovell-Davies. The circle had become a dizzy spiral, feeding upon itself. Suspicion now hardened against the *Daily Mail* as the paper most likely to print the story and nothing that Bernard Donoughue or I said could shake their conviction that it existed. Wilson wanted it stopped, come what may. We declined to help and so he asked Albert Murray to tell a senior official of the printers' union that the *Daily Mail* intended to publish a 'scandal' in the week before polling day. The union leader said firmly that it wouldn't. Should such a story be prepared for publication, he said loyally, there would be a strike to prevent the press from interfering in the democratic process; what's more, he added, there would be a strike in any paper which tried to publish and if an attempt was made by the BBC to do so, 'the plugs would be pulled out'.

There was no story and no strike, but disruption at the *Mail* the weekend before polling day led to a lengthy front-page article in the paper on the Monday protesting that it had no plans to expose anything.

This was all an element in a deteriorating situation within our office where matters had been going from bad to worse for several months. No matter that the prime need was to win the second general election of 1974; the need to score points within the office was greater. During the summer, I heard that Marcia had taken the decisive step to get rid of me. She had told Wilson I should be supplanted as an influence in his kitchen Cabinet by Lovell-Davies; if she were to make a graceful concession, it would be no more than that I should remain as a toothless and spineless cardboard cut-out of a press secretary. Foolishly, she had said it in front of a witness, who promptly told me. She thought she had chosen her time well to make her move; as she knew, I was about to borrow a friend's telephone-less cottage in the small hamlet of Ardentinny, in a remote part of Argyllshire, for a two-week break. That would have given Lovell-Davies (who may well have known nothing about the scheme) a chance to move in. But the holiday played in my favour, not hers, and frustrating the scheme was child's play. Before I left for Argyllshire, I told the story to Gordon Greig, a close and loyal friend who was shortly to succeed Walter Terry as political editor of the *Daily Mail*. After I had been away for some days, he ran the story in the paper's gossip column. When I returned from holiday, Wilson vehemently denied the story to me. We both knew it was true but we avoided another crisis by both pretending it wasn't. What was amusing was that neither Wilson nor Marcia, both of whom regarded themselves as expert practitioners of the black arts, ever suspected I had anything to do with the *Mail's* story. After all, I had been in Argyllshire for ten days and the story carried not the by-line of Gordon Greig but of Nigel Dempster, then regarded as an inveterate enemy of Marcia's, though many years later he was to claim a close friendship. That put a stopper on the plot for a while, until Marcia tried another tack.

When the election campaign was about to begin, and while Donoughue and I were waiting outside the Prime Minister's study for a strategy meeting which he had called, we discovered he was holding the meeting in his flat without telling either of us. No doubt we were then expected to arrive at the flat, looking sheepish for being late for a meeting we hadn't been told about and where we weren't wanted and automatically relegated to a junior and defensive position. Instead, we went back to our offices. Our departure from the study area was immediately reported to the Prime Minister; within minutes we were summoned to the flat.

The atmosphere was strained, but Terry Lancaster, who was already there and who possessed a rare talent for crashing in where others dared not tread, jovially started the conversation with: 'Joe will write the speeches, of course?' There was an uncomfortable silence. The Prime Minister raised his eyes, looking at no one in particular but concentrating on an unremarkable part of the ceiling, and said: 'Under Marcia's direction . . . the speeches.' Putting Marcia in charge of the speeches – hadn't she been in charge of the party conference speech which had been left on the floor? – was about as constructive as asking a dyslexic to compile the New Oxford Dictionary. His words only confirmed what we knew all along: that Lovell-Davies and his close friend, Denis Lyons (both of them present that day and both to be made peers in the following year) had been identified by Marcia as putative speechwriters. Later, Wilson told me Lovell-Davies and Lyons would be 'having a shot' at the first speech, but asked me to look at it when he had finished. The final draft which emerged from several hours of hard work was laboured and unspeakable, in every sense of the term. I wasn't surprised. Lyons had submitted a bizarre memorandum to Wilson in June setting out a mythical message to Ted Heath from a well-wisher in Tunbridge Wells which attacked Labour and put the Tory case very well. The purpose of the memorandum was to rectify Labour's 'abysmal failing' in putting over its message. Heath might

DAILY Mirror

BRITAIN'S BIGGEST DAILY SALE 6p   Monday, February 7, 1977

WORLD EXCLUSIVE
The incredible story
of Lady Falkender

MARCIA : The truth about that honours list

Begins today:
The most explosive
story of influence
and power inside
No 10—see Pages 15, 16 & 17

LADY FALKENDER—the former Marcia Williams—drew up Sir Harold Wilson's main resignation honours list on her own lavender notepaper.

Many of the peers and knights on the list were her nominations. The names appeared in her own handwriting. And the Prime Minister made few changes.

These astonishing revelations about the controversial honours were made by Joe Haines, who was Sir Harold's Press Secretary.

In a book out next week he describes the sweeping scope of Lady Falkender's influence at No 10 Downing Street.

He charts her rise from shorthand-typist at Labour Party headquarters to a unique position of power as Sir Harold's personal and political secretary.

Haines says: "She possessed a remarkable personality which, at its peak, was overpowering ... Had she gone into the House of Commons she would have forced her way into the Cabinet at an age when most single women were still hoping to get married."

Yet her power, says Haines hung "like a baleful cloud" over the heads of the Downing Street staff.

Haines's book is called

By TERENCE LANCASTER
Political Editor

"The Politics of Power." Today the Mirror starts serialising major extracts from it.

The former Downing Street Press chief reports on the tears and tantrums at No 10. He talks of

● Marcia the "telephone tyrant," whose calls so often ended in shouting matches.

● The time when an angry Harold Wilson banned Marcia from coming into the office because

CONTINUED ON PAGE 2

INSIDE NO. 10: SHE was fiercely loyal. HE needed a match for his own political genius

How the *Daily Mirror*'s political editor Terence Lancaster first reported
The Politics of Power on 7 February 1977.

༄༅། །ཏ་ལའི་བླ་མ་ཆེན་དང་། གནས་མལ་ཡོ་གནས་རྫོགས་ལ།
བཀྲ་ཤིས་བདེ་ལེགས་སུ།། །།

With Season's Greetings
and
All Good Wishes
for a Happy
and
Prosperous New Year

The Dalai Lama

With Very Best Wishes and
God's Blessings
for Christmas and
throughout the New Year

from

AL-HAJJI FIELD MARSHAL IDI AMIN DADA, V.C., D.S.O., M.C.
PRESIDENT

State House, Entebbe. Uganda.   Christmas, 1975.

Some of the Christmas cards to Harold Wilson thrown into a waste paper basket by Lady Falkender. Clockwise from top left: the Dalai Lama, 'Field Marshal' Idi Amin 'VC', Archbishop Makarios of Cyprus, and the Secretary-General of the United Nations, Kurt Waldheim.

With Best Wishes
for Christmas
and the New Year

Archbishop Makarios
of Cyprus

MERRY CHRISTMAS
AND A
HAPPY NEW YEAR

THE SECRETARY-GENERAL AND MRS. KURT WALDHEIM

The author with Harold Wilson in happier days.

"Y'know, Marcia, I've just realised that Joe Haines' book will be published on February 14th ..... St Valentine's Day."

McLACHLAN

McLACHLAN

MARCIA: THE TRUTH ABOUT THAT HONOURS LIST

"It makes you wonder what else she influenced Sir Harold to do"

How some of the cartoonists saw the Wilson–Falkender relationship. Opposite page: McLachlan; right: Keith Waite; and below: John Kent.

Not a happy day: Lady Falkender, Harold Wilson and Joe Haines walking grimly from Wilson's home in Lord North Street to Labour headquarters in Smith Square during the February 1974 general election campaign.

Lady Falkender (right) with the billionaire James Goldsmith, knighted in Wilson's last honours list, and Lady Annabel Goldsmith.

Joe Haines, Harold Wilson and Dr Bernard Donoughue (Senior Policy Adviser) leaving Labour's HQ in Smith Square.

Lady Falkender (left) and Lady Wilson at the memorial service for
Lord Wilson in July 1995.

have been encouraged by it but I wasn't. Rightly or wrongly, it looked to me like another attempt to undermine my position. Nothing came of it.

Lyons was a huge man and Lovell-Davies very thin; they were known irreverently within the office as Laurel and Hardy. But this wasn't funny. I was not prepared to give them lessons in speechwriting, nor was I willing, if it were possible, to try to improve their draft. Raising the *Titanic* would have been easier and I saved far fewer words from it – one adjective, in fact – than there were survivors of that unfortunate ship. Anyway, the issue was too serious for games. Instead, I told both men I intended to go on holiday, reinforcing what Bernard Donoughue had told them earlier. There was a whiff of panic in the air. Lovell-Davies asked me: 'Do you think we are being used by Marcia against you?' I said I thought that was possibly so. Lovell-Davies then said he wasn't a speechwriter and Lyons said he was a busy man. Their retreat from the action was at a speed once derisively reserved for the troops led in the Libyan desert by General Graziani. When Wilson later asked me what their first speech effort was like, I replied: 'No good.' 'You do them, then,' he said, and that was the end of that particular plot.

Throughout that summer, Marcia had been determined to do anything she could to break what she thought was my stranglehold on the Prime Minister's speeches, except let him write them himself. Finally, after he retired, it was done retrospectively. He was full of praise at the time for a speech I wrote for delivery at the annual dinner of American correspondents in London. It was a rather dramatic attack on the IRA which won front-page headlines about 'blood on the shamrock.' After resignation, he was to describe the speech as a mistake, admitting that he didn't write it himself, which meant it was my mistake, not his. But the most important speech of his second premiership, in his eyes, was one delivered to the National Union of Mineworkers at Scarborough on 7 July 1975. In his book, *Final Term*, Wilson wrote: 'Never, in thirty years in Parliament, had I prepared a speech with such care – dictating, writing, amending, inserting, discarding and drafting again . . .The work went on – according to the No. 10 diary – "until just before Sunday midnight". In that last hour, I rewrote the final appeal, stressing how much was at stake for the industry, for the mineworkers and for Britain . . .'

That last paragraph consisted of the words: 'What the government is asking for the year ahead, what the government has the *right* to ask, the *duty* to ask, is not a year for self, but a year *for Britain.*' Wilson's description of his writing and rewriting was fantasy. That particular passage about a year for Britain was suggested by Geoffrey Goodman, industrial editor of the *Daily Mirror,* who had been seconded to the government to run the newly-established Counter-Inflation Unit, and, had been discussed by a small group, including me and Lord Jacobson, once editorial director of the *Mirror* group, several days beforehand. Wilson may have 'tickled' the final appeal, to use newspaper sub-editors' jargon, but that was his usual practice and that was all.

Wilson's other references in *The Final Term* to that Scarborough speech were nearly all untrue. The main body of the speech was written by me. Of course, there were changes to my first draft; there always were. Indeed, I toughened it myself, at his request. Wilson wrote the historical passages relating to his knowledge of, and friendship with, miners' leaders of the past and to his 1945 book, *New Deal for Coal.* But he wrote across my note submitting that first draft: 'This is your best ever.' Why he should have claimed what he did, I do not know, unless he was made to or unless the clouding of his memory had gathered apace. After all, everyone concerned with that speech knew that what he had subsequently written was not true.

There were other, more provable, lapses of memory concerning this period in politics. On Friday 27 June, ten days before the Scarborough speech, Wilson had sent a memorandum to the Chancellor, Denis Healey, telling him to instruct his officials not to waste their time on either a fully voluntary incomes policy (which would have meant abdicating the policing of it to the TUC, which couldn't be relied upon) or upon a statutory policy which would, inevitably, mean that trade unionists who defied it would end up with criminal sanctions being taken against them. This memorandum was a reaffirmation of a decision taken some weeks earlier during an all-day Cabinet meeting at Chequers, the Prime Minister's country residence. An attempt by right-wingers to force Wilson to adopt a compulsory incomes policy looked liked being successful until Bob Mellish, the Chief Whip, scuppered it.

Several ministers had opted, with varying degrees of reluctance, for a compulsory policy, with Reg Prentice the most enthusiastic, adamant that election promises would have to be broken and a legally-enforceable policy introduced. Barbara Castle was seethingly against and, at the end of the debate, Wilson turned to Mellish and asked his opinion: 'I'm not one of your effing intellectuals round this table,' said Mellish, 'All I know is, I'll never get the effing thing through the House.'

'I think that settles it,' said Wilson. But it didn't. Within weeks, the Treasury was back, insisting that a compulsory policy was the only one with a chance of success and there were ominous signs that Wilson was preparing to concede to their demands. On Monday 30 June, Bernard Donoughue and I had a stand-up battle with the Prime Minister outside the Cabinet room after a meeting of ministers had moved menacingly towards a legal pay limit. The argument between us went back and forth, but the one uppermost in Wilson's mind was that the pound had dropped to only $2.17 that day (compare that with 1998's average of around $1.66, which manufacturers moaned was too high, or the figure for 2002, which varied between $1.39 and £1.59). Wilson had been speaking at Stoneleigh, in Warwickshire, that morning. By the time he returned to Downing Street, the Treasury was on hand to propose a statement by the Chancellor to the Commons the following day which would announce a compulsory incomes policy, despite Wilson's express instruction three days earlier to rule out such a step. It proposed a legal limit of ten per cent on pay rises, which sounds generous today but wasn't then. The trouble with percentage increases was, and is, that those earning the most get the most and those on the poorest pay get the least. Percentage pay increases are spuriously equal; they merely widen the real income gap between the better and the worse-off.

At the end of a long debate between Wilson, Donoughue and me, the Prime Minister said wearily: 'Joe, the trouble is that when old problems recur, I reach for the old solutions. I've nothing to offer any more.' But, stubbornly, he wouldn't retreat from his inclination towards a compulsory policy because he couldn't understand our alternative, which was a voluntary policy with a statutory back-up if the unions, as was their custom, broke their word.

The Treasury, sensing the Prime Minister's uncertainty, played its hand for all it was worth. It spent the day fine-tuning a statement which was to be submitted to the Cabinet the following morning and for which Wilson asked its members to attend an hour earlier than usual – 9.30 a.m. instead of 10.30 a.m. There was a dinner, followed by reception, for the Belgian Prime Minister, Leo Tindemans, that evening. The Treasury's proposed statement finally came over at ten minutes past midnight – a single copy for the Prime Minister. None for me and none for Donoughue, despite firm promises earlier to the contrary. The draft was nothing less than a complete reversal of government policy, economically questionable and politically impossible. It would never have got through the Commons except with Tory support, and for that the opposition would have exacted a price. It would almost certainly have brought down the Prime Minister, if not his Government. All this in pursuit of a policy obsession of unelected civil servants whose own salaries had been so substantially and disastrously increased only a few months before. It was a classic case of 'don't do as I do, do as I say'. Bernard Donoughue and I attached our objections to the Prime Minister's statement so that he would see them before he went to bed and we then left. Wilson phoned me before I got home, leaving a message with my wife that I should call him immediately I got home. We spoke just before 2 a.m. He said that he agreed with our objections and had given instructions that the Treasury draft was not to be given to Cabinet ministers. In addition, he had put back the Cabinet meeting to its usual time, though his decision was too late to reach many members who turned up at 9.30 am.

I have written about this episode before, but it is necessary to repeat it in view of Wilson's subsequent version of events. He wrote in *The Final Term:* 'Without a legal framework, indeed, one backed by criminal sanctions, we were told, sterling would go. At 1 a.m., ministers emerging from the Cabinet room were so advised. In this respect, Mr Joe Haines's book reproducing his note to me on the midnight Treasury demarche is accurate.'

But that wasn't what I wrote at all. There was no meeting of ministers that night, in the Cabinet room or elsewhere. Wilson went to his study just as I and the last of his a hundred or so guests were leaving at 12.50 a.m. There had been a meeting earlier in the day which authorised the Treasury to produce a draft (after which our row outside the Cabinet room took place), but no other. Only those who knew just how formidable Wilson's memory was would realise the importance of his faulty recall of this occasion. He hadn't been at a Cabinet at all that night. He seemed to have forgotten altogether that there had been an official dinner and that he had been entertaining M. Tindemans and his other guests until well after midnight.

Eight
Time to Go

In January 1975, Wilson went to Canada and the United States. Our party hurriedly left Ottawa, without formal ceremony, as the rain began to freeze upon the VC10's wings in the sub-zero temperature; we arrived in Washington in gale-force winds and a temperature of seventy-seven degrees. Our first attempt to land at the Andrews Air Force Base came close to disaster, with the plane rocking violently when little more than fifty feet above the ground. Members of the crew told us that air traffic control had given the wrong instructions to the pilot. It was a harrowing experience. Had things gone cataclysmically wrong, British politics would have been radically changed, for the others on the plane included Jim Callaghan and Denis Healey, Wilson's two most likely successors. My attention, as the pilot wrestled to get the aircraft stable, was distracted by my assistant being sick next to me; the young secretary sitting next to Bernard Donoughue clasped his hand so tightly that when he stepped off the aircraft, his palm was bleeding in four places where her fingernails had dug in.

Apart from that, it was not a particularly memorable trip. President Ford, who had taken over from Nixon after the disgraced President had resigned the previous August, was a nice man, but not much more. We travelled home, gratified that no harm had been done, even if little had been accomplished. When we arrived at Heathrow, there was an imperative message for the Prime Minister: Marcia wanted to see him urgently and was on the way to the airport. Only the first part of the message was true, in that she wanted to see him, though the urgency remained a mystery. For the rest, she had no intention of leaving home until she knew that his plane had landed. Why she had to come to the airport was another mystery, since it would have been more convenient and more private if he had called in on her at her home on his way back to Downing Street, or if she had visited him there. No one would have seen anything unusual in that. But Wilson accepted her terms and decided to wait until she arrived. After forty minutes, with all-round embarrassment growing by the second and no sign of Marcia, he said he was leaving and told all of us still there, officials and advisers, to go home. He was driven away and then we left. But he merely instructed his driver, Bill Housden, to circle the airport and then return to the VIP lounge to wait for Marcia's arrival. Eventually, she turned up, but Housden didn't overhear what was afoot. Nothing ever emerged to satisfy our curiosity. I think that, yet again, it was no more than an exercise in humiliation, deliberately inflicted. Wilson had been parading on a world stage; now he had to be brought down a peg and the entourage who had paraded with him had to learn that, compared to her, they didn't count. Come to that, nor did the American President.

There was a similar episode on one of our many visits to Paris. A dinner at the British embassy was delayed for forty-five minutes, with officials desperately making excuses to the guests, while Marcia harangued Wilson over the telephone with another grievances, real or imagined, to which she insisted he should give attention, culminating in a demand that he should return to London at once. That Wilson would be damaged by the private opinions of influential guests about his apparent rudeness – or shocked by his haggard appearance when he eventually turned up – was of no account. Towards the end of that visit, I went to the Elysee Palace to pick up Wilson after a meeting with the French President, M. Giscard d'Estaing. He looked concerned. When we got into the back of the car, he told me he had had 'a heart flutter' and said that as soon as we returned to the British embassy he would go to his room and I was to get his doctor, Joe Stone, immediately.

When Stone came out of the room he told me the Prime Minister had to rest and that I was to concoct a story justifying his absence from Downing Street. He needed a week off, said Stone, and after that he would be all right. Sometimes, press secretaries have to be more than economical with the truth; they have to dispense with it altogether for what they perceive to be the greater good. It was reminiscent of Winston Churchill's stroke in 1953, when No. 10 lied about his illness when he hardly had the strength to get into the car which took him to Chartwell and his officials were uncertain whether he would be alive when he got there. On this occasion, I said Wilson had influenza, an illness everyone understands and accepts. Had I said his heart was giving him trouble, the political and financial consequences would have been huge. And he did recover.

On yet another European occasion, this time at a European Community summit in Rome, work in the British delegation was temporarily suspended while Wilson dealt with a telephone call from Marcia in London, again demanding that he return home immediately. He, of course, refused. But it staggers the mind that she could have thought for a moment that the Prime Minister of Great Britain could abandon a summit of European leaders on the instructions of his secretary in order to deal with her personal crisis at home. A temporary illness was one thing, but no press secretary yet born could have plausibly explained a sudden return home on that occasion and I know I would not have tried.

These visits abroad were becoming an increasing worry. No one knew better than Wilson that he had wavered under pressure on the pound and it worried him. Though he wouldn't have buckled under Marcia's insistence on his returning from European summits, yet it had its own temptation. These meetings had begun to bore and depress him. No sooner did they begin than he longed for them to end. Once, he would have tried to dominate the gatherings. Now, all he wanted to do was leave.

The Rome summit in 1975, chaired by the Italian Prime Minister, Aldo Moro, was one of the worst. No more than three delegates from each country were permitted to attend the working sessions of the EEC. This meant that only the Prime Minister and the Foreign Secretary and a note-taker (an FCO official or the Secretary to the Cabinet) could be at the conference table. It also meant that the Prime Minister had to be in attendance nearly all the time, while the rest of us hung about in the marbled halls of the Barbarini palace, where the summit was taking place. Occasionally, Wilson or Callaghan would come out to give us a brief progress report or, more likely, to stretch their legs.

Finally, on the first day, Wilson came out at 4.45 p.m. and said: 'God, what a bore. Still, it's nearly all over. I'll pop back in and see you all at five.' He didn't come out again until nearly 7 p.m. I know how Wilson felt about the tedium. The boredom of those of us who had exhausted all our small talk through the long hours of the afternoon was indescribable. 'I thought you were going to finish by five,' I said to him.

'So we were,' replied a fed-up Wilson, 'but bloody Moro decided he would sum up and he took an hour-and-a-half to do it.' 'Do you mean,' I said, mock-indignant, 'that for all their Moros we gave our today?' He smiled wearily, for the only time during the day.

A meeting with the German Chancellor, Helmut Schmidt, was disturbing in a different sense. I went to Chequers late one Sunday evening to prepare for it and to leave Northolt with Wilson early on the Monday morning. When I got there, Wilson was distressed. He told me he had 'the squitters' and might have to call off the visit. This wasn't the first time he had been so afflicted. The 'squitters' were becoming a familiar indisposition when difficult problems had to be faced. I have very little medical knowledge but I suspected that these illnesses were emotional rather than physical. I told him he couldn't call off the meeting; nothing creates more uncertainty domestically than the belief that a Prime Minister's health is failing. We had had to deny too many false stories about his physical decline to start issuing true ones. Fortunately, next morning, he pronounced himself fit and we set off for Northolt.

On the way there, for want of something to do and hoping to stop him pumping pipe smoke into the confined space every few seconds, I pointed out a magpie to him in a nearby field. Wilson sat bolt upright. 'Only one?' he asked. 'Yes,' I replied. 'That's unlucky,' he said, and slumped back gloomily in his seat. I was astonished. I had been with him for six years and had never before been aware that he was superstitious. A minute or two later, he sat upright again. 'Look over there,' he said, pointing. 'There's a white horse. That means everything's OK.'

He may have been reassured. I wasn't. He had been a man of supreme self-confidence, or optimism, when dealing with foreign statesmen. He never had any need to look for omens, good or bad. Had he not himself always reserved the white horse for Roy Jenkins? He had an unhappy time in Hamburg and had difficulty in coping with the questions of German reporters, most of whom spoke impeccable English. All he wanted to do was to get away.

Wilson had intended, if he had won the 1970 election, to retire after two years. Only defeat made him carry on. His post-1974 victory talk about his being a deep lying centre-half rather than a centre forward, because he had a team of stars, was only his way of publicly expressing his private desire. He had had enough. He feared that scoring goals was getting beyond him. Being Prime Minister was no longer what mattered most. He knew his old flair and inspiration were declining. In minor ways – the repeated styes under the eye (although an antibiotic was found to cure them), the tennis elbow which ended his golfing and one cold after another – his health had deteriorated. He felt he had been around too long, suffered too much strife and was tired of fighting what he saw as the wreckers in his own party. He forgave none of those who had betrayed him over *In Place of Strife* and, though he treated them with his usual generosity, he forgot nothing and discounted nothing. That he eventually sided with Jim Callaghan as his successor was not so much out of admiration as out of necessity. He had said his only debt was to the Labour voters who had put him back in office and two more years there was enough to pay off the debt. The remark by the insufferable William Rees-Mogg that George Brown was a better man drunk than Wilson was sober was probably the most inaccurate judgement made by an editor of *The Times* since Geoffrey Dawson persisted in seeing the better side of Adolf Hitler. The truth was that Harold Wilson off-colour was still better than his Cabinet colleagues in their most brilliant plumage. Some of those who criticised him so severely, in and out of office, won't reach his shoulder when they stand side by side in the pantheon of British political history.

After the successful introduction of the new incomes policy, and the remorse he felt at not himself seeing that there was a way through to it, Wilson's yearning to leave office became the dominant theme of his life and ours. In late summer, he toyed with the idea of announcing his departure at the party conference at the end of September. Both Marcia and I immediately dismissed that with the cry of 'Macmillan and the Tories in 1963,' when the Conservative conference was reduced to an electioneering shambles by the announcement that the then Prime Minister was stepping down. Wilson knew the argument's strength and instantly abandoned the thought. His next idea was to go during the Christmas recess, a quiet time for politics. That proposition was squashed by Marcia (who was determined, if she could, to put off his resignation for as long as possible) who told him how unpopular he would be if he were responsible for all Labour's MPs being torn from Christmas with their loved ones, whoever they might be, in order to hold an election for a new leader. At that point, he settled to go in the late winter of 1976, the announcement and the final departure to straddle his sixtieth birthday on 11 March. At 1975's party conference at Blackpool, Wilson's growing detachment from government was more evident. As we talked in his hotel room one night, he handed me a number of memos from ministers seeking his decisions. 'You deal with them,' he said. He had never acted like that before. It was one thing to seek the advice of the unelected people close to him; it was another to delegate matters to them totally. What they all were I cannot now remember, except one which Tony Benn might recall: his memorandum sought the Prime Minister's agreement to his spending £2 million or so on a project which was being resisted either by other ministers or civil servants. It seemed to me Benn's case was impeccable and so I drafted a reply for Wilson, authorising him to go ahead. Wilson signed it without question.

He then asked me, in great secrecy, to draw up a timetable, in co-operation with his principal private secretary, Kenneth Stowe, for his resignation in the following year. He told me to date it from the afternoon of Wednesday 25 February, because the monthly meeting of the party's National Executive Committee would be held on the morning of that day and, he said, 'I'm not having those buggers interfering with it.' In fact, other constraints, cautiously outlined in my memorandum on the timetable, made that date seem impossible at the time. In the event, I was far too cautious. The announcement was delayed for three weeks without causing the problems I envisaged, but it was still impossible for the 'buggers' to do anything about it. Wilson was obsessive about security, repeatedly remarking that no one outside our very close circle – Marcia, Bernard, Albert and myself – and now Stowe, had any inkling that he was retiring and that if anyone else got to hear of it, it would leak. At about this time, I drew up a list of those who knew his intentions, and it came to twenty, which was testimony to the loyalty of those who worked for him and whom he unjustly suspected. In any case, he had already told George Thomas and Lord Goodman and, of course, his wife, as well as dropping heavy hints to Harold Lever. In pursuit of this mythical security, he stressed that I should make no copies of the document I was to draw up and that the original should be handed to him. That was too much to ask. I knew he would possibly lose, mislay, or inadvertently destroy the original and then ask me for a copy of it. I made just one copy, thinking that if he didn't require it, posterity might.

In the end, the timetable I included in the document (see below) had to be compressed. By late February, ominous signals were coming from the financial markets; sterling was falling very close to an exchange rate of $2 (happy days!), reckoned to be a confidence level, and a new crisis was brewing. If, while it was still on the hob, the Prime Minister resigned, it would be certain to boil over, so he decided to postpone his announcement until mid-March. The crisis eventually broke on 5 March, when sterling dipped below the $2 level. As Wilson wrote dramatically later, with his love of military metaphor: 'The Maginot Line had been breached,' or, as he described it a few paragraphs later: 'The Rubicon had been crossed,' finally adding, for good monarchical measure: 'The Emperor had no clothes.'

The perennially suspicious Foreign Secretary, Jim Callaghan, with the insight of an ex-Chancellor, had already approached Wilson in late February to ask him whether the Treasury was aiming to drive the pound down. He was about to go abroad, but requested a meeting should be held on his return to discuss his fears. Wilson assured him he was watching events, but both politicians knew that the Treasury had a mind and will of its own. It was, after all, a Treasury man who later rose to the heights of his department who once said to me that, 'Top Secret means that we don't tell the Chancellor.'

Despite assurances from Denis Healey that the fall in the value of the pound was temporary, caused by the Bank of England overselling sterling, it continued to drop and hovered a little above $1.90. Here again, in *The Final Term* Wilson misremembered, to put it politely, the history of his times. He wrote about the crisis: 'Apart from national considerations, this was worrying news to me personally. I had set Tuesday March 16 for announcing my resignation from the premiership' and later added: 'By that autumn [of 1975] 1 had set March, 1976, as, the time, on or around my sixtieth birthday on 11 March.' That was simply not true. The document I drew up demonstrated it; so did his agreement to give Marje Proops, the *Daily Mirror's* legendary columnist, an interview for publication on his birthday. That was to be his valedictory interview. When the crisis forced him to put off his resignation, I urged him to cancel his meeting with Marje. He said he could not without arousing suspicion (forgetting that the paper's political editor, Terry Lancaster, had been present in March 1974, when he said he would serve no more than two years). In the event, Marje's final question was the inevitable one: 'How long do you intend to carry on?' He replied to the effect that he would stay for as long as there was a job for him to do, an answer for which Marje never forgave him. The fall in sterling's value led to the Chancellor,

Denis Healey, becoming embroiled in a brutal Commons battle with the left, resulting in a defeat for the government. Healey long believed that that row scuppered his chances in the subsequent leadership contest, but I never thought that he could win. Like Roy Jenkins, his popularity was greatest among those without votes – Fleet Street and the broadcasters.

Though the final timetable was shortened by three weeks (we had envisaged lengthy ballots and re-ballots which never took place), the date of his departure was on schedule. My memorandum to Wilson, incorporating much of Ken Stowe's thoughts, read:

Arrangements for the handover.

1. The Prime Minister will want to hand over the leadership in such a way as will leave the authority and capability of the government as strong as possible. This note sets out some of the essential points that need to be taken into consideration for that purpose under four heads: personal, party political, constitutional and governmental

Personal

2. The reason for – and timing of – the handover must be presented as cogent and persuasive, and the decision must be a clear initiative by the Prime Minister, which pre-empts speculation about personal, party, or governmental crisis. The reasons are:

a. The present Cabinet is the strongest and most experienced for generations;

b. There must be opportunity for the most able to succeed in his prime;

c. The Prime Minister, having seen the country to a definitive conclusion on the EEC, and to a sound policy for dealing with inflation, judges that the time is right for a new man;

d. After nearly 30 years on the Front Bench, 13 years as Leader of the Labour party and nearly eight years as Prime Minister, the approach of his sixtieth birthday marks a point at which he can reasonably retire;

[ie. A new Prime Minister must be given the maximum opportunity to shape his government and be given an adequate opportunity to succeed before another general election is necessary. He should assume office while the present Parliament still has the larger part of its statutory course to run.]

3. Early 1976 could be exceptionally difficult for a handover; sterling, the economy, Northern Ireland could all create crisis conditions which would/could be aggravated by uncertainty over the leadership. It follows:

a. The Prime Minister's options must be kept open by maintaining secrecy.

b. The final decision must be able to be taken and implemented quickly.

Party political

4. Each of the two main parties now has an electoral process to find a new leader; neither is speedy unless in response to the first ballot there is a rallying of support for the front-runner which makes further voting unnecessary. This cannot be assumed. The procedure for the Labour party is, presumably, for the Liaison Committee to decide, though they would no doubt accede to the wishes of the Prime Minister if they have general support within the Parliamentary party. A measured procedure might be as follows:

[I then set out a voting schedule lasting three weeks altogether, which, in the end, was hopelessly pessimistic.]

5. This three-week timetable allows only three ballots. If there were a large number of candidates, the process would need to be speeded up; it would be hardly conceivable to allow more than three weeks.

6. The announcement of intention to resign would need to make clear that a three-week long electoral procedure would follow (but that would require, would it not, the Liaison Committee being brought in before the announcement?) in order to dispel misconceptions and talk of a 'leadership crisis'.

Constitutional

7. The constitutional position would be:

a. The Prime Minister would tell the Queen at an early date of his intention to stand down [in fact, Wilson later claimed that he had already told the Queen, during his annual visit to Balmoral in September 1975 of his intention to go within six months]; and

b. He would, on Day 1, tell the Queen that he had set in hand the procedure for choosing his successor as Leader of the Parliamentary Party.

c. On the day when the new Leader is known . . . he would go to the Palace and advise the Queen to send for him.

8. An alternative position would be that the Prime Minister actually resigned on Day 1 and was then invited by the Queen to continue in office until a new Leader had been elected.

9. All that is essential is to ensure that it is well known and understood at home and abroad that the Prime Minister and the Government remain in office until the Party elects a new Leader.

Governmental

10. This is the difficult aspect. In February, March or April we shall probably, at some point still unforeseeable, move from the simple anti-inflation £6 pay policy to some degree of inflation [this was a mis-typing by me for 'reflation']. If the question of selective import controls has not then been settled, that remains as an element in this 'spring

package.' The Chancellor will need to have room for manoeuvre on timing – from end January, say, to a Budget introduced just before Easter, e.g. Budget Tuesday 6 April for debate before the Recess (Good Friday 16 April).

11. The desirable interval is for the new administration to have three-four weeks in hand before the last day for a pre-Easter Budget, i.e., if the Budget were April 6, then Day 1 of the handover would be Tuesday, April 24. A Day 1 after this comes near to compelling the Chancellor to defer his Budget until after Easter. All the political pressure, especially in respect of unemployment, is likely to be for an early Budget, or at least an early packet of measures for reflation.

12. It is not possible now to plan a firm path through these uncertainties. The inference to be drawn is that since any move towards a package of reflationary measures will itself be likely to be preceded by a period of uncertainty in the foreign exchanges, it would be desirable to have disposed of the leadership issue before the Government began seriously to move in that direction – otherwise it would be preferable to have disposed of the leadership issue until after the 'reflation/Budget' action. The obvious difficulty about all this is that the Chancellor, unwittingly, becomes the determinant of the timetable for the handover by his judgement of the timing of his 'reflation' measures. If he has not acted by the third week in February, that becomes the time to set the handover in motion, the Chancellor then having to defer any measures for a few weeks.'

My memorandum was dated 6 November 1975, some five-and-a-half months before the decision to retire was announced. Had I been able to release it at the time, all the acres of newsprint devoted to speculation, mainly sinister, about the resignation 'mystery' might have been saved.

Rumours about his departure were eddying round Westminster for some months before it was finally announced. The Queen knew and so, I imagine, did members of her senior staff' Lord Goodman knew' George Thomas knew' Harold Lever knew' Jim Callaghan knew, almost certainly, Gerald Kaufman knew. Wilson couldn't keep it to himself.

But what shattered me was to discover than on 8 January 1976, Wilson and his wife and Marcia went to dinner at David Frost's house to discuss a TV series for Yorkshire Television and a book to be published by Weidenfeld and Nicolson, both on the theme of 'A Prime Minister on Prime Ministers'. Those present included Sir (soon afterwards, Lord) George Weidenfeld, James (soon afterwards Sir James) Goldsmith and Yorkshire TV executives. Lady Falkender was to be appointed as a 'consultant' for the series at a fee unknown to me. It was outrageous that people with a commercial interest in Wilson's retirement should be discussing with him matters of mutual profit when most of the Cabinet, nearly all of the parliamentary party and virtually every member of the party in the country had absolutely no idea that he was about to depart for greener pastures.

When I obliquely raised the question of the dinner and its purpose with Wilson he assured me that no one there that evening had been told of his intention soon to resign. They didn't need to be. None of them was born yesterday. Prime Ministers don't start making detailed arrangements for post-premier life when they are only fifty-nine and the next election is more than three years away unless they have it in mind to go quickly.

A small example of Wilson's growing failure to cope with routine govern-mental matters came early in 1976 when the parliamentary under-secretary at the Department of Education and Science, Joan Lestor, resigned over cuts in the education budget. He was uncharacteristically disturbed by Miss Lestor's going, though in his past he had taken in his stride many resignations of much more moment than a junior minister's. He was agitated when he raised with me the question of finding her replacement. He feared that because Miss Lestor had resigned on 'a matter of principle' no one else would take the post – which showed his grasp of political realities was loosening – and that the left would be in revolt. Given that Jennie Lee had once swallowed the reintroduction of prescription charges, the very issue on which her husband, Aneurin Bevan, had left the Attlee government, I told him his fears were groundless. 'But who do I get to replace her?' he asked. 'Give the job to another left-wing woman,' I said and suggested he should appoint Margaret Jackson, former Transport House employee, MP for Lincoln, parliamentary private secretary to Mrs Judith Hart at Overseas Development and at that time holding about the lowest job in the government as an assistant whip. 'I don't know her,' he said, 'do you?' When I told him that I did, he asked me to sound her out, but not to say that he had asked me to do so. Once again, we were in a position where, if Margaret spurned the offer, it was only a piece of unauthorised private enterprise on my part and no one could write that Wilson had been snubbed. So, through Jean Denham, her closest friend, I invited Margaret to No. 10 for coffee.

She was suspicious from the moment coffee was served. 'What's this all about?' she demanded. My feeble-sounding excuse that I thought it would be nice to meet again was brusquely dismissed and her question repeated. I told her that we had a problem over Joan Lestor's resignation and that I was thinking of recommending her to the Prime Minister for the vacancy, if she was interested, without, of course, any guarantee that he would listen to me. 'I know nothing about education,' she replied. 'You went to school, didn't you?' I asked. (In fact, she attended a high school in Norwich and the Manchester Institute of Technology.)

After a little more banter, she agreed that if she was offered the post, she would accept it; when she had left the building, I dashed up to Wilson and told him he could go ahead and appoint her, which he did, with relief out of proportion to the problem. Joan Lestor, an old friend, was never very friendly to me again after that. In later years, I was pleased with my talent-spotting. Margaret married Leo Beckett and, in her new name, became deputy leader of the Labour party under John Smith, acting leader when Smith died, President of the Board of Trade in Tony Blair's first Cabinet, Leader of the House of Commons and then Secretary of State for the Department of Food and Rural Affairs. Not even Barbara Castle ever held such a clutch of eminent posts.

The first inkling I had of new horrors to come was a few weeks later, when Ken Stowe showed me a shortlist of peerages proposed to be granted in the Resignation Honours List. It included David Frost, Wilson's favourite TV interviewer. I objected strongly; firstly, on the grounds that the dinner to exploit Wilson's retirement had been at Frost's house and that he might have a financial involvement; secondly because a peerage to a man whose reputation was founded on his role as a TV satirist would be greeted with derision to the Prime Minister's detriment. I had no idea at that stage that the Honours to be granted in the Resignation List in May were such that, by comparison, Frost was eminently suitable.

One phrase used by me in criticism of that final cascade of Honours stuck in the minds of headline writers; I said the list was written on Marcia's distinct lavender notepaper and it became notorious as 'the lavender list'. Marcia was to say later that the notepaper was pink; my wife said that what I called lavender was really lilac. But lavender it has remained.

Marcia was to claim that the list was all Harold Wilson's. She had merely written down the names which he gave her. Certainly, Wilson carried around odd scraps of paper on which he wrote such names as Len Murray, general secretary of the TUC, and a few other political worthies. But that list was Marcia's: Weidenfeld (to whom I also objected, knowing of the contractual arrangement which Wilson had made to have another book published by him), Kagan (to whom she looked for financial assistance), Miller (to whom she had become romantically attached), Lew Grade and Bernard Delfont (part of her showbiz obsession) and James Goldsmith. Wilson had told me Goldsmith intended to offer her a directorship. Goldsmith was a well-known contributor to Conservative party funds; the previous autumn, Wilson had asked me to make any excuse to get him out of a dinner, arranged by Marcia and David Frost, with Goldsmith and James Slater, on the grounds that he had always opposed those who made money rather than earned it. In an indiscreet moment when we were discussing his Resignation Honours (I wanted to make sure that a promise to make Albert Murray a peer was not reneged upon), Wilson muttered: 'Why should I give anything to Goldsmith? I hardly know him.' The bulk of that list was Marcia's. The names which brought the most odium were those thought likely to bring her the most reward, though in many ways the most bizarre peerage was the one given to John Vaizey. Vaizey was not a Labour supporter. He had been virulent in the past about Wilson. He wrote to Albert Murray after Murray lost his seat at Gravesend, rejoicing in his defeat. His sole qualification for a title was the assistance he gave to Marcia in finding a public school for her sons.

In later years, Marcia was to write to another peer saying that her finances were in a poor state, and asking him, seeing that she had been responsible for his peerage, whether he could help her. The answer was short and sharp. He refused, saying that he was well aware that Roy Jenkins had nominated him.

An embarrassment for Wilson, as his retirement day drew nearer, was an approach from the French President, Giscard d'Estaing, and the German Chancellor, Helmut Schmidt, asking if he would agree to their asking Roy Jenkins to become President of the European Commission. Schmidt explained that his preference had been for Denis Healey but that the French would not accept Healey (a fluent German speaker), who was seen by them to be too pro-German. Wilson was in a dilemma. He did not want them to speak to Jenkins, have him accept the post and then find that Wilson had retired a few weeks later. Wilson thought Jenkins would believe it was a deliberate manoeuvre to stop him from becoming Prime Minister. He stalled.

Wilson's final European conference was at Luxembourg at the beginning of April. We travelled in an aircraft of the Queen's Flight, with other ministers nearby sitting with the Prime Minister. He left them and joined me at a table for two and asked me if I would accept a peerage. I told him, as recounted above, that I wanted to abolish the House of Lords, not strengthen it. He then asked me if I would like a knighthood. Again, I refused, saying I regarded such honours as worth no more than regular invitations to cocktail parties. In any case, I added, my wife had already told me that if I took any title which forced her to be called a Lady she would issue a statement dissociating herself from me. I think he was relieved at my refusals. Mine wasn't a name already inscribed by Marcia on her lavender, pink or lilac list and if I had accepted, he might have had a fight upon his hands, though it might have tied my hands for the future.

My outstanding memory of that period was not Wilson's final day but the Cabinet meeting on 16 March which I had attended. He announced it to the astonishment of some and to the consternation of others, such as Barbara Castle and his deputy, Ted Short, who said: 'The Prime Minister's announcement fills us with a very great sadness.' An odd tear was shed and kind words were spoken all round the table, especially by Jim Callaghan, who must have been sure he would succeed: 'Harold,' he said, 'I think history is going to deal much more kindly with you than your contemporaries. It is no crime to endeavour to reconcile the different strands of thought that exist in our party. You have always done that and I believe in doing that you have served not just the party . . . but . . . the country well.' Wilson light-heartedly said that there would be 'one or two celebrations' before he finally left and Callaghan interrupted: 'It will be a wake, Harold, not a celebration.' But, then, he didn't know what I knew, which was going to make it harder for history to be so generous or for celebrations to be so heartfelt.

Before the Cabinet meeting ended, I left and hurried to the Lower Press Gallery at the House of Commons, immediately behind where the journalists sat and where there was an array of telephones. One political reporter, speaking to his office, spotted me and popped his head out of the door. 'Anything happening?' he asked. 'The Prime Minister's resigned,' I said.

'Don't muck about,' he protested.

'I'm not,' I replied.

His face went white, but like a good professional he snatched up the phone to his office.

Now it was nearly all over. But there was still one moment of pure, if black, comedy to come. Wilson had told me in the days before his announcement that the Queen had consulted him about the timing of another, very different, announcement: that Princess Margaret and Lord Snowdon were to divorce. The Queen was worried about the inevitable publicity which would follow. 'Don't worry,' said Harold cheerfully. 'Announce it on the day that I make my statement and my going will blanket it.' The Queen, he said, had taken his advice. I had my doubts about it, and rightly so, as it turned out; far from Wilson's retirement blanketing Margaret's divorce, the reverse happened in the tabloids and Wilson's news had second place.

After Callaghan's triumph on a second ballot, Wilson went to Buckingham Palace and tendered his resignation and I left Downing Street as a workplace for the last time. Like him, I felt a certain sadness. It is still the centre of power in our country. But, also like him, I felt an enormous relief; I discovered it was possible to sleep for eight hours without being woken. I hadn't experienced that luxury for more than seven years.

Nine
Why? Why? Why?

In 1977, Andrew Roth published his biography of Wilson, *Sir Harold Wilson, Yorkshire Walter Mitty*. Carefully researched though it was, Wilson and his wife issued a libel writ against Roth, which was settled out of court for the sum of £10,000, a promise that no further copies of the second edition would be distributed and a further promise that there would be no paperback edition. The settlement was generous, because a good many of the statements to which exception was originally taken fell by the wayside and could have been proved in court had they been persisted in. There were others, though, which, while not necessarily untrue, might have lacked proof enough for a jury. Publishers are reluctant to feed their usually meagre profits to a phalanx of lawyers and they weren't prepared to run the risk of losing the action.

The last paragraph of Roth's book read: 'When he announced his resignation in March, 1976, under the surface admiration floated the recurrent question: "What is Harold up to?" But after the Marcia-backed names on his Resignation Honours List "leaked", the recurrent question became: "What is her hold over him?"'

Apart from changing the tense, that is still the question and one which, after more than two decades of occasional thought, I cannot, with certainty, give an answer. In the language of today, she was undoubtedly a control freak. But that isn't an explanation of how she became his San Andreas Fault. Did she really know something which would ruin him? Had he been indiscreet, perhaps, in a letter to her? Or worse? Was there an undisclosed financial impropriety – always the dread of Labour leaders about their colleagues – or the indisputable evidence of an affair? My conclusion, after so many years of pondering, is that it is in the latter where the solution lies.

In the mid 1960s, an American newspaper published a picture of Wilson and Marcia together and the story beneath was headlined: 'The Other Woman in Wilson's Life.' The 'other woman' had only one connation in most people's minds, and Wilson sued for libel. After initial resistance, the paper paid up; I believe in the region of £35,000. But if Marcia's announcement to Mary Wilson that she had slept with her husband in 1956 was true, then Wilson was guilty of perjury in denying it. As Jeffrey Archer subsequently discovered, judges are apt to take perjury in libel cases seriously.

If that theory, or it in combination with any others, is right, then everything becomes explicable. The hold that she had, the contents of the handbag which she so frequently claimed could destroy him, was the real atomic bomb: not the allegation of an affair, but the proof of it.

Marcia's career with Wilson can be roughly but conveniently divided into three phases. In the first, between 1956, when she became his secretary, and 1964, when he became Prime Minister, she did more to help him reach 10 Downing Street than anyone else. But by 1964, her private life was already beginning to be a problem for Wilson. She had a passionate affair with the most unlikely of men, John Scofield Allen, son of a former Labour MP and an honours graduate, which seemed to be the only thing the two had in common. Allen was sweaty, overweight and married. He giggled incessantly and was one of nature's most successful freeloaders, usually to be found at the elbow of whoever was buying the drinks.

Apparently, at the height of the affair in the mid-60s, during a major financial crisis, Allen was summoned to No. 10 late one evening and handed, by a private secretary, a note, personally written by Wilson, informing him that he had to make up his mind about whether he was going to marry Marcia. To help concentrate his mind, he was to be sent to West Africa for some months to think about it. Three months later he returned, his fare paid by Joe

Kagan. The relationship with Marcia appears to have cooled after that, not least because he had no intention of marrying her. When, in the early 1970s, after the end of his first marriage, he decided to marry again, he was foolhardy enough to drop an invitation to the wedding on to her desk while she was out of the room. At that moment, she came back in. Allen's nerve broke; by the time she had read it and was chasing after him, he was running down the Commons corridor behind the Speaker's chair at a remarkable speed for one of his size and unaccustomed to exercise.

The second phase took in her subsequent and long-lasting affair with Walter Terry, political editor of the *Daily Mail*, who was also married; after the births of her two sons, between which I became her colleague, her concern was more with what Wilson could do for her, rather than what she could do for Wilson.

The final phase, from February 1974 until Wilson's retirement in April 1976, was destructive to the point of being catastrophic; there was abuse of public and private funds, obsessive suspicion of civil servants and a distinct sense of corruption in the award of honours. The good she might have done in her earlier days was swept away by the damage she did in the latter ones.

She was never, in public, other than fiercely loyal to Harold Wilson – a loyalty which, forced or not, he amply reciprocated – but in private she sought constantly to control him, often by disparagement and the wounding Walter Mitty comparison. In so doing, she distracted him, demoralised him and depressed him. Lord Goodman, who knew of Wilson's intention to retire the following spring, held a dinner at his flat in December 1975, for Wilson and selected newspaper editors. The purpose of it was for Wilson to drop hints about his intentions, so that when the resignation was eventually announced in March, the editors would not be able to say it was a sinister surprise. Unfortunately, the hints were so obscure – for example, Wilson saying loudly to Goodman: 'By the way, Arnold, I spoke to the Queen about that matter we discussed' – that none of the editors picked them up and they still asked three months later: 'Why has he so suddenly and surprisingly resigned?'

Halfway through our main course that December night, Goodman whispered to me: 'Mr Haines, he will not go down in history as one of the great Prime Ministers, but if it had not been for *that woman*' – he almost spat out the words – 'he would have gone down as the greatest.' Goodman was over-flattering his client to me as he was wont to do. I believe history will rank Wilson as a good Prime Minister and, usually, a kind, decent and generous man, but neither his insecurity nor the circumstances of his premiership made it likely he would be called the greatest. The claim was too large. Goodman was also overlooking the further question which her admirers would have asked: could Wilson ever have been Prime Minister but for her? I suspect Goodman may have known the answer to the central riddle of why she held such power, which would account for the vehemence of an unvehement man.

In terms of elections won, Wilson was certainly Labour's most successful leader. His four victories – 1964, 1966 and February and October 1974 – were as many as all the other Labour leaders up to Tony Blair put together. But in her boastful private moments, Marcia often claimed to have made him, as if he were a knitted toy; to have transformed him from a dull dog, a parliamentary bore, into a sparkling, and for a while, irresistible politician, one who today would inevitably be called charismatic. The case for her claim is strong, but not unassailable.

By the time they met, Wilson had been an MP for eleven years after being one of the most successful Oxford graduates – triple first-class honours – of the inter-war years. He was in the government before he was thirty and a Cabinet minister at thirty-two. Any politician who had reached – unaided, on his own merits and against the hostility and envy of older men – the Presidency of the Board of Trade by that age had the right to expect, or hope, that the premiership was within his eventual grasp. All this he achieved at a time when he was surrounded not by the mediocrities who swarmed into the Cabinets of later years, but by political heavyweights, actual and potential. He sat in the Cabinet of Clement Attlee, still Labour's most revered Prime

Minister, alongside such men as Sir Stafford Cripps, Aneurin Bevan, Herbert Morrison, Hugh Gaitskell and Ernest Bevin (whom he hated: he told me the best news he ever heard about Bevin was the announcement that he was dead); a coalition of political giants whose equal has not been seen since. On the backbenches, or with a toehold on the front bench, were the likes of Roy Jenkins, Jim Callaghan, George Brown and, later, Denis Healey, all of his generation but, in terms of youthful achievement, not in his class. But he *was* a dull dog; he *did* bore; he was noted far more for his grasp of statistics than for his sense of humour. He was never a wholehearted member of any group, not even the Bevanites, despite resigning from the government at the same time as Bevan. He belonged to a trade union, because that was what Labour leaders were expected to do, but, unlike Callaghan or Brown, he was not at heart a trade unionist. He travelled frequently to the Soviet Union of Josef Stalin – who had yet to emerge as the world's biggest mass murderer after Hitler – and Nikita Kruschev, and he was welcomed there, a cause of lasting suspicion by right-wingers later in his life. He was on the edge of the inner circle of politics but not part of it. He didn't socialise, host dinner parties at his home – Mary Wilson wouldn't have them, anyway, but it was not his style – or give cocktail parties for the great, the good or the influential.

Whether Marcia was Wilson's mistress, however briefly, can never be known for an absolute certainty, because though she said she was, he said she wasn't. In the absence of a camera or witnesses, both impossible, the fact will always be in dispute. In 1997, I was told from two different sources that Marcia had deposited the typescript of a book with a London publisher, with an embargo on publication until the death of Lady Wilson. If that is the case, then it might contain Marcia's version of what the relationship was. Even so, it would remain her word against his, unless there is irrefutable documentary evidence.

That she was an enormous help to Wilson in her early years is undeniable. When I first knew her, she had a mind which could cut like a laser through jargon and confused thinking. But given that, and assuming, for argument's sake, that she slept with him, whether in 1956 or later, it still isn't enough to explain her influence upon him, which grew, if anything, once he became the Prime Minister. Few mistresses, girl friends, participants in one-night stands, secretaries or even wives, ever held such a powerful personal sway over their bosses or spouses. It was a sway which never diminished with the years. It was as potent when he left office in 1976 as it was in 1956 when they first embarked on the path which was to lead them to No. 10.

One former member of my staff at No. 10 claimed she saw Wilson and Marcia 'in a clinch' late one evening in 1969. Possibly, she did. But as Marcia was at that time deeply into her affair with Walter Terry and was soon expecting her second child by him, a consoling hug for a woman under stress might easily have been misunderstood for a romantic embrace, especially if one was looking for the latter. If there had been anything between them physically, it was certainly over by then.

Personally, though I never saw any sign of it, I have to conclude that the weight of probability of an affair is heavy. An ambitious politician, just forty; a secretary, just twenty-four, equally ambitious for him. Thrown together hour after hour, day after day, and often in hotels in Britain and abroad, the mix has proved deadly often enough before and since. But was it enough to give her a lifelong hold? Not by today's standards it wasn't.

In very private and violent moments, witnessed again and again by those who worked closely with Wilson and, perforce, her, she would also threaten to 'destroy' him, which accorded with her destructive personality. In effect, she was declaring that what she had created she could uncreate; she could bring down the man she had raised up. Her language and actions never changed in the reiteration of that threat. It was her invariable reaction to personal, as much as to political, adversity. She would lift her ever-present handbag, tap it with a hidden and unexplained significance – the clear implication being that it contained some awful, unknown, documented and earth-shattering revelation – and declare: 'One call to the *Daily Mail* and he'll be finished. I will destroy him.'

That scene was part of every crisis, large or small. Was its underlying menace the key to his continually forgiving or excusing outrageous and intolerable behaviour? She never said with what she would slay him, only that she could. No one could know whether it was fantasy or for real. She never said it to Wilson's face if anyone else was present, but we were all to understand that she could do it.

One particular afternoon in 1975, in her office at 10 Downing Street, was typical of the violent threats she would utter against Wilson. She had sought my advice about a libel writ she had issued against the London *Evening Standard* over her involvement in the land deals affair. The paper had offered £500 in settlement of the action and she asked me whether she should accept. I told her that £500 was usually an insufficient amount to compensate for a serious libel, but if the *Standard* refused to increase it, acceptance might be preferable to the alternative: that was, that the case would go to court where she would be subjected to cross-examination in the witness box. I warned her that the *Standard's* QC might be allowed to range widely in his questioning of her. 'Why?' she demanded. 'What can he ask me?' 'He might,' I said, 'ask about your children.' Her face darkened, as always when she was in a temper, and she exploded: 'If he does, then I'll destroy him', and she slapped her handbag. 'Him' was Wilson, not any QC the *Standard* might have hired.

There was another problem had she undergone cross-examination, which I didn't mention to her, but of which we were both aware. She wore a locket around her neck which contained tranquillisers prescribed by Joe Stone, Wilson's personal doctor, who had a deep loathing of her. Stone did not believe she could last for a long period under stress without recourse to the pills, which, in the circumstances of a High Court action, might not have been possible. He once said to me that if ever she appeared in court there would be a real risk of anything happening under cross-examination, including her storming out of the witness box and the court precincts.

Joe Stone was a good friend to all the staff around Wilson. He would willingly examine any who had fears about their health and soothe their anxieties. He was also utterly devoted to Wilson. He, more than anyone, knew the problems which Marcia created for the Prime Minister. He had overseen her two pregnancies and supplied her with the medication which enabled her to get through the day. He also despised her for the damage he believed she was doing to Wilson's reputation and ability to do his job. One day, after the 'slag heaps' row had gone off the boil, Joe walked into my spacious office fronting Downing Street, having just left the Prime Minister. Sitting down, he asked, in his usually slightly excitable voice, whether we could discuss ways of taking the weight of Marcia off the Prime Minister. I said I thought nothing could be done, even if the Prime Minister wished it, which I doubted.

Joe then said that he could 'dispose' of her in such a way that it would seem to be from natural causes. He added that he would sign the death certificate and that there would not be a problem. As Agatha Christie and the redtop tabloids might have put it, that was an invitation to murder; to be an accessory before and after the fact, even if not during it.

I told him there was no way in which I would 'go down that road' and he dropped the subject. Some days later, I confided in Bernard Donoughue and found that Joe had approached him, too, about the possibility of 'disposing' of Marcia.

His reaction had been the same as mine. Shortly afterwards, as the three of us were strolling through the main square of Bonn at a moment of leisure during an official visit to Helmut Schmidt, the German Chancellor, Joe offhandedly raised the question again. We both squashed it and that was the last we ever heard of it.

There was nothing to be done about Joe's suggestion, except to reject it. There was no question, for example, of reporting it to the police. Joe could have laughed and said he was joking. The Prime Minister would not have believed us. Our positions would have become impossible and Joe's would have been compromised. A bad situation would have been made worse. There was never any chance that Joe would have acted independently because he had already shown his hand.

Charming though Joe was, his proposition was crazy and wicked. When Wilson wanted the assassination of Idi Amin, the deranged Ugandan President who was killing thousands of Asians each week, I was ready to go along with it. But whatever Marcia had done, she didn't deserve that kind of end. The sack was the only punishment I ever had in mind.

Even supposing our consciences had allowed us to go along with her killing, which they would not, how would we have lived the rest of our lives? always in fear that one or other of the co-conspirators would break. Supposing there *had* been suspicions? After all, she was only 42 at the time. Wouldn't the truth have put Watergate and every other post-war scandal into the shade, destroyed the Prime Minister, destroyed his government and, no small matter, destroyed us as well?

Joe was, in every other respect, an honourable, upright and well-liked man. He and his wife are now long dead and neither Bernard Donoughue nor I would ever have breathed a word about it while they were alive. I recount it now only because it is part of the Wilson–Marcia history and because it illustrates just how far a man we all admired was prepared to go to ease a situation we all found intolerable.

Marcia's conventional upbringing and appearance – she was always smartly, even elegantly, dressed and would not have been seen dead in a genderless boiler suit and trainers – effectively hid a nature which was volcanic and neurotic (her description of herself). One had to know her, to win either her trust or earn her indifference, before she allowed herself to explode.

In the early 1950s, she married an aeronautical engineer, George Edmund (Ed) Williams, who emigrated to the USA in 1957, the year after she joined Wilson. In 1961, they were divorced. According to Andrew Roth, Wilson secretly visited Ed Williams in Seattle in 1960 to try to persuade him not to divorce Marcia. The only purpose of such a trip must have been to guard his own back against scandal, seeing that Marcia did not want to join Williams in the USA and wasn't insisting he should return to her.

Indeed, apart from bestowing upon her the best known of her three surnames, he made so little impact on her life that she didn't mention him in her *Who's Who* entry or in either of her books. Wedded bliss, such as it was, according to her, was brief. She told me she realised she had made a mistake soon after boarding the train taking her and her husband on their honeymoon. She gained an Honours degree in history at Queen Mary College, London, and later became a lay Governor there. She went to secretarial college and was a highly competent shorthand typist. But beneath her shy exterior – which, often, was not a pose – smouldered an ambition which led to Downing Street, a personality intent on breaking those who interfered with her, and a temper whose exercise was to provoke fear, terror, hatred or unquestioning love among those with whom she worked.

Gerald Kaufman, who for several years after Wilson became Prime Minister acted as his political press secretary until becoming Labour MP for Ardwick in 1970, remained devoted to her for more than thirty years, ready to forgive her for anything and everything. But even he once described her to me, with tears in his eyes, as 'a wicked woman' after he had been a victim of her lacerating tongue. He said he would never speak to her again until she apologised. The next morning, he appeared unasked in her office and kissed her.

Harold Wilson, who had grown skilful in ducking below the parapet when she was on the rampage, would at times go to great lengths to avoid her. On occasion, as Prime Minister, he would take refuge in my Downing Street office, knowing it was one of the few rooms she was unlikely to enter uninvited; on other days, he would take the lift down from his flat, rather than walk down the stairs and be seen passing her office. Yet, no one defended her more loyally and constantly than Kaufman and Wilson. That's why they were irreverently mocked as Wilson, Kaufman and Marcia after a music hall turn known as Wilson, Keppel and Betty.

Occasionally, Wilson would strike back. In opposition, Marcia once refused to hand over a box in her possession containing private papers which Wilson wanted and was determined to have. He came into the office in triumph one Monday morning, telling me that he and Tony Field had broken into Marcia's garage at the weekend and recovered the box and his documents. The immediate thought I had, no doubt selfish, was that I was the press secretary to the leader of the Labour party and former Prime Minister who had that weekend burgled a home owned by his political and personal secretary, even if it was only to recover his own property. How would I explain that away if he were arrested? The possibility chilled me to the core.

Civil servants, almost without exception, hated her. The feeling was mutual. A very senior Foreign and Commonwealth Office official, in his time chairman of the Joint Intelligence Committee, told me bluntly that he and the FCO believed she was an Israeli spy, but didn't, or couldn't, offer any evidence. It is also true that at that time, the FCO was almost totally populated by Arabists and they were not objective on the subject.

She was certainly totally committed to the Israeli cause, as was Wilson, whose attachment to Israel was of long-standing and which was part of the cause of his hatred of Ernest Bevin, who was pro-Arab. Over more than twenty years he was instrumental in getting large numbers of Soviet Jews safely to Israel. It was as a consequence of that support that Jewish businessmen in Britain were the principal contributors to the running of Wilson's office where she controlled the finances. Virtue was not its only reward.

Israeli officials based in London frequently came to No. 10 to see her, not the Prime Minister. She arranged private meetings with Israeli ministers – including a secret conference with the then Israel Prime Minister at a London hotel in the mid 1970s – without the Foreign and Commonwealth office being told. Indeed, she did everything she could to prevent the FCO, or anyone at No. 10, from knowing what was going on. Those contacts were often intended to determine the attitude taken by Britain in UN Security Council discussions on the Middle East. The Foreign Secretary, James Callaghan – who, like Roy Jenkins, had a regard for her abilities which was not reciprocated – was furious about the Prime Minister's independent links with the government in Tel Aviv but could do little about it, except protest and exact a promise from Wilson – which was not kept – that he would not interfere again in Security Council matters.

However, the Israelis were not exempt from her scorn. I have recounted before (in *The Politics of Power*) how, shortly after the Soviet government granted exit visas, at Wilson's prompting, to two dissident ballet stars, the Panovs, a lunch at the Israeli ambassador's home in London was interrupted by a telephone call for the ambassador, Gideon Rafael. 'Yes . . . Yes . . . Of course,' he spluttered. 'No . . . No . . . No . . . Of course I would like you to meet them . . . Yes . . . No . . . Of course not . . . Not trying to exclude you . . . Please . . . They're here tomorrow . . . 5.30 . . . Please come.'

Rafael was a brave man who, despite his age, had fought as a volunteer on the Golan Heights during the 1973 war. But I doubt if he came under such sustained attack from the Syrian army as he did that lunchtime. He put down the phone and said to me: 'That was Lady Falkender.' 'I know,' I replied. I had heard it all before.

However, when Mrs Golda Meir came to No. 10 and was introduced to Marcia, the Israeli Prime Minister treated her with noticeable coldness and disdain, nodding and then turning away from her when Wilson formally introduced them; it was as close to a snub as was possible without being overtly rude.

Domestically, while Wilson was Labour leader, no one ever took on Marcia Williams and won. Sometimes a draw, honourable or otherwise, might be fought, but even those limited successes were few. She held an unassailable sway over Wilson and to defy her was often suicidal, as more than one civil servant found out. Sometimes, Bernard Donoughue and I were able successfully to intervene with him on behalf of an unjustly accused civil servant, as we did in the case of Robin Butler. Others were not so lucky. Middle Eastern affairs apart, she had little lasting influence upon government or party policy, though she would sometimes, if only for a moment, cause Wilson to veer wildly from reality before returning to sanity. The central charge against her is not that she changed the course of events but that she constantly harassed a

Prime Minister who was in a position to do so — she wore him down, she wore him out and she put her own crises — ranging from love affairs and her children to tax arrears or the installation of a telephone or TV set — before his and the country's.

Her appointment to the Upper House broke the established convention, especially within the Labour party, that anyone created a life peer should be a working peer. She never made a speech in the Lords. Her excuse, at the beginning, for her silence was that she could not speak while she was the Prime Minister's political secretary, which was true enough. But that inhibition lasted for less than two years, until his resignation in 1976. In the years which followed, she didn't make a speech, either. If she collected her expenses, she didn't sing for her supper, though she frequently voted.

In his latter years as Prime Minister, Wilson had few of the Parliamentary triumphs which were once so readily accorded him. But after one particularly effective speech, viewed, unusually, by Marcia occupying one of the privileged seats under the public gallery, he was sitting in his Commons office with senior officials, Donoughue and myself, basking in the pleasure of his success. Suddenly, the door burst open. Marcia stood there, scowling. 'I suppose you think you are clever?' she sneered. We all left, without Wilson having to ask us. No one wanted to stay and witness what was bound to follow.

Even on the most mundane level, humiliation of him was her constant aim. Often, Wilson could not use his official driver, Bill Housden, on a Friday morning because Marcia required him to take her shopping, sometimes in the Prime Minister's car. The other Downing Street drivers deeply resented having to attend on the Prime Minister because she was using Housden for her domestic purposes. On the fewer and fewer occasions she came into the office, Housden was required to collect her from Wyndham Mews in the late morning — again in the PM's car — and to take her home again in the early afternoon. Apart from anything else, that was a misuse of public money. Housden, an unstoppable gossip and unending source of information about her affairs, domestic and sexual, was, nevertheless, terrified of her. After

Wilson's retirement, he approached me and asked if I could get him £15,000 from someone for his reminiscences. He told me that for years he had been recording his daily adventures on tape and was ready to sell them, though not for publication until after he retired. I spoke to James Margach, political editor of the *Sunday Times*, who said his paper would willingly pay the money and give a guarantee not to use them until Housden said so. I passed on to Housden what Margach had promised; shortly afterwards, I heard through Albert Murray that Housden had told Marcia that I had offered him £15,000 for his memoirs. I was disappointed in him and could only assume he was afraid that word of what was happening might get back to her and he decided on a pre-emptive strike. Although he was a civil servant, she was paying him £15 a week for his services as a chauffeur; I imagine he feared that if she found out what he was proposing she could have exposed him, perhaps prejudicing his job or exciting the interest of the Inland Revenue.

It is necessary to emphasise what I have said before: her overall effect upon policy was minute. That is one advantage of Cabinet government and, in any case, Wilson would draw the line there. For example, one day in January 1975, when a temporary ceasefire had been ordered by the IRA, John O'Connell, a Labour member of the Irish Dail, called Marcia's brother, Tony, whom he had got to know when he accompanied Wilson and me to Dublin three years earlier. O'Connell wanted to pass on the current views of the IRA directly to Harold Wilson, by-passing the Northern Ireland Office, which they distrusted. Highly excited, Marcia phoned Wilson while I was with him in his study, told him of the call, said that the truce was about to break down and that she was going to Dublin herself to see O'Connell. Wilson was rough with her. He told her she would do no such thing. 'You are ignorant,' he said. 'You don't know what you are talking about.' The situation, he added, was far too serious for her to interfere. The foot was firmly down and she knew when to back off. But, even so, Wilson would not ignore her entirely. He had to do something and, in the end, I met O'Connell in London and received the IRA's message, but that's another story.

It was her effect on personal relationships and the personality of the Prime Minister which was profound, and wearying beyond the belief of those who have never undergone such relentless nagging, day after day, year after year; it was a torrent that never stopped, a volcano which always heaved, lightning always likely to flash across a clear blue sky. While I knew them, nothing he ever did received her unstinting praise. Every success had to be demeaned. Every failure was represented to be worse than it was.

Later, during Wilson's second term, her sister, Peggy, who was strikingly attractive, struck up a friendship with a man who told her he was a hospital registrar. Marcia, who believed that there was always someone seeking to penetrate the fortress of her privacy, telephoned the hospital where the man was said to work – and found he wasn't employed there at all. The relationship ended after that.

What was so appalling and galling about these and the endless other episodes which, at worst, were almost daily occurrences, was the time which her or her family's affairs consumed – if only in listening to them – in what was a tiring and relentless schedule. Almost nothing had greater priority than settling her down. When, like all of us on our return to Downing Street, she was required to undergo positive vetting, she point-blank refused to do so. The specious ground was that she didn't see confidential papers and therefore there was no need to be vetted. We all knew that wasn't true. She did see confidential papers, if only when the whim took her; she discussed the most secret matters with the Prime Minister when it entered her head to question him on government policy, and it was impossible to be in No. 10 and not know about matters that were kept from the public eye. That particular episode dragged on for months. It was finally dealt with by the Prime Minister signing a certificate on her behalf to meet the requirements of trustworthiness. She had been vetted when she first entered Downing Street in 1964, but the examination had to be regularly renewed, as mine was. I suppose she did not want to be questioned about her children.

Sometimes, Wilson knew what a nonsense it all was, but said, in effect: let's go along with her. When she insisted upon better accommodation at a Blackpool party conference than the best hotel there could provide – not an impossible task – Albert Murray was sent out to find a luxury flat and to rent it, even though Wilson knew she had no intention of travelling from London. It was better to waste the money than risk a change of mind and a sudden arrival, demanding to know where her flat was.

A few days free of her demands, her suspicions, her conspiracy theories – a chance to do the work for which Wilson and the rest of us were employed – were cherished. But these were periods of remission, not recovery. Always there was the fear that the next piece of nonsense would find its way into the newspapers. And we all knew that, inevitably, the sun would go down again and darkness reign.

My personal objection was that I was always being called in to deal with or advise on matters for which I did not have the necessary expertise or the inclination and which were nothing to do with me or the government. My knowledge was about journalism and politics, not counselling. Donoughue was in the same position, though he was more skilled than I in soothing ruffled feelings. There was a time when Wilson frequently turned to Donoughue to help placate Marcia in the belief that he had at last found in him the elixir for a trouble-free life. One night, he called Donoughue out of a dinner party and asked him to go to Wyndham Mews to calm her down. 'She's threatening to phone the papers,' he said. 'Tear her phone out of the wall if you have to.' She repaid Donoughue's willingness to help by successfully demanding that Wilson should not let Donoughue accompany him to the 1975 Commonwealth Conference in Jamaica, despite the fact that Donoughue had prepared the bulk of the briefing papers for it. During the early months of 1974, the *Sunday Mirror* received a tip that a Cabinet minister was involved in orgies at a large block of flats near the West End. The editor, Bob Edwards, told me of it only because the rumours were around and because he thought I ought to know. He also told me that his reporters had carefully checked and that there was absolutely no truth in the story. I wasn't surprised. No member of the Cabinet of that time was less likely to take part in such sexual misbehaviour than the one named.

Nevertheless, I told Wilson because he had a right to know; he, in turn, told Marcia because he was an incurable gossip. Of course, that ought to have been the end of it. But then . . .

One warm day during the summer of 1975, the front door of Marcia's home was surprisingly left open. A handbag belonging to her sister, Peggy, which was lying on a table just inside the house, was snatched by a prowling thief. A few days later, Marcia received a phone call from a man who said he had found the handbag and asked if she would care to collect it. The address he gave, unfortunately for him, was the very block of flats where the Cabinet minister had supposedly misbehaved. All the alarm bells rang. Marcia's immediate conclusion was that an attempt was being made to lure her and Peggy into one of those orgies. (There weren't any, but that was beside the point.) The Special Branch was alerted and a squad of detectives descended upon the bewildered porter at the block. It was yet another false alarm. The poor man had found the handbag − empty, except for an address and telephone number − wasn't able to return it because he was about to go on duty and out of the goodness of his heart had telephoned the number inside the bag in the expectation that the owner would want it back. He got more than he bargained for.

Paranoid behaviour of this kind grew more frequent during Wilson's last few years as leader of the Labour party and especially his last two years as Prime Minister. When a lock-up in Buckingham Palace Road was broken into and various papers and boxes disappeared, Special Branch, under Detective Chief Superintendent Roy Ranson, was called in by a hysterical Marcia who claimed that 'very valuable papers historically, letters of congratulation, etc' were missing. As I pointed out, the papers in part consisted of scores of copies of old speeches. I didn't endear myself by saying I couldn't even give them away when they were new. As for the letters of congratulation which were historically important, it hardly tallied with the fact that in a fit of temper she threw away a number of Christmas cards (some soiled by teacups being stood upon them) sent to Wilson by foreign heads of state, including Messrs Podgorny and Kosygin of the Soviet Union, Mrs Indira Gandhi, the Dalai Lama, King Olaf of Norway, the King and Queen of Belgium, Constantin Karamanlis of Greece, Archbishop Makarios of Cyprus, Mrs Bandaranaike of Sri Lanka, Kurt Waldheim, secretary-general of the United Nations, President Husak of Czechoslovakia, President Honecker of East Germany, Chou En-Lai and Al-Haji Field Marshal Idi Amin Dada, VC, DSO, MC, as he grandiloquently (and falsely) described himself. That list included as fine a collection of mass murderers seen since the Nuremburg war crimes' tribunal. Idi Amin's card, ironically, arrived at Christmas, 1975, the year in which Wilson contemplated ordering his assassination. Albert Murray rescued the cards from the wastepaper basket, and I still have them.

Jeremy Thorpe, the struggling Liberal leader, was a beneficiary of this intermittent hysteria. Despite knowing that Wilson had been prepared to expose Thorpe's affair with Norman Scott, that back in power Wilson had instructed the Department of Social Services to give him a copy of Scott's National Insurance records, and that Thorpe was deeply in trouble because of his connections with a failing secondary bank, the London and Home Counties, Marcia insisted Wilson should leap to Thorpe's aid when the South African-born Peter Hain – a Young Liberal activist, before joining Labour and becoming a minister in Tony Blair's government – gave him a dossier alleging a conspiracy by BOSS, South Africa's intelligence service, to blacken Thorpe's name.

At the time, to be fair, Hain said he doubted its worth. The central question about such a conspiracy, which even believers in it would be hard put to answer, was what possible interest South Africa could have in destroying Jeremy Thorpe, whose influence, such as it was, was waning even in his own party? He was hardly a major figure in Britain – the high tide of the Liberal vote in the first 1974 election had receded in the second – and was never likely to be one to the outer world. And why assist in Thorpe's political demise when he was making such admirable progress in doing it himself? The theory that BOSS wanted to destroy Thorpe because, ten years earlier, he had advocated the bombing of Ian Smith's Southern Rhodesia wasn't worth a second thought and nor was the dossier.

Nevertheless, Marcia, who liked Thorpe, seeing him as a fellow-sufferer from the conspiracies which abounded in her world, demanded that Wilson should defend him in the House of Commons, which, uncomfortably, he did. Thorpe was pathetically grateful to clutch at any straw but his inevitable downfall followed soon afterwards and Wilson was left with more needless egg on his face.

I first met Marcia in the mid-1960s when I was a reporter in the Commons Press Gallery. She was an attractive, witty blonde, enjoyable company unless one started to talk politics to her, at which point her guard would spring up. Although I had been a colleague and friend of Walter Terry's for several years – I had spent four years on the *Scottish Daily Mail* and for a while worked in the same room as he – I knew nothing of his relationship with Marcia; the first hint came when Mavis, the wife of Walter and smaller and much more attractive than Marcia, asked me what I thought of Wilson's secretary. I uttered a few words of praise and immediately realised I'd said the wrong thing. Mavis detested her, and rightly so, as it turned out.

But at that time, I did admire what I knew of her and that continued for a long time after I joined No. 10. Unfortunately, what was good was what I knew; what was bad, I didn't know. I saw her frequently at first; she regarded me as an ally against the civil service, against the Tory press and against those who were enemies of Harold Wilson. Later in 1969, 1 saw less of her, which is my only excuse for not realising that she was pregnant. Her first child, a son, had been born the previous August; the second, another son, conceived aboard *HMS Tiger* off Gibraltar at a time when Terry was covering the abortive talks with Ian Smith, was born less than a year later.

It was incredible, looking back on it, that the two pregnancies completely escaped the notice of the press and, indeed, almost everyone at Downing Street and in the Cabinet, though Michael Halls was told; he, poor man, as I outlined earlier, had to bear the brunt of anything that ever went wrong and, in the view of his wife, Marjorie, that contributed to his sudden and early death.

At the end of 1970, apart from occasional visits, Marcia ceased to come into the office. Months went by without our seeing her. If Wilson wanted to see her on other than routine matters, he had to travel to her home. She still controlled the office by telephone, but I soon grew adept at hanging up on her. This, strangely, she did not resent, provided always that the person who put the phone down was the one who picked it up to renew normal office collaboration. But my fragile relationship, occasionally interspersed with bouts of politeness or even cordiality, went on fracturing over the years as I ceased to pay her the respect she demanded. Inevitably, this almost led to disaster.

I had been banned, for reasons long forgotten, from playing any part in Wilson's conference speech at Blackpool in 1972, which meant that passages I had prepared for it before we left London had to be claimed by him to be his own. It was to be the last major speech whose final drafts were prepared only by him and her. Predictably, it went wrong.

Wilson wrote and rewrote the speech, finally going to bed at about three in the morning, seven hours before he was due to deliver it, leaving Marcia to check the numbering of the pages of the final draft. She did not like to hear Wilson speak and so I was readmitted to the fold for the purpose of accompanying him to the Winter Gardens conference hall.

It was the custom in those days for the leader to make his speech immediately after the announcement of the results of the elections to the National Executive Committee, which are of little importance today compared to what they once were. The disadvantage of this arrangement – which Tony Blair rightly scrapped – was that the hall would still be buzzing and scrutinising the results as the leader rose to his feet and little attention would be paid to his first words.

Wilson would occupy himself while the NEC results were being announced by underscoring any passages in the speech to which he wanted to give greater emphasis. The 1972 speech was intended to win back some of the lost support on the left by announcing that the next Labour government would introduce a programme of land nationalisation.

Without that passage, there was nothing much in the speech. And as he underscored, he suddenly discovered he was without it: Marcia had not included it in the final draft. Fortunately, I was standing near the front of the platform. He spotted me and sent Shirley Williams, then a member of the Executive, scurrying off the platform to tell me what had happened. Luckily, Bill Housden was a few yards away and he drove me at speed the mile or so to the Imperial Hotel. I left the Winter Garden just as Wilson was rising to his feet.

The floor of the workroom at the hotel was literally covered with discarded drafts. It was impossible to walk into the room without treading upon them. Housden and I each snatched at handfuls of paper in a search for the missing nationalisation proposals. After about five minutes, I found a version of them, but it was impossible to know whether it was an early or a late one, since most of the drafts were unnumbered and all were on white typing paper – two basic, elementary errors in the preparation of any document needing more than one draft. I placed the pages in order as Housden drove me back to the Winter Gardens. We re-entered the hall twenty minutes after leaving it. I beckoned to Shirley Williams, who slipped off the platform, collected the missing pages and placed them in front of Wilson.

At the back of the hall, I asked Terry Lancaster how the speech was going. 'All right,' he said, 'but he's a bit slow.' Once again, disaster had been courted and then averted only by luck. Either Marcia or Wilson or both recognised how close he had been to the shortest and emptiest conference speech on record; she never took part in those speech consultations again, nor did she ever again attend a party conference.

But the underlying fault was always there. The office was the most ineffi-cient of any office in my experience, which, seeing that during my working life I was employed by several newspapers, is saying a lot. The girls in it were terrified of Marcia's wrath and they carried out her instructions to the letter, without deviation. All post arriving in the office, most of it addressed to Mr Wilson, had to be opened and taken by Housden to Wyndham Mews, where Marcia would dictate an answer to every one, even to those whose scribblings in red and green ink, with Biblical quotations and extensive underlining and make up a significant part of a politician's post which can safely be binned. (Apart from anything else, replies provoked even longer letters by return of post and usually registered.)

When the day's mail was answered – not necessarily or even usually on the same day or even in the same week – it would be taken back to Westminster by Housden, without any priority accorded to any of it and distributed to the girls for typing. When that was completed all the letters would go out to Wyndham Mews again for Marcia's signature if satisfactory or for amendment if not. Letters seeking interviews with Wilson would first be acknowledged by Marcia; when the acknowledgement was typed and signed, she would dictate a further note, this time to me, saying, 'I have acknowledged. This is for you to deal with.' As that note, too, needed to be typed and signed, the original letter would once more be taken to Wyndham Mews, along with her note to me, before finally arriving on my desk. By then, it was often too late for the journalist's request to be met.

On one occasion a request from a visiting American columnist to interview Wilson was seen by me ten days after it arrived and several days after he had returned to the USA. It was useless to speak to Wilson about this nonsense. He would only say that Marcia was under a great deal of pressure, that the typists were no good and ask me to bear with her. In any case, letters for him to sign were treated in exactly the same way. All I could do was to tell journalists to phone me or write to me personally. At worst, I could say 'No' more quickly. One day, after one of her many resignations, Wilson asked me if I would deal with the general post. With two secretaries taking dictation, every letter was answered and signed by 3 p.m. Her resignation was promptly withdrawn and I was never asked to answer the post again. Colonel (later Lord) George Wigg buttonholed me in New Palace Yard, Westminster, the day after the 1970 election defeat and said (wrongly, as it turned out): 'Until Harold gets rid of Marcia, the Labour party will never be in office again.' Wigg was a voluble, argumentative character who believed in conspiracies, probably because he was often a participant in, or instigator of, them. In the early years of the 1964 government when he was close to Wilson, he fed the Prime Minister's appetite for the cloak and dagger life. To him, nothing was straightforward. He specialised in exposing incompetent army 'brass' and inhabited the murky world of military intelligence. He was instrumental in the parliamentary manoeuvres which brought down John Profumo, the Tory War Minister whom he asserted jeopardised national security by sharing a mistress with the Soviet naval attaché in London. He was appointed Wilson's Paymaster General in the 1964 government but was universally known as the Spymaster General. Wigg kept in touch with me occasionally long after I left No 10. He was an invaluable contact during the Falklands war, frequently phoning me at home with news of our task force which was invariably denied by the Ministry of Defence but which was more accurate than not. During each of those calls, he turned the conversation back to Marcia. He always hated her and, fatally for his career, he was never afraid to show it. On one celebrated occasion, he was said to have refused to divulge secret information to Wilson while 'that typist' – Marcia – was in the Prime Minister's study. When, reluctantly, she left the room, Wigg apparently turned the key in the door from the inside so that she could not come back in. It was a deadly insult and he paid for it. Wilson removed him from government office and made him chairman of the Tote, the state's bookmaking service. Many years after his retirement from that post, he was arrested and found guilty on a kerb-crawling charge. Whenever he phoned me, he would protest his innocence and allege that he had been 'set up' at the instigation of Marcia. The last time we spoke I told him I didn't think that was possible and I still don't, but he grew very angry and I never heard from him again. What was undoubtedly true and done to defend Marcia's public reputation was that in the summer of 1974 a private detective, hired through Labour's former Chief Whip and Local Government Minister, John Silkin, a wealthy Jewish solicitor and loyal ally of Wilson's, was put on Wigg's tail. Wilson told me Wigg was writing a book (which I assumed was to be a second volume of the autobiography which he had published in 1972) which was, reportedly, to include an all-out attack on Marcia and reproduce copies of the birth certificates of her children. The purpose of the private detective was to gather information which might persuade or compel Wigg to change his mind. One night, the detective watched Wigg enter a one-bedroomed flat, occupied by a single woman. He did not leave until the following morning. The woman had a grown-up son. The inference drawn was that Wigg was the boy's father.

A journalist friend calling on Wilson around this time was met by a gleeful Prime Minister who exclaimed: 'We've got him.'

'Who?' inquired the journalist innocently. 'Ted Heath?'

'No,' said Wilson. 'Wigg.' He didn't explain himself to the journalist, but later he told me the story of the private eye and handed me a piece of paper on which the woman's address was written. I was supposed to hold it for safe-keeping, but I lost it. Wilson later told me that Wigg's book had been toned down considerably from its original draft; nothing, however, was ever published and yet another threatened public personal disaster, real or imagined, for Marcia had been averted. It was a shabby, demoralising experience and it was about then, for the second time, I seriously considered resigning from the press secretary's job. But the arguments of my wife and close friends like Albert Murray – that staying was the greater good for the party, prevailed. Had I gone, the private detective might have been given further, if frustrating, employment. More to the point, it would not have been possible for me to go silently and I would probably have decided to get my blow in first.

The junior staff, both at No. 10 and in opposition, suffered the most from the interminable tantrums. These rages were not passing storms. In 1970, Jane Cousins, a research assistant was recruited from Martin Gilbert, the historian. She came under fire for allegedly leaking office gossip to a journalist, Andrew Roth, because she took a phone call from him asking for copies of Wilson's speeches. The greater truth was that she was photographed shoeless at the Labour conference in 1971 and was also remarkably pretty – gross offences which in previous centuries might have earned the curses of a wicked witch. There was no room for two female stars in Marcia's sky. In the end, Jane got fed up with Marcia's constant sniping and the distrust of her that it engendered in Harold Wilson and she left, eventually to become a successful author.

Marcia's young personal assistant, Susan Lewis, was cruelly used by her, especially at the Labour conference in Blackpool in 1970. The first draft of the conference speech had been prepared in London, where Marcia had decided to stay. Susan had to travel to Blackpool with Marcia's amendments to the speech; amendments whose meaning and purpose were rarely apparent or logical.

She was sent on the Friday overnight train arriving early on Saturday morning at our headquarters in the Imperial Hotel, by which time Wilson and I had prepared the second draft. She returned to London with that and was then dispatched back to Blackpool on the Saturday evening train, arriving on Sunday morning and returning to London later that day with the next amended draft, only to return to Blackpool again, via a third night on the sleeper on Monday morning. Marcia then phoned Wilson with instructions that Susan was once more to return to London, though by the time she would get back it would be too late for further amendments to the speech to be considered. Susan, whose mother was a Labour party employee and in Blackpool for the conference, refused to go and said she was staying where she was. She was sacked by Wilson in my presence.

Apart from the distress caused to Susan, this would be just one more example of pettiness, no doubt replicated in other offices and other businesses in other parts of the country, though today industrial tribunals exist to remedy such unfair treatment. But this was more than small-time bullying and Jane and Susan were only the most prominent of the young women who suffered from Marcia's intolerance. It was symptomatic of a personality which increasingly demanded instant, complete and unquestioning obedience, whether by a member of her staff or by the party leader himself, and to whom No was not a word to be uttered; a personality, too, for whom the line between right and wrong had become blurred.

One employee who did not bend before Marcia's rantings was a choleric Transport House employee, George Caunt. He was described in newspapers as a party official who served in Wilson's private office from 1964 until 1973. That surprised me, because I only ever met him once and that briefly and I joined at the start of 1969. He wrote a book, which was not published, recounting a large number of incidents concerning her, including one in which he threw her on to a sofa after a blazing row. If there had existed the political equivalent of the Victoria Cross then he would have deserved it for that action. But I don't know the truth of that nor his countless other allegations and, in the main, I have tried in this book to write of only those matters of which I had first-hand knowledge. Nevertheless, he would certainly have had a close experience of her during the time, however long or short, that he worked in the office.

I was not, at first, aware of her increasing desire for the luxurious material things of life. It was only natural, after the birth of two children, that she should want a larger house, especially as her mother and sister, Peggy, lived with her, too. But Wyndham Mews was in the wealthiest part of London; she was assisted financially in moving there by Joe Kagan, later Lord Kagan. After receiving a peerage from the Queen he was to become an inmate in one of her penitentiaries, in surroundings considerably less opulent than he was used to. I knew of his help to Marcia because I was present when she berated him for not doing more. She said in a statement in 1975 that she did not own the house in the Mews, only rented it, but at some point, she also gained either by rental or purchase, the use of the house next door, too. At the same time owned a home in Buckinghamshire. Wilson always insisted to me that her salary was no greater than mine; indeed, on one occasion he told me she was earning £1,000 a year less. That led me to ask my wife – after we had started to draw upon our small capital in order to pay our mortgage and other current expenses – why the two of us were not able to manage on £5,000 a year when Marcia could run two houses (I didn't know about the third), two cars, two children and employ up to five Filipino servants – without, according to Housden, paying their National Insurance dues – on a salary which was allegedly no more and on occasions said to be worse than mine.

On the other hand, I had heard, through Housden, that of the £240,000 or thereabouts Wilson had received in 1971 from the *Sunday Times* for serialisation of his memoirs, Marcia had received half and that in addition, the paper had agreed to pay a salary to Peggy for five years. Even so, that did not seem enough to finance such lavish lifestyle, especially if tax was paid upon it.

Wilson told me bitterly that the father of Marcia's children had made only one payment of £500 towards their keep. I asked Walter Terry outright if that was true. He was shocked. He had given her £5,000, and after that she had refused to accept anything more. I unhesitatingly accepted his word because he was not an untruthful man and because Wilson's denials weren't convincing when I took it up with him. I don't doubt £500 was the figure he had been given by Marcia, but I suspect he didn't wholly believe it. She often preferred the grievance to its remedy.

But money had to come from somewhere and after the defeat in 1970, and later, the number of dubious characters who grew closer to the office increased to join one of the most dubious of all, Kagan, who Wilson had made famous by wearing his highly successful Gannex raincoats. By the time I joined Wilson's staff, Kagan came into Downing Street and, later, the opposition leader's office, more often to see Marcia than to speak to Wilson.

What these businessmen gave was a closely guarded secret. A trust had been created to provide finance for the office, but whenever it met Wilson always found reasons for not wanting me around, telling me to have an early night for a change. Marcia would always come in for its meetings. Lord

(Wilfred) Brown was the chairman, the ubiquitous Lord Goodman was its secretary and Lords Plurenden and (Sammy) Fisher of Camden were members. That part of the *Sunday Times* money which Wilson retained went towards paying his staff and was presumably included in the funds which the trust controlled. Lady Falkender was later to write that the trust was to help finance the office of all leaders of the Labour party and that Wilson was only the first beneficiary; were he to be ousted or retire then the trust was there for future leaders to benefit. That was nonsense, as Jim Callaghan showed when he became leader and an entirely different and more open scheme was set up to pay for his political office. All the members of the trust were, she wrote, so discreet that, although Wilson knew of its existence (!) neither he nor anyone else knew the full details, nor who exactly contributed to it. This claim, no doubt, was meant to show that it was a 'blind trust' of the kind later to be popular with Tony Blair and some of his Shadow Cabinet. However, it doesn't square with the fact that the trust met in Wilson's office and he not only knew of its existence but attended its meetings. A trust that didn't discuss income and expenditure in the presence of its only beneficiary doesn't sound plausible. Marcia would, amazingly, often make assertions like that which could easily be disproved.

One weekend, I was called to Chequers to be with the Prime Minister to prepare for an early take-off from Northolt the next day on a visit to yet another European capital. I arrived early and found several people gathered around the piano in the Great Hall, enjoying a singsong. They included Lord Brown, Lady Falkender, Jarvis Astaire, the impresario, Lords Plurenden and Kagan and Eric Miller. The jollity stopped abruptly when I walked in and Wilson suggested that the party should adjourn to the Long Room upstairs, while I stayed downstairs. Albert Murray, as office manager, went with them. He told me afterwards that each of the guests was asked to contribute £1,200 immediately towards the cost of running the political office and that Miller had said that was not enough and proposed a higher figure. Miller was subsequently knighted, Plurenden had already received a knighthood and a peerage and Astaire, a genuine Labour supporter, was recommended for a knighthood by Wilson, who later withdrew the nomination after it met strong resistance in Whitehall.

The trust operated for as long as Wilson was Prime Minister during his second term. During the second election campaign of 1974, Marcia balked at my suggestion that I should stay at St Ermin's hotel (along with many senior Labour party staff), saying that she wasn't going to have the office paying for me to have breakfast in bed and suggesting instead that I should stay at the Churchill hotel, where the rooms were more luxurious, the charges considerably higher and where breakfast was undoubtedly served in bed. It just happened to be owned by Eric Miller's company and, therefore, no bill need be expected. Miller had already loaned us the use of his private plane for the first election when we were in opposition. He was a genuinely generous man and provided all the presents for a Christmas party for disabled children which was held at No. 10. But my doubts about the unassailability of his honesty had grown enough for me to refuse that particular offer of hospitality; there's no such thing as a free breakfast in bed for a government official.

In the event, Marcia raised my intransigence with Wilson. He retorted: 'Why are you the only one who is right?'

These connections with questionable businessmen plagued us throughout Wilson's second term. On 9 October, the eve of polling in the general election, a cashier at the London branch of the International Credit Bank of Geneva – which closed its doors two days earlier on the pretext of it being a Jewish holiday, but in fact because it couldn't meet its obligations – told the London *Evening Standard* that he had a story which would 'blow the election open.' That story was to the effect that Wilson had an account at the bank and that he had sought, just before closure, to withdraw his money – implying that Wilson had been tipped off that a collapse was imminent and was getting his money out while he could. There was an account there – or two, to be precise: a current account with £50 in it and a deposit account with £1,450 – but Wilson had made no attempt to withdraw his money. But how did it get there? The Press Office at No. 10 was given a prepared statement to answer any queries. It said that the £1,500 was contributed by a donor sympathetic to the Labour party and was a contribution towards the running expenses of Wilson's office while in opposition. The donation came through a friend of Dr Arieh Handler, the managing director of the bank (in fact, it was probably Dr Handler himself who was the benefactor) and, as it 'was not immediately required' and at Dr Handler's suggestion, it was put on deposit at the London branch in Mr Wilson's name. That statement raised more questions than it answered. Not required? But weren't we so short of money that Wilson allegedly had to go on lecture tours to raise my salary? When there wasn't enough in the kitty to pay a £300 hotel bill for me? And why had so skilful a politician, one who was super-sensitive to any suggestion of financial scandal and who had helped build his career on the back of his attacks on 'the gnomes of Zurich,' been so foolish as to have an account in his name at a Swiss bank?

Fortunately, the cashier who made the allegations and who was, apparently, under great stress, retracted his claim and the affair died down. But it would never have come alive in a properly ordered office whose effective controller was not obsessed with raising money.

There was, undoubtedly, a real problem about the financing of the leader's office and it still hasn't been solved to this day: the annual contribution from Transport House, the party headquarters, towards the expense of running the leader's office was more than niggardly; it was downright mean, amounting to about £6,000 a year. At one point, the office of the General Secretary, Ron Hayward, even refused to pay Mary Wilson's train fare when she accompanied her husband on party engagements. Wilson defeated that manoeuvre by telling Hayward that his wife was more popular with the voters than he was and if she couldn't go there was no point in his going.

The public and press are quick to condemn private contributions towards politicians and parties because, rightly, they know givers expect to be receivers. But in the same breath they reject any suggestion that the state should make the major contributions. As long as the taxpayer and the press want to have it both ways then the dangers of corruption will exist. But nothing will ever eliminate it altogether; the greedy will still be greedy.

Bill Housden, an incorrigible gossip, came into my office at No. 10 one day with a large brown envelope. 'Guess what's in here?' he said, tapping it. I told him I couldn't begin to guess. 'Four £1,000 watches,' he exclaimed triumphantly. 'John Cordle [a Tory MP who was thought by most of his fellow MPs, including those in his own party, not to be trusted 100 per cent, and who had become a regular escort for Marcia] sent these over and told Marcia to choose one of them for herself.'

'What are you going to do with them now?' I asked. 'I'm taking them back to him,' he replied. 'Marcia asked Harold which one she should have and Harold told her that there was no way that she could have any of them.' After being in his employment for nearly twenty years, and knowing the sensitivity which relates to politicians and their staffs accepting gifts, she ought not to have needed reminding of that fact. Had it become public knowledge that the Prime Minister's secretary was receiving expensive gifts from a Tory MP – or from anyone else – there would have been another public scandal.

But at least Cordle remained on the fringe. Others, like Kagan, Brayley, Rudi Sternberg (Lord Plurenden), and Eric Miller were very close. (Rudi Sternberg should not be confused with Sir Sigmund Sternberg, a loyal and active supporter of the party and an open contributor to it. He was a decent and honourable man and everything he did was above board.)

The omniscient Housden told me one day in opposition that Brayley had arrived at the Wilsons' house and handed over a brown paper parcel. After he left, it was found to contain some £7,000 or £8,000 in notes. There was no rule of parliament against accepting such a gift and no requirement then to register or disclose it. The Wilsons did not know what to do with it and Mrs Wilson said she had better put it into the bank. The street-wise Housden was horrified. 'You can't do that,' he protested. 'How's it going to look if it leaks out that you've handed over all that money in used notes?'

The money should, of course, have been returned, though I'm certain Wilson did not profit by it personally – he didn't have that regard for wealth. Instead, it was used to pay his office staff, which accounts for the fact that for the next year Wilson paid me each month in £50 notes.

Rudi Sternberg was the kind of man classically portrayed on film by Peter Lorre. He had about him that air of sinister mystery which Lorre uniquely conveyed. When I went to Ceausescu's Romania with Wilson, it was no surprise to find Sternberg, coincidentally and apparently independently, standing at my elbow at the hotel's reception desk. He had a freedom to move within the Soviet empire unlike anyone else I knew or heard of, even Robert Maxwell. When Wilson decided to make him a peer, a shocked Foreign Office official protested to me, knowing I would tackle Wilson about it, that Sternberg was a Soviet spy. When I raised it with Wilson, he said cheerfully that he had always thought so, too, but that when he checked with the security services he had been told Sternberg was a double agent. I had no answer to that and the strange peerage went ahead. It was a peerage not for his contributions to charity or the national good, but to the Wilson office accounts.

Eric Miller, knighted in the Resignation Honours List, was another regular contributor; a handsome, often likeable and engaging man who enjoyed his wealth while feeling slightly embarrassed about it. When he came to No. 10, it was usually in a taxi, which waited across the street, meter running, from the front door. In fact, the taxi belonged to him and the taxi-driver was his own chauffeur; he thought it less ostentatious than arriving in his Rolls Royce, especially at the home of a Labour Prime Minister. Marcia was to develop a torrid passion for Miller, writing in indiscreet terms to Albert Murray about it, though Miller's wife was soon to put an end to that. In retaliation, Marcia prevented Albert and his wife, Anne, from travelling to Israel for the barmitzvah of the Millers' son, Robert.

Miller was a highly successful businessman, taking over a small company, Peachey Properties, and turning it into a large one. Unfortunately, his failure to distinguish between what was his and what was the company's – like flying off to Rio with his friends for a jolly weekend in the company's plane – led to the police investigations and his eventual suicide before he could be arrested. But before that, he had been made treasurer of the Socialist International – a ridiculous appointment – and when the SI met in London, it was at the Churchill hotel.

The embarrassment which Miller caused to Wilson was to continue long after the businessman's death. In March 1978, Mr S. D. Samwell – of the chartered accountants Josolyne Layton-Bennett and Co. – one of the inspectors appointed to look into the affairs of the Peachey Property Corporation, Ltd., wrote to Wilson asking him to attend a meeting at the accountants' offices, suggesting he might set aside three hours for the interview, to which he could if he wished be accompanied by legal advisers.

They listed a number of matters on which they wanted to question the former Prime Minister and to discuss ways in which Miller may have spent the company's money to its disadvantage. These included the alleged supply of office equipment, such as a typewriter costing £4,000, an expensive computer, shredding machine and filing cabinets, the use of a helicopter and aircraft for the February 1974 general election, chartered planes to the Scilly Isles, donations to the Labour party and banquets for the party and the Socialist International at the Churchill hotel. I knew nothing about the office equipment (not my department) or of any planes to the Scillies, but I certainly flew on Miller's private plane during that February and attended a meeting of the SI at the Churchill. Whether Miller donated company money to the Labour party I do not know: he certainly donated it to Wilson's political office.

Mr Samwell was also concerned about allegations that Miller was unavailable for the company's affairs because of 'inordinate time' spent at 10 Downing Street, especially in early 1975. I frequently saw him there, but I never understood that he was calling on Harold Wilson. The inspectors, who were anxious to stress that they sought to negate all 'false rumours', were also looking into a sum of £13,500 originally paid to Goodman, Derrick (the firm of Lord Goodman, Wilson's solicitor) on 30 May 1975, and then transferred to another law firm from whom they were waiting to receive a satisfactory explanation of its disposal. Presumably Sir Harold, as he then was, was able to satisfy them; the climate then was different from today's.

Not every businessman who contributed to the maintenance of Wilson's political office was dubious. One very rich man who helped out financially refused a knighthood when it was offered to him because he wanted nothing for himself. Regrettably, those who said 'No' were few and far between. A small contractor from south London who made his contribution had his minor honour delayed for six months because no one could think of a plausible reason for awarding it.

Marcia was often to protest that she was 'only' a secretary and had very little money of her own. But she was constantly in touch with businessmen. Lord Arwyn, for example, wrote to her in March 1976, in somewhat mysterious terms: 'My dear, I am in close touch with Tony and we may bring it off before he goes to Saudi Arabia end of this week. I have been sorting out the 'Cardiffian'. I had to agree that if the sudden disastrous slump had not occurred in the property market almost overnight just after Tony's investment, he would have made a good profit. The forecast is now a revival in values and boom conditions by September. So get ready! . . . 'When you become a Member of Lloyds, I will transfer all insurances to you.'

Only the reasonably wealthy could become a Member of Lloyds; it was not a 'club' open to the average well-paid secretary without £75,000 to spare. She protested that she received no money from the slag heaps deal; she said she got virtually nothing from the father of her children; she claimed in 1970 to be earning only £30 a week; Wilson, at a later stage said at first that she earned £5,000 a year and then amended it to £4,000. As she was employed by him and not by the state, she was only paid in salary what he could afford. Where did the money come from? How could she afford to send her two children to an extremely expensive private school, employ five servants, have two cars and rent or own three houses? Where the money came from and what hold she had over Wilson are separate questions, but maybe inextricably mixed.

Ten
Taking Over

On the spring day in 1969 when I finally became Press Secretary to the Prime Minister, the safe in my new office, the bow-fronted room which looks out upon Downing Street to the right of the famous door, was ceremoniously opened by my Higher Executive Officer, Doris Knight. She handed me a top-secret file which detailed my intended role in helping the nation survive in the event of a nuclear war. Under what parliamentary authority, if any, I was to operate I do not know, but the file showed that I was to assume complete control of the television and radio output of the BBC as well as ITV (there was then no satellite broadcaster) and of all of the national press. I imagine I would have had to close down all the newspapers and produce a *British Gazette*-type sheet of the kind master-minded by Winston Churchill during the general strike of 1926. The file demonstrated the obsession of the civil service for making plans to cope with any conceivable circumstance, whether or not those plans bore any relationship to the situation which would exist when and if the time came. Had I finished reading it, I would no doubt have discovered where and how my newspaper would be printed, where the paper and ink supplies were, how it would be circulated and my complete freedom to choose who would write and edit it (presumably not me as I would be busy doing other things, perhaps writing the news for a single service TV channel). Even for a journalist with a lamentable dictatorial streak, the glittering prize of total control of all the media was not worth a nuclear holocaust. I handed back the file, saying that its contents were based on a fallacy, the assumption that in the event of such a war I would come into the office.

In 1969, in any case, I had more immediate matters on my mind, principally the standing of the government, which was at a record low for modern times, and what, if anything, I could do to improve it. I did want to reflect upon how governments handled the release of official information, how political parties' press officers worked, or should work, with the government machine, what the relationship between government and the media should be and how I would do the job differently from the way it had been done in the past. But not yet. That would all have to wait for another time. There was no point in planning the next cruise while clambering into a lifeboat. In the event, I did very little. Short-termism is a major defect of democratic government.

I made little perceptible public impact in my first spell at No. 10. What good, if any, I did for Wilson was done out of the public gaze. I had taken over a press office which seemed indifferent to or unaware of the Government's unpopularity. Traditional and theoretical impartiality insisted that the well-being of the Government had little or nothing to do with them; reality demanded that it did. The office had no political feel; those in it were doing a job for which most of them were unfitted and unfocused and it was, consequently, a handicap rather than a help to the Government's survival.

My predecessor, Trevor (later Sir Trevor) Lloyd-Hughes, a former political correspondent — our desks adjoined in the Press Gallery when we both worked there — had held firmly to the view that the civil service had to be impartial at all times. It served governments not the government, ever ready to remain in post as the current government departed to be replaced by a new one. It was an attitude both admirable and unreal. Trevor exemplified this outlook by wanting to stay on as a civil servant under the 1970 Heath government and would have served it as faithfully and impartially as he did Wilson's had Heath agreed, which he didn't.

In the short time I was his deputy, we disagreed sharply on more than one occasion about the direction in which the office should go. He told me once:

'You are too political' – a complaint echoed, curiously enough, at about the same time by a junior press officer at the Department of Employment when I tried to inject some sparkle into his ministry's lifeless 'popular' version of *In Place of Strife*. That junior was Bernard Ingham, who was later to receive a knighthood for many years of what he no doubt regarded as distinguished impartiality as Mrs Thatcher's press secretary.

When Trevor was offered 'promotion' to overall supervision of the government's information services, two months after my arrival, he feared, rightly, that he was being thrust upwards but aside to make way for me and that would mean the office would be politicised. I respected his view on the political neutrality of the press secretary, which was theoretically correct, if unreal. It wasn't one I shared, nor did the Prime Minister. I never asked my staff to make party political judgements, to speak from a party political standpoint or to disclose to me their political allegiances – one who was quick to do so, I never trusted – but I did want them to be politically aware. With the exception of three – George Holt, who was my deputy in 1969-70, Janet Hewlett-Davies, who filled that role in 1974-6 and Jean Denham, who I recruited from the Labour party – they were not. On one notable occasion when I was choosing a new member of staff from a list of four candidates, I finally took the only one who knew on which days the Prime Minister answered questions in the House of Commons. On the other hand, I had been steeped in politics from the age of eleven. I even read *Mein Kampf* at that age, though I can't pretend to have understood it. Everyone with whom I was likely to deal knew where I stood politically. It would have been hypocritical for me suddenly to assume the role of political eunuch, even though, to conform to the civil service's proclaimed public face, I had to resign my seat as a Labour councillor.

Like me, many of the members of the Lobby correspondents' group believed the twice-daily meetings between the Press Secretary and the reporters – in the mornings at No. 10 and in the afternoon, always at the Lobby's invitation, in a little eyrie on the top floor of the Commons – had become a farce. Some went because the meetings were part of the tradition of the House; some, after consuming a good lunch, to bait the No. 10 spokesman; others, because they regarded it, in a vaguely old school tie way, as their duty to the Lobby. Few went in the belief that they would learn anything. As a reporter, I had long given up regular attendance after a squabble about press accuracy, which at the time I defended with a misplaced zeal. Trevor Lloyd-Hughes had criticised certain newspaper stories for their mistakes and added, pointing to a clock on the wall whose hands had not moved in the memory of the oldest inhabitant: 'even your clock doesn't work.' I retorted: 'At least it's right twice a day, which is more than you are.' They were unkind words which I later regretted when I found myself confronted with the same problems in which he was daily enmeshed.

In June 1975, I solved the problem of those meetings when I abolished them altogether, amid screams of outrage from the Lobby, which failed to see that I was doing it a favour, not inflicting a punishment. Subsequent press secretaries restored the meetings, and a fat lot of good it did them. The fact was that the Lobby, whose members at its founding could easily have sat round a decent dining room table, had grown far too large, and far too partisan.

Members of the opposition were regularly told by political reporters what I had said at supposedly non-attributable Lobby meetings; confidentiality had ceased to exist. The final straw came when, after listening to blatantly misleading statements in the Commons from a Tory spokesman about a future debate on the steel industry, I instructed Janet Hewlett-Davies to disclose to the Lobby some of the behind-the-scenes dealings between chief whips on the issue. Within the hour, Labour's chief whip, Bob Mellish, told me that his Tory opposite, Francis Pym, had complained to him that I had broken the rules of secrecy by which the whips' offices conducted their business. Perhaps I had. But so had the three Lobby correspondents who had left Janet's Lobby meeting and gone straight to the Tory whips' office to report what had been said. That was enough for me. I wrote a Dear John letter to the chairman of the Lobby (whose Christian name was John) ending the meetings from that moment on, thus attracting to me the kind of publicity which I believe press secretaries should strive to avoid. Every disgruntled reporter blamed Wilson's dislike of the press, principally because they could see no fault on their part, rather than accept it was a matter on which I felt strongly and had done for years. However, I was in no way unique in my attitude. President Gerald Ford's press secretary, Ron Nessen, writing to me at Christmas in 1975, said he had been having more problems than usual with criticism of his office at the White House and added: 'As I told you at Rambouillet [a French chateau outside Paris where an economic summit had been held earlier in the year], I envy your ability to call off your daily briefings. I often wish I could do the same. But with the mood among the press in America, I think I would get too much criticism for hiding or stone-walling.' His caution was not mine.

My first public 'political' act in my first spell at Downing Street was to attend the annual Labour conference in 1969. It seemed to me absurd that I should be the Prime Minister's press secretary for fifty-one weeks in the year but in the one week when, more than any other, he was at the forefront of the nation's attention, the week in which he made his most important speech of the year, I should, by civil service custom, rules and tradition, be stuck in London handling nothing more significant than press notices about the appointment of vicars to hitherto unknown livings in obscure parts of East Anglia. Meanwhile, I would have had to leave the Prime Minister's press relations to the press office of a Labour party whose executive was frequently at odds with, or hostile to, its leader.

The British press may have understood the artificial difference between Prime Minister and party leader, but the foreign press, which descends upon party conferences by the hundred and whose requests for information took up a considerable part of my office's work, did not. What I regarded as a sensible and realistic innovation was abandoned by my Tory successors and Ted Heath's, Mrs Thatcher's and John Major's press officers stayed away from the conferences. The ridiculousness of that policy of intermittent virginity was demonstrated when the IRA attempted to blow up Mrs Thatcher and half her Cabinet in the Grand Hotel, Brighton, bombing of October 1984. That was in every sense a national and international story, not a party political one, but her press secretary was not at the seaside to handle it.

Of course, had he been there, he might, regrettably, have been one of the casualties. Nevertheless, the principle is unaltered. Sensibly, Alastair Campbell, Tony Blair's spokesman, revived the practice of attending party conferences in government and took on a more overt public political role after the general election victory of 1997 than I was ever allowed to do. The party leader in government is first and foremost the Prime Minister, even on party occasions. Not to accept that, or to quibble about what proportion of the spokesman's pay and expenses should be met by the civil service and what by the party, is one of those arcane constitutional squabbles so beloved by the British press and the tame academics it can call on when the occasion arises.

That obsession was illustrated for me one rainy day in 1974 when Wilson was meeting the Liaison committee of the Labour party inside No. 10. That meeting on government premises was perfectly proper and legal, provided that any refreshments offered to the participants were paid for by the Prime Minister; however, it was deemed improper for the Prime Minister subsequently to meet the press there because he would be speaking not as Prime Minister but as leader of a political party. But it was bucketing down outside and those reporters waiting on the doorstep of No. 10 who considered it unmanly to carry an umbrella were being drenched. Out of a misplaced goodness of heart, I asked that No. 12 Downing Street, the Chief's Whip's Whitehall workplace, should be opened up and the journalists saved from a further wetting by placing them in the conference room there until our meeting was over. At the end of that meeting, as the downpour showed no sign of easing, I suggested to Wilson that he meet the press in No. 12, rather than all of us traipsing over to Transport House, more than half a mile away, and condemning the journalists to a further soaking. 'What will they say about a party meeting in a government office?' asked Wilson. 'They won't say anything,' I confidently replied. 'They're only too grateful to be in out of the rain.' Inevitably, the first question, of course, was: 'Mr Wilson, why are you using government accommodation to hold a party press conference?' When the reporters had dispersed, I told Wilson I was sorry. 'Next time,' he growled, 'let them drown.'

I had made a basic mistake. For the one and only time in my press secretarial career, I had forgotten that I was employed to serve the Prime Minister, not the press. By helping them, in what they probably regarded as an untypical display of humanity and in a physical rather than informational sense, I had let him down.

The first change I made in the role of the Downing Street press office was not popular with journalists, though it was approved by some of Whitehall's chief information officers. When I arrived at No 10 beginning work at 10 a.m. rather than the 7.30 a.m. which is the modern practice – I found that the outer office staff over whom I was to preside until I succeeded to the No. 1 job were all engaged from an early hour telephoning every other government department's press office to find out their current line upon every minute detail of their ministers' work and plans. This ring-around would go on until just before the morning Lobby arrived for their briefing at eleven o'clock. This was a crazy system for several reasons. First, the other information departments resented No. 10 answering on their behalf and snatching away their best stories. Inevitably, they would sometimes keep back their choicest tit-bits, leaving No. 10 to look ignorant, untruthful or out of date.

This undercurrent rivalry was bad for the morale of the information service, which was the Cinderella of Whitehall, anyway. After I joined, several senior civil servants gleefully repeated to me the mantra that if a recruit to the civil service was honest but not bright he was given a post in information. That may have engendered a feeling of superiority among the ambitious Oxbridge graduates but it caused resentment among the press officers.

Second, the policy of ringing round made No. 10 the central clearing house for all government information, which, with a staff of five or so, it was totally unfitted to do. Third, it was taking up the time of that staff when it could be better employed on the Prime Minister's immediate concerns. Fourth, which mattered a lot to me, it was a recipe for lazy journalism. Instead of spending their mornings making their own inquiries from the different ministries, evening newspaper journalists would have a leisurely coffee break before drifting into No. 10 expecting all their questions to be answered on any subject by me or my deputy. As a recipe for inefficiency, it could not be bettered. The Whitehall departments, with their inbuilt sense of inferiority, were rightly jealous of Downing Street's automatic assumption of superiority, even though it was a fact, and also of my privilege in announcing their news, even though I didn't want it.

Though I was already developing a belief in the need for autonomy for departments, there were times when No. 10 had to be a long-stop. After I had been at No. 10 for only a few weeks, Bob Carvel, the London *Evening Standard's* peerless political editor, asked me for technical help, seeking an estimate of the space his paper would have to devote to a digest of the forth-coming White Paper on industrial relations. I had once worked on an evening newspaper I understood the problem and I gave him my estimate. Within the hour, the Ministry of Labour's chief press officer was on the phone complaining about what I had done. For the past week, he said, he had been refusing to answer that same question from the paper's industrial correspondent, Alan Johnson, who had just been on to him to protest that what he had refused, I had given. 'Why did you refuse it?' I asked, and put the phone down.

On another occasion, a Ministry of Health spokesman told me that his department would not be giving political correspondents the usual advance copies under embargo of a Royal Commission report they were publishing. 'Why not?' I asked. 'Because John Grant [later a Labour government minister in the 1974 administration, but then the *Daily Express's* industrial correspondent] got a leak on it and we are paying them back,' he replied. I told him, clearly, colourfully and at dictation speed, exactly where he was wrong and where I thought his future might lay if the report was not distributed in the customary way. He was indignant, but did as he was told.

Soon afterwards, Wilson and I met Trevor Lloyd-Hughes in the long corridor of No. 10 that leads from the front lobby to the Cabinet room. 'I'm glad Joe's with you,' Trevor said to Wilson, 'because I have had some complaints about him.'

'What kind of complaints?' asked Wilson.

'He's been rude to civil servants,' replied Trevor.

'Good,' said Wilson. 'Anything else?'

It was difficult, however, to make any positive moves to turn the press office operation into the kind of machine which was needed; my time seemed to be spent more on preventing things from going wrong than devising a structure which might assist in helping them to go right. The tradition of secrecy ran deep in all aspects of the civil service. Some senior officials operated the 'need to know' criterion to excess. If there were confidential matters which they did not wish to see in the press, then the press offices of their departments were not told, on the grounds that if, by definition, secret questions were not for publication, press officers did not need to be informed of them. Chief information officers only saw the record of Cabinet decisions which directly affected their departments, whereas at No. 10 even the most junior press officers saw the complete Cabinet minutes after I had finished with them. This meant that only No. 10 saw the whole picture. Even there, an unconscious desire not to tell even the Press Secretary what was happening ran strongly. Time and again in my early months, information was kept from me, either deliberately or because the thought of informing the press office didn't occur. There was a practice whereby I was able to read all the papers put in the Prime Minister's red boxes, but if I was too busy to do that two or three times a day then I might miss something vital; or a private secretary might place a final batch of papers in a box just as he (there was never in my time a she in the private office staff except young duty clerks) locked it for delivery to the Prime Minister. Inevitably, I suspected that sometimes documents were placed in the boxes at the last moment in order to prevent me seeing them.

Above all else, at a time when the government was not always synchronised with its party, and when ministers were not always in tune with each other, I saw my role clearly as to answer for the Prime Minister, no one else, which meant I had to know what he knew. The fact that I did not answer for the ministries, though, did not mean that they were free to be independent; that path led to disarray and disunity. I wanted to know what they were doing, but I did not want to do it for them. If they stepped out of line, then they had to be pulled back. Ministers, too, had to be restrained. Dick Crossman, who was first Housing Minister and then Secretary of State for Health and Social Security, was a disaster not only waiting to happen but one which frequently did. One Monday afternoon he announced to the Commons increases in denture and spectacle charges by his department which dismayed and infuriated Labour supporters. An angry Harold Wilson demanded to know why he had made his announcement only three days before the annual local elections in which we were bound to do badly in any case. Crossman innocently replied that he hadn't realised that the elections were taking place. It is frequently said that ministers grow out of touch with the electors; there was never a better case. One consequence of that debacle was that all ministers were instructed to submit to No. 10 – in effect, to me – at least forty-eight hours in advance any statement they intended to make to the Commons, so that I could ensure they did not repeat Crossman's blunder. Only emergency statements were exceptions to this rule and, on the whole, it worked.

The professional civil servants were not normally a problem; but a few special advisers who saw their role as the promotion of the policies, and often the personalities, of their ministers, potentially were. However, Bernard Donoughue kept a constant overall eye upon them and so, more haphazardly, did I. They could promote their ministers' policies provided those policies were the government's. What they could not do, under pain of instant dismissal, was to trash the policies or blacken the names of other ministers. It was a lesson which Tony Blair's government was slow to learn or, if they already knew it, to enforce, though they did in the end.

There were occasions, such as the Department of Health episode, when it was necessary for No. 10 to use its heavy boot; failure to give the newspapers time to prepare a considered report might have led to an unfavourable press for the Royal Commission – an absurd outcome to a press officer's pique (and, incidentally, justifying the jibe about their lack of intellectual calibre).

For the same reason, I did, very occasionally, chair the weekly meetings of Whitehall's chief information officers, but I preferred to leave them to my deputy – in my four years in Downing Street I had three admirable deputies, first, George Holt, a very able journalist-poacher-turned-gamekeeper; Charles Birdsall, steeped in civil service traditions and loved by all, but with an irritating habit of knowing every reason why I could not do something and no reasons why I could; and Janet Hewlett-Davies, whom I had first met when she was a young chief reporter on the Tonbridge *Kent and Sussex Courier* and I was a local councillor. They were all trusted by civil servants because they were all civil servants. They were all trusted by me, too.

A further problem with which a Wilson press secretary had to deal was the attitude of the Prime Minister himself. He devoured every word of the political columns. Until his memory grew faulty, he recalled every wound, every jibe, every inaccuracy which was ever penned against him. By the time I got in each morning, he had read every newspaper and would fire questions and judgements at me as soon as I sat down to talk. If there was one paper I hadn't read, that was the one he wanted to discuss. He was proud of the fact that the *Guardian* had once offered him a job and never realised that he was not temperamentally suited to be a journalist. He liked the company of journalists: especially the cynicism of Terry Lancaster of the *People* and, later, the *Daily Mirror*, and the gentle but firm questioning of James Margach of the *Sunday Times*. As a journalist, I frequently travelled on his plane on foreign visits; he would wander down the aisle, look over our shoulders and ask: 'What are you chaps up to?' From my point of view, this was unnerving, especially if I was writing critically about the results of the trip. The fact was that the privilege of being a passenger on the Prime Minister's aircraft was inhibiting. My journalistic mentor, Harold Hutchinson, always preferred to make his own way to a foreign capital and would be waiting at the airport for the Prime Minister to arrive, just in case, as he would explain, the plane crashed on landing. As a press secretary, I found the presence of journalists interfered with our work, too, and I ended, as far as I could, the custom of offering seats on the aircraft to journalists, even though they paid the full commercial fare. No subsequent press secretary agreed with me and some used the convenience of travelling on the Prime Minister plane which they offered to journalists to exert an influence upon them, or to shut out those who were not members of the Lobby and who were not to be influenced.

Wilson undoubtedly tried in his early days as leader of the Labour party and Prime Minister to be friendly with and helpful to the press. He invited them to receptions at No. 10. He knew their first names; he remembered wives when they accompanied their husbands to functions at No. 10. But it is a mistake for politicians and journalists to be too friendly. The correct relationship should be a distant one. I made it a practice as a political reporter never to invite to my home, or visit the home of, MPs whom I did not know before they became MPs. Priggish, perhaps, but it saved me heartache when I found it necessary to criticise them.

It was not a view Wilson understood. One Christmas time, Ian Aitken, ex-*Tribune*, ex-*Daily Express* and *Guardian* political reporter was in hospital for the removal of an eye. Wilson, then Prime Minister, suddenly and unexpectedly arrived to visit him, causing, I was told, a flutter among the nursing staff. Some years later, Aitken was trenchantly critical of Wilson in the *Guardian*. 'How could he write that?' Wilson demanded of me. 'I went to see him when he was in hospital.' I've always thought since that that reaction was a warning to every reporter. Just as journalists don't offer free lunches, politicians don't do free kindnesses. Wilson was not peculiar in this regard; every Prime Minister or political leader I have known has had the same attitude towards the press. They are fascinated by, even when despising, the creators of the written word and, consequently, they have an insatiable desire to manipulate or control them: 'Some do it with a bitter look/ Some with a flattering word/The coward does it with a kiss/The brave man with a sword!' In his time, Wilson employed all of these methods and his approach has been shared by those who are attached, or who attach themselves, to party leaders.

In the late 1960s, Wilson adopted the bitter look approach when he had lunch with Roy Thomson, owner of many British newspapers including *The Times* and the *Sunday Times*, and caustically criticised *The Times's* political editor, David Wood; according to Wood, in a later outburst to Wilson which crossed the border into hysteria and which I witnessed, he had demanded that Wood should be sacked, thus making at least one more enemy for life. This is an intolerable approach to problems with the press, even when a reporter's behaviour might justify a sacking; what's more, it is guaranteed to unite the press against the politician.

Harold Macmillan's fatal encounter with the press and his subsequent downfall owed more to the jailing of two reporters after the Vassall inquiry of 1963 than to the Profumo affair which followed a few months later. John Vassall was a homosexual cipher clerk at the Admiralty who in 1962 was jailed for eighteen years after being caught selling secrets to the Soviet Union. Like other *Daily Mail* journalists at the time, I contributed to a fund for Brendan Mulholland, a *Mail* reporter who was sentenced to six months' imprisonment for failing to disclose to a judicial inquiry his sources for alleging a link between Vassall and a junior Navy Minister, Thomas Galbraith. I knew Galbraith well and Mulholland hardly at all; I never for a moment believed that Galbraith, vain and supercilious though he was, could have been a homosexual. There was a widespread view among journalists that the reason the two reporters did not disclose their sources was because they didn't have any and that in the fevered atmosphere of the time they allowed their imaginations to run riot. Nevertheless, sending then to prison, the direct result of Macmillan setting up the inquiry, alienated the body of journalists as a whole.

It's a tribal thing: he may be a liar, but he's our liar. Using the power of the state to exact revenge was unacceptable to every journalist. Using the privilege of a powerful position to go direct to a proprietor was in the same league, even if the possible punishment was not. Never in my life did I complain to a proprietor about the conduct of a reporter, although as a journalist I thrice suffered from that kind of treatment by politicians, each time, ironically, from prominent figures in the Labour party.

In 1986, for example, I experienced the most serious of these when Robert Maxwell owned the *Daily Mirror* and Peter Mandelson was Director of Publicity for the Labour party. Mandelson wrote to Maxwell complaining about the paper's failure to ensure the proper (i.e., lengthy) reporting of a speech by Neil Kinnock, then the Labour leader. As political editor of the paper, that was my responsibility; it was fair enough that Mandelson should be incensed at my judgement, though it was widely shared by other newspapers, and had he written to the editor to complain rather than take it up with me, I would have been irritated, but little more. But writing to the proprietor was of a different order of seriousness: editors tend to defend their reporters against the protests of the powerful, but proprietors tend to placate the powerful at the expense of the journalist. Editors are concerned with how many readers their papers have; proprietors are more interested in who their readers are. Mandelson's letter, therefore, as he must have known, was an attack upon me and even upon my employment.

Fortunately his complaint was first seen by Peter Jay, the former British ambassador to Washington and Maxwell's chief of staff. Jay did the perfectly proper thing: he had to show the letter to Maxwell but he sent it to me first. By the sort of unusual coincidence which happens so often as to be usual, I was reading Mandelson's poisonous letter at the very moment when he telephoned to congratulate me on the leading article which I had written for the *Mirror* that day. I exploded and accused him of hypocrisy; so vehement must I have been that he had no contact with me for the next two years, a period which covered the general election of 1987, when the *Mirror* was the only national newspaper of electoral consequence which supported the Labour party. I wouldn't suggest for a moment that Mandelson's decision to cut himself off from the *Mirror* affected the election result in the slightest but, at the least, it was injudicious and resulted from a failure to understand how journalists behave.

Wilson's major effort at flattering the press was to try to establish an elite corps among the Lobby members, the so-called 'white Commonwealth' consisting of the leading political journalists on national newspapers. Had I been at Downing Street at the time, I suspect it might have been a resigning issue for me. The Parliamentary Lobby are, or were then, a tightly knit group. Rival reporters worked alongside each other in large rooms. They ate together, they drank together and many of them played golf together at the weekends. It was not possible for the major members of that community suddenly to disappear from the Press Gallery (the meetings were held at No. 10, or the Prime Minister's room in the Commons) without everyone quickly becoming aware that something was afoot. Their equally sudden return and the appearance the next morning of stories sourced to 'circles close to the Prime Minister' told even the most junior political reporter what was going on. It became a point of honour to expose the 'white Commonwealth' and it did not long survive the light of day. After devaluation, Wilson retreated to his bunker, which is more or less where I found him when I agreed at the end of 1968 to join his staff.

Wilson's hatred of the press by this time knew few bounds, perhaps because he had loved it so much and had been jilted. He felt betrayed by the hostile coverage of his activities because at heart he thought he was one of them. This attitude caused me difficulties. At a European summit meeting in Rome, I asked him, after a lengthy and testing session, what I could say to the press. 'Say nothing,' he snapped. That was easier said (by him) than done (by me) but it was what he wanted, so that was what they got: nothing.

Nevertheless, there were issues on which we were wholly in agreement and one of those was the need for a law on privacy. I did not then, and I do not now, accept the press's arguments of the public's right to know everything about the private life of a public person, whether politician, vicar, actor or chairman of a quango. After a committee headed by Sir Kenneth Younger failed to come up with a definition of privacy, Wilson asked me to supply one and I did: 'Newspapers shall accord to the general public the same right of privacy as they accord to their proprietors.' That seemed to me a good polemical start to any agreement we might have made with Fleet Street, though any law based upon it would have virtually excluded every report about everybody. Bernard Donoughue and I had a meeting at No. 10 with Harold Evans, then the editor of the *Sunday Times*, in which we offered to act upon some of those substantial matters which concerned editors in return for a significant step forward on the right to privacy. What we had in mind – and which Wilson much later incorporated in a speech – was to reform the laws on contempt of court, always a dangerous minefield for newspapers, and libel, always an expensive minefield, in favour of the press. Wilson was later to add the question of amending the *sub judice* rule, which had long prevented the *Sunday Times* from reporting the thalidomide scandal in the 1960s and 1970s, to the list of the improvements in press freedom we were prepared to make, but it was to no avail. Evans promised to consult among his fraternity of editors and the word came back from him that there was no hope of getting their agreement to a new law on privacy. Wilson wanted to propose, and later did, a voluntary code of practice but that, in effect, existed already in the Press Council which, like its successor, the Press Complaints Commission, was a toothless watchdog which fled to the hills at the first sight of an intruder. It howled but couldn't bite.

Turning down our approach was a classic case of the press preferring to remain restricted in the name of freedom. We could easily have met most of the objections to a privacy law by ensuring that it would not apply to elected representatives or to those appointed to serve on public bodies if a public interest argument could be sustained (e.g. if an MP publicly promoted family life while keeping a mistress or advocated the importance of National Savings while salting away his money abroad he would not be protected by a Privacy Act).

But we got nowhere. Since then the position has greatly worsened. When I first went to work in the Press Gallery as parliamentary reporter of the *Bulletin*, an obscure Scottish tabloid for middle-class, middle-aged spinsters and long since dead like most of its readers, I was its youngest member. Yet I quickly learned of two affairs which today would be blazoned across the front of every newspaper in the land: Hugh Gaitskell's discreet affair with the wife of Ian Fleming, creator of James Bond, and Bob (Lord) Boothby's indiscreet affair with Harold Macmillan's wife, Lady Dorothy. Had they become public knowledge, both men would have been ruined politically, one because he was an adulterer and the other because he was a knowing cuckold. In which case, the Labour party would have been deprived of the best Prime Minister it never had and the Tory party would have been denied one of the best Prime Ministers it ever had. These affairs would unquestionably have been of interest to the public, but would their exposure have been in the public interest?

One of the errors firmly entrenched in the public mind is that it is only the tabloid newspapers (tabloid is a description of size, not of content or quality) which are the scandal sheets, not the broadsheets like the *Guardian*, the *Daily Telegraph, The Times* or the *Independent* or their Sunday sisters. That is not so.

During my term at No. 10, I heard of an ambassador to the Soviet Union who had resigned after tempting a Russian chambermaid into his bed. (Seeing that she was believed to be a KGB agent, not much tempting, if any, would have been required.) The ambassador instantly realised that his foolishness might compromise him and resigned. Some years later, the *Daily Mirror* was given the story by an informant. The paper's then editor, Mike Molloy, asked me if it was true and, when I reluctantly confirmed it, sent a reporter to interview the ambassador, who was living quietly in retirement. The ex-diplomat admitted the indiscretion but asked the reporter to handle it with sensitivity, as his wife did not know of it. When the *Mirror* man reported back, Molloy said simply: 'He's admitted it and we are not in the business of ruining him.' The *Mirror* didn't publish the story. A year or so later, the *Sunday Times* did.

In 1983, during the Labour party conference at Brighton, I was approached by a reporter on the *Observer* with a story which his paper, a broadsheet, would not publish but whose publication I would defend: the affair between Cecil Parkinson, chairman of the Tory party whose election campaign that year, as ever, had upheld family values, and Sara Keays, his secretary, who was expecting his child. The *Observer* man wanted £500 for the details. I immediately went to Tony Miles, the Mirror Group's chairman and former editor of the *Daily Mirror* and told him of the offer. He did not jump for joy, as I half expected. Instead, he told me that the *Mirror* had had the story for some weeks but that he and the editor had decided not to publish it, apparently on the grounds that it was not the role of a Labour-supporting newspaper to lead the way with a story of that nature. Within days, every newspaper in the country splashed the scandal, including the *Mirror*, but we had deliberately decided not to be first. Personally, I always disagreed with that decision, but it demonstrated an editorial standard which had ceased to exist a decade later. On the other hand, I believe the *Mirror* would always have published the photographs of the Duchess of York half naked with her 'financial adviser'. If she wanted to be a member of the Royal Family, to enjoy its privileges and to live, in part, off public largesse, then an affair with an American entrepreneur was not something which should, or could, have been kept quiet. I mention these instances of Parkinson and Fergie only to show that newspapers would have had little to fear and much to gain had they seized the chance of doing a deal with the Wilson government.

The upshot today is that the balance, uneasy and uneven though it was, between the press and politicians has dramatically changed for the worse, largely, I believe, because the newspaper publishing business has changed beyond recognition. There was a time in the 1960–85 period when I was inclined, when consulted by doting parents about the prospect of their offspring making a name in Fleet Street, to suggest they steered their loved ones into a more secure career, like sky diving. The newspapers were heavily controlled by the printing trade unions. Managements couldn't, and didn't, manage. Corruption was rife. After the settlement of one dispute, a union negotiator brutally told a newspaper management that he didn't want any more cases of whisky. His garage was stacked high with the stuff. From then on it was to be strictly cash. One *Mirror* manager, responsible for the nightly production of his paper, wouldn't go near the presses without a pocketful of fivers to distribute in case of trouble. Robert Maxwell sacked one union man on the Scottish *Daily Record* for instructing printers to break the paper reel – enough to put a machine out of action for forty minutes, always a calamity when minutes are precious – and his union promptly ensured that another newspaper took him on. With a circulation of over four million, the *Daily Mirror* was losing money in the 1970s. Maxwell and Rupert Murdoch smashed the newspaper unions and transformed the prospects and profitability of the papers. I know of no other newspaper owners who could have done it. But that success brought other problems in its wake.

When newspaper proprietors like Beaverbrook, Kemsley, Lord Hartwell and the Rothermeres owned the bulk of the national press, profit was important, but not all-important. None of them owned newspapers in order to keep the wolves or shareholders, from their door. They were driven by their political ideology or beliefs and the luxury of power, not commerce. When Beaverbrook and Rothermere were branded as 'harlots' by Stanley Baldwin for demanding the right to approve his Cabinet, they were not concerned with profits but with control.

Now that has all changed. It is a poor proprietor who can't make money from newspapers today. Profit is the motive force and circulation its engine. Sensations sell newspapers. Sleaze, real or imagined, sells newspapers. Sex, even heterosexual sex between consenting adults, sells newspapers. Scandal in its broadest sense has real commercial value. When, in January 1999 the *Mirror* decided not to publish the news of the forthcoming engagement of the

Queen's third son, Prince Edward, every other newspaper editor must have though the *Mirror* was mad, and, no doubt, so did quite a few of its shareholders. Intrusion, taste and prudence are controlled not by innate senses of decency but by whether a particular story's aid to circulation is sufficiently strong to outweigh the adverse publicity it might engender for the newspaper.

This decline in standards – or liberation of the press, depending upon where the reader is standing – is not confined to Britain. It is worldwide, which is why I don't believe anything can be done about it, at least voluntarily.

A friend told me that Mario Cuomo, one-time Governor of New York State and often tipped as a future Democratic presidential candidate, rejected running for the White House on the grounds that any boy of Italian descent who grew up in New York was bound to have had friends or relatives with connections to the Mafia, and he did not want their lives crawled over and damaged by a press determined to sling mud.

The relentless scrutiny of the press, relevant or not, is a consideration every ambitious politician has to take into account before he first seeks to be a candidate or to be drafted into a government. In Tony Blair's first administration, two businessmen, Lord Simon and Lord Sainsbury, whose very wealth, apart from their own honesty, made them unbribable, must have wondered whether serving the public good was worth the aggravation of having their shareholdings and their probity investigated as if the presumption was that they were up to something venal. Who wants it? Geoffrey Robinson, who resigned as Paymaster-General at Christmas 1998, was a wealthy man, much of whose money was legally lodged abroad and who was linked in some business matters with the late and hated Robert Maxwell. After a year's hounding, he was forced out of office before anything was proved against him. If the Maxwell connection was a prime cause of his downfall, then many other politicians, in all Britain's three main parties, as well as bankers and businessmen, might look at Robinson and say: 'there but for the grace of God and the fact that the papers didn't know, goes I.' To varying extents, the same might apply to a good many of Maxwell's twenty-five thousand employees.

Innocence has nothing to do with it. Guilt by association is all. I write with feeling, for I was one of those at whom the mud was thrown and intended to stick. If, on the other hand, Robinson's political demise was due solely to his being rich, then, by definition, all Labour politicians who have been successful in business are to be excluded from government, to be replaced, presumably, by men and women who have made an outstanding financial failure of their life. But there is more than wealth and knowing Maxwell to bring a man down today. Homosexuality is said now not to be a bar to a man's career. Up to a point, Lord Copper. Did Mr X ever have an under-age homosexual affair at public school or behind the bike shed at a state school? If he did, he won't become Prime Minister. Is there a former mistress or lover waiting to cash in with a lurid tale of youthful liaisons, especially if whips or other forms of sado-masochism are involved? Then he might be safer becoming a lawyer. Did he/she ever accept a gift which in today's light might look like a bribe even if it were not and was never intended to be? Did he/she borrow too much for a house too grand? Accept hospitality from a would-be government contractor? Send or receive a Christmas present to or from a man or woman who subsequently turned out to be, or became, a crook? Know a foreign diplomat too well? All those sins disqualify him from ever becoming Chancellor of the Exchequer, let alone Prime Minister.

But what do we want? A government of Pope Johns and Mother Teresas, staffed by monks and nuns? If we did have one, does anyone think they would be safe from scandal? The homosexual vicar used to be the staple diet of the Sunday papers and a homosexual vicar in government would bring those days back with a flourish, cartoons and all.

It is the proper role of newspapers to be irresponsible. It is not their job to save the face of any crooked politician or anyone else in public life. The question is where the line is drawn. There is nothing wrong with muckraking if there is muck to be raked. But when muck-raking becomes mud-slinging, when smoke is created without fire, when innocent actions are portrayed as sinister, when honest mistakes are splashed across the front pages as crimes of malicious intent, when generosity is seen as corruption and charity is portrayed as base, as all are today, then the balance between the right to publish and the public good has become too uneven. The inevitable consequence, one day, is that a government not of liberal intent will bring in a law which will punish newspapers for the slightest infraction of what, in its judgement, it believes to be best, and then we will all be losers.

One sentence of Lord Macaulay's review of Thomas Moore's biography of Lord Byron is usually quoted when the press is under attack for exposing the alleged sins, usually sexual, of politicians and others: 'We know of no spectacle so ridiculous as the British public in one of its periodical fits of morality.' But there was more to the passage than that and it is equally relevant:

> *Once in six or seven years our virtue becomes outrageous. We cannot stand the laws of religion and decency to be violated. We must make a stand against vice. We must teach libertines that the English people appreciate the importance of domestic ties. Accordingly, some unfortunate man in no respect more depraved than the hundreds whose offences have been treated with lenity, is singled out as an expiatory sacrifice ... If he has a profession, he has to be driven from it. He is cut by the higher orders and hissed by the lower. He is, in truth, a sort of whipping boy, by whose vicarious agonies all the other transgressors of the same class are, it is supposed, sufficiently chastised . . . At length our anger is satiated. Our victim is ruined and heartbroken. And our virtue goes to sleep quietly for seven years more.*

Long before the tabloids of today, Macaulay understood how they would operate; only his timetable was wrong: for six or seven years read six or seven days. Those in public life who live by the spoken word may easily be condemned to die by the written one.

If the change in newspapers has been dramatic, it has been even more so in broadcasting. Profit, too, is the motive for the commercial companies and I have no complaint about that, even though it has led to Channel Four, for example, under the flag of liberty, liberalism and freedom of expression, to make vastly increased surpluses through a relentless portrayal of pornography, hard and soft. But profit is no excuse for the British Broadcasting Corporation, feather-bedded as it is by a licence fee which rises every year, seemingly in direct proportion to the decline in its standards; rather than pounds it chases ratings. Its profit margin is its audience figures and it is the BBC, rather than ITV or Sky, which shows the most remarkable fall in objective reporting.

This was never more starkly demonstrated than during the second Gulf war which began in March 2003. In its early days, the collective culture of the BBC seemed to relish every apparent or alleged setback for the coalition forces; its dismay was palpable as, day after day, doleful forecasts of another Vietnam or another Stalingrad were disproved by advancing troops who failed to kill the tens of thousands, even millions, of citizens whose fate had been so carelessly estimated by politicians and so gleefully quoted by the broadcasters.

The BBC was once the flagship of Britain. Now it's a rust-bucket, wallowing in a sea of inflated vanities. It has been coming for a great many years. It is difficult to see it sinking further without disappearing altogether as a serious and trusted voice of Britain.

Current affairs presenters, even those who are little more than glorified newsreaders, earn huge salaries and have acquired egos to match. Should an interviewee dare try to continue speaking while the interviewer is interrupting, his/her voice will be drowned out. Presenters bark: 'Answer 'Yes' or 'No'' to ministers and others, asserting their right to choose the form of words in which an answer is made. Should anyone have the temerity to suggest that the interviewer might, conceivably, be wrong, even, perhaps, talking rubbish, angry offence knows no limits. Hell has no fury like an interviewer refuted.

After more than seventy years of broadcasting, the age-old dispute over whether the purpose of the medium is to inform or entertain is no nearer being resolved. But it is in the current affairs presenters that the anarchy of the journalist and the vanity of the entertainer are so perfectly joined. They are today's Torquemadas: they claim to carry the banner of democracy, yet they are appointed by their own kind, elected by no-one, responsible only to those who share their arrogance, and exhibit their sublime belief that every idol has feet of clay. They are indignant to order, superficially omniscient, momentarily omnipotent, more expert than the expert, more wise than the philosopher, more conceited than any politician. The height of their ambition is to provoke, create or invent a controversy which will lead the later news bulletins and even be taken up the following day by the newspapers. Superficiality runs deep and frivolity is their serious business. For them, the issue of education, say, is about whether the Prime Minister's children have missed a day's schooling, not inequality of opportunity: housing is not a question of homes for the homeless but the size of this or that public figure's estate. The public finances boil down to the question of how many bottles of wine were consumed at a Foreign Office party; war is about how many votes there might be in it. There are no morals in public life, only immorals. A rich man is rich because he is greedy, not because he is clever. The BBC fosters not so much envy as resentment, confident that the worlds of politics and business are peopled by knaves on the one hand and fools on the other. The transition from reporting the news to making it is complete and, because of the power of television to enter every living- or play-room, more dangerous, more sinister, than any of the worst excesses of the press. They behave like ill-mannered tabloid columnists but they haven't their skill.

This substitution of rudeness for intelligent interrogation is not a new phenomenon, but it has grown immensely over the years since I first became involved. Harold Wilson was one of the first politicians to recognise the power of broadcasting and one of the first to attempt to steer or control it. His choice of Lord Hill, the former Radio Doctor and National Liberal and Conservative minister, to be chairman of the BBC was designed to achieve that end. Not that he gave instructions to Hill; it was just that he believed that a politician was the man to do the job for politicians. He didn't reckon on Hill going native.

Before the 1970 election, Wilson thought the BBC needed to be sorted (Iain Macleod, the Tory Chairman at the time and who knew the cowardice of the BBC's upper brass, was to think the same and shrewdly announced the Corporation was so pro-Labour that he wouldn't appear on its programmes, thus ensuring, temporarily at least, a pro-Tory bias). Wilson asked Lord Hill to come to No. 10 for a private talk, with only me present to take notes. The three of us gathered in Wilson's study on 9 December 1969. More through incompetence than malice, the BBC had invited Ted Heath to discuss the Queen's Speech for the last session of Parliament, against their then practice of not discussing issues under debate, or about to be debated, in the Commons. I had discussed with the BBC's Secretary, Kenneth Lamb, who I had known as a friend for many years, an invitation for Wilson to appear on *Panorama* in order to achieve a balance to Heath. But the arrogance of BBC staff permeated the whole Corporation, including those who never appeared on the air. The mild-mannered and gentle Lamb, a devoted worker for good causes, especially in my home area of Rotherhithe in south-east London, was a different being wearing his BBC hat. He told me it had been decided that as a mistake had been made in inviting Heath, they would not compound that error by inviting the Prime Minister.

It was the second time in six weeks that the BBC had decided not to have Wilson on. After a one-sided programme about Wilson's policy over the civil war in Nigeria, the Governors of the BBC concluded that it couldn't be balanced by a Prime Ministerial interview on the same subject because of the 'no interview while a debate is pending' rule. What was happening, Wilson told Hill, was that neither the chairman nor the director-general, Charles Curran, knew what was going on in the BBC 'lower down the line.'

Hill defended the Corporation by repeating that it was wrong to invite Heath, therefore it would have been wrong to invite Wilson as a balance; his voice, as always was grave in tone, but there was a twinkle in his eye. He had defended enough bad policies in the House of Commons to know the difference between a sound point and a debating one. Nevertheless, he bewilderingly repudiated Lamb's approach in his talks with me, saying that he didn't accept Lamb's line. Wilson became more angry and accused the BBC of 'sheer political bias.' When Hill denied that, Wilson asked why his wife, Mary, was banned from appearing on the BBC (she had not featured in any programme since *Woman's Hour*, five years previously). He said he had told Curran that this was monstrous; Curran said he would think about it, but added that Mrs Wilson could not be on more than once before the general election (theoretically April 1971). If that wasn't a political ban, Wilson said, he did not know what was. (Unsaid by either side, of course, but in the minds of both, was the fact that Heath was unmarried.)

The discussion went round in circles. Hill said there was no 'common attitude of hostility' to either the Prime Minister or his wife, to which Wilson retorted: 'Then why isn't she on?' Wilson complained there was 'a vassal state' within the BBC with a Duke of Burgundy somewhere. There was a lack of control which allowed this to happen. Hill said that a dinner which Wilson had given for Curran on the previous Sunday had promoted in the director-general the confidence and assurance that he needed – until Wilson had lost his temper with Curran the following night over *Panorama*. Hill, astonishingly, asked Wilson to repeat his meeting with Curran. Wilson ignored the request. He was not about to play counsellor to a director-general with an inferiority complex, not least because he thought Curran was inferior. Hill went on to say he was in despair at the Prime Minister's remarks. Wilson retorted that he was in despair, too. Hill accused the Prime Minister of saying that the Current Affairs and News divisions of the BBC were politically corrupt. There was no conspiracy against the Government. Wilson said he agreed there was no conspiracy. Conspiracies were organised and this was disorganised. The meeting ended with Hill saying he was 'disturbed and disheartened.'

So far as Wilson was concerned, he believed he had stopped a rot which looked like spreading. He was neither disturbed nor disheartened. Neither man ever alluded to the fact that Hill had been appointed by Wilson in the first place to do the job which Wilson complained was not being done. Setting a thief to catch a thief is not always the simple process it appears to be.

The armistice between Wilson and the Corporation did not last for long, perishing in a famous interview when the June 1970 election was under way. Wilson and I arrived at the BBC TV studios at Lime Grove one warm summer's day to find that under the studio lights it was warmer still. He was always prone to sweat when temperatures rose and was uncomfortable even before he took his chair to be interrogated. Inevitably, shortly into the interview, he began to perspire. Beads of sweat could be seen running down his face. Equally inevitably, the Conservative press, which was most of it, portrayed him the next day as an evasive politician sweating because the questioning had found him out. The heat in the studio was bad enough, but when the floor manager, a kindly woman known to everyone as 'Mum,' tried to placate him by apologising for the conditions, she unfortunately added: 'I don't understand it. When Ted Heath was here yesterday it was freezing cold.' That, for Wilson, confirmed that there was a deliberate plot among unnamed executives at the BBC to lose him the election. He swore he would never forgive them.

At first after the election was lost, there was little desire by the Corporation to invite him to appear on TV or radio apart from the minimum necessary to achieve the balance required of them. Consequently, when on 5 November 1970, he received a letter from David Dimbleby, a young TV reporter in a hurry to make a name independently of his more able and famous father, to cooperate in a programme whose working title appeared in the letter to be *Her Majesty's Opposition*, his first instinct was to reject it. I thought that would be a mistake and I persuaded him to agree to see Dimbleby and the programme's ambitious young producer, Angela Pope. The fight-back had to start some time and I saw much merit in making a start with a factual programme about the opposition in action. The programme was to have been one in a series of *Tuesday Documentaries*, serious looks at public affairs, which carried much prestige even if they enticed few viewers. Dimbleby told us that the programme was to be 'political and personal.' When I asked him what that meant, he said he would ask Wilson about the personal impact of losing the general election and what change it had made to his life: in particular, problems that arose from needing to find a house, to establish an office, to acquire a car. They seemed to me perfectly proper questions and after Dimbleby had gone I convinced Wilson he should take part and to encourage his colleagues to do so. In the event, Wilson was right to be suspicious.

Dimbleby's original concept, it emerged much later, of filling the *Tuesday Documentary* slot was dropped a couple of months after he had first approached us, he and Pope deciding, 'we didn't want to do it, too dull, too difficult, too boring.' But his superiors insisted that the programme should go ahead, as the pair of them had already discussed it with the intended participants. It was agreed, however, that it would occupy a slot in *24 Hours*, a programme carrying less prestige and whose editor would not be directly responsible for it. Needless to say we weren't told of the change.

The first warning, which I ignored, came when the Sergeant-at-Arms at the Commons ejected Pope and a TV crew from the Palace of Westminster after they had been discovered filming scenes in the House of Lords. Pope told the Lords' authorities that the Sergeant-at-Arms had given her permission to film there, an obvious nonsense to anyone who knew anything about the Palace. The Sergeant-at-Arms's writ did not run in the Lords, nor would he have wanted it to. There was never any possibility that he would have given Pope the authority she claimed. The Sergeant-at-Arms was furious. He said that she had never approached him, that she had falsely used his name when challenged and that he would not have her back in the Commons. That, with hindsight, would have been the most fortunate outcome because it would have ended the 'documentary' there and then. But when I explained that to exclude her would be a severe embarrassment to Mr Wilson, he relented. I wish he hadn't.

In January 1971, the home of the then Conservative Home Secretary, Robert Carr, was bombed by the Angry Brigade. There was a fear that this marked the start of a series of attacks on the homes of politicians. The address of Wilson's new home at Grange Farm, near Great Missenden in Buckinghamshire, was not widely known. It was fairly isolated in a country lane but with easy access to the main road for any potential terrorist. The Wilsons' holiday home in the Scillies had already been filmed, which I regretted, but the strong police advice was that Grange Farm should not be. I told Pope of the police view and insisted that under no circumstances could Grange Farm be identified (Wilson was regularly receiving threats to his life during this period and on one day alone there were four). Pope did not accept my or the police's reasoning. She appeared at times to have been brought up on a diet of American B movies, asking me at one point in this particular dispute to 'get off my back, Joe. Give me an easy ride', requests which, if taken literally, were incompatible. The issue was not resolved until I told her that unless she agreed we would take no further part in the programme. Apart from the risk to the Wilsons, there was also the question of the safety of their housekeeper, Mrs Pollard, who spent most of the week alone at the house. At that point, Miss Pope backed down, or so I thought.

Some six weeks later, a man was seen climbing into the garden of Grange Farm. When he was challenged by an electrician working there he said he was a BBC photographer and had Mrs Wilson's permission to take pictures. That was untrue. Mrs Wilson had given no such permission; and if she had, why was he climbing over the back fence?

Dimbleby's interview with Wilson, supposedly to be about the role of the Leader of the Opposition, took place on 11 May. After some serious but not enlightening questions about the Common Market, Africa and the like, it turned into an interrogation about Wilson's income, which was clearly the point of the whole episode. Dimbleby said that Wilson's book about the 1964–70 government had made him rich, which was absurdly superficial. Wilson lost his temper and said the filming had to stop. It did, after a few moments, but the audiotape continued to run while the two men continued to argue. There was, of course, a row with the BBC executives. John Crawley, who was the special assistant to the director-general, Charles Curran, telephoned me to say — and I took a shorthand note of his words at the time — that the whole of that section would be 'destroyed formally, lost sight of, and forgotten.' Angela Pope had told Wilson immediately after the interview that the film would not be used and Dimbleby promised that it would not be leaked. Later that month, Curran met Wilson at a cocktail party and confirmed that the section of the interview to which we objected would not be used. He added that 'heads will roll over this'. He then sent Wilson a tape, which came to me, of the row, saying that it was the only one in existence.

We were still labouring under the impression that the programme would be called, *Her Majesty's Opposition*.' We did not know that the title had been changed to *Yesterday's Men* until it was listed as such in the *Radio Times*, although it turned out to have been the working title inside the BBC from the beginning. I spoke to the BBC's Head of Current Affairs, John Grist, about it. He said the film had been completed and the title could not be changed. I then said that I took it the conversation between Wilson and Dimbleby and the identification of Grange Farm would not be in the programme. He became rather formal in his conversation and said he would have to refer me to higher authority, meaning Curran. I reminded him of the promise we had been given at the start of the project that I would be given a private showing of the programme before it was transmitted. I was told that I could attend the press preview. Grist was uncomfortable and clearly acting under orders; he had always been straight with me before. I was encountering part of a depressing pattern of cowardly behaviour, completely betraying undertakings given on behalf of the BBC. There were to be others.

My first instinct was to refuse to attend the press preview because it would be impossible for me to object to anything in the film without the press knowing it. But a BBC staff member sympathetic to Labour telephoned Transport House, Labour's headquarters, to warn that it would be a damaging programme, so I went along. It was not a serious documentary, but a send-up, with a pop group, hitherto unknown to me and appropriately named The Scaffold, singing a specially-composed song called, 'Yesterday's Men.' They had been hired for the task months before and recorded their contribution before Dimbleby had seen Wilson. And, appallingly, there was a photograph of Grange Farm.

Soon afterwards, before the film was broadcast, the tape of the Wilson–Dimbleby row was leaked and splashed in most of the newspapers.

Two national newspaper critics telephoned me (and one took me to lunch) to name the leaker of the tape, a man still prominent at the BBC today. Unfortunately, I had no independent proof and neither was prepared to make the accusation on the record. Worse than the leaking of the tape, however, was the identification of Grange Farm, the most outrageous betrayal of all, as it might well have put in jeopardy the life of an elderly housekeeper and/or the Wilsons. Lord Goodman and I met Charles Curran and Huw Wheldon, head of TV programmes, in the early hours of the morning of 17 June 1971, in Lord Goodman's flat near Broadcasting House. Curran and Wheldon seemed to me to have been drinking a lot, though I was told later that Curran was a teetotaller. If so, he must have been sitting for some hours close to someone exuding alcohol fumes. Both men certainly appeared to be merry or consumed with a mixture of bravado and guilt. We went over all the promises broken, all the deceits in which the programme was conceived and brought to birth and I singled out, in particular, the promise not to show Grange Farm. Curran said it was impossible to remove the photograph (later, a BBC producer was to tell me nothing would have been easier). But the reaction of Wheldon, whose reputation as a man of integrity was higher than any at the BBC, in an age when that was a supreme tribute, was a disgrace. Waving his hands vigorously, as some people of Welsh descent are inclined to do when excited, he exclaimed: 'Ah, Mr Haines, we promised we would not film Grange Farm, but we did not promise we would not *photograph* it.' If any politician was to utter such a shameless, hair-splitting defence of an unprincipled act, he would be hounded from office by the press and BBC, and rightly so. It was the most disreputable sentence I ever heard spoken by a man in public life. In magisterial fashion, Lord Goodman told Wheldon that, on reflection, he would regret what he had said. But at least we now knew what that photographer had been doing. The BBC continued to quibble about what promises had been made to me, arguing that when John Crawley said the 'whole of that section' would be destroyed he meant that only a third of it would be. Lord Hill, who had a record of aggressive defence in government and a reputation for general fearlessness, scuttled like a rabbit into his burrow. When Marcia Williams tried to reach him at the BBC so that Wilson could speak to him, he instructed the telephone operator to tell her that he had gone home.

Marcia then said she would phone Hill's home in an hour's time – that would have been about 1 a.m. Hill promptly telephoned his wife and told her not to answer any calls during the night. He wrote in his diary: 'My purpose in all this was to avoid being put into the position of having pressure applied to me,' as barefaced and craven as any excuse ever put forward by the Corporation to avoid justified retribution or facing up to its responsibilities.

In a further diary entry, for 17 June, Hill gave the game away, writing: 'When the incident . . . concerning Harold Wilson's income from his memoirs was reported to me by the Director General [Curran] two or three weeks' ago, he told me that questions on this subject were to come out, Wilson having been so assured. Today, he said the assurance given to Wilson…was that it was only the third question that should come out and that the television people proposed to include the first two questions and the answers.'

Part of the purpose of the Goodman-Haines confrontation with Curran-Wheldon was to threaten an injunction against the BBC to prevent the programme being broadcast. After the BBC bosses had made a shame-faced and more sober departure, I asked Goodman if he would be handling the legal proceedings for us. 'Oh, no, dear boy,' he said. 'I'll be at Royal Ascot, as a guest of the BBC.'

No action was taken to obtain an injunction, but Goodman and I prepared a lengthy dossier for the BBC governors to consider when the inevitable inquiry into the programme took place on 7 July. Addressed to the Chairman and Governors of the BBC, it was sent on 22 June, fifteen days in advance of the inquiry. The night before they were due to meet, I telephoned Tom Jackson, one of the governors and general secretary of the Post Office Workers' Union, to gauge his reaction to our document. He had neither seen nor heard of it. I went to see him on the morning of the meeting, but there was no time for him to do more than glance briefly at our submission. None of the other governors saw our complaint until the meeting itself, despite the fact that it had been in the BBC's possession for ten days or so. Instead, they were handed a draft statement by Hill refuting all our allegations against the BBC's conduct. The governors' whitewash was predictable and inevitable, though they did conclude it was 'an error' to transmit a laudatory programme about Ted Heath on the evening following *Yesterday's Men*. A month later, the BBC broadcast an apology for suggesting that Wilson had made 'advantageous use of privileged or secret documents in an unjustifiable fashion,' in writing his memoirs.

The controversy slowly faded away, though the effects never did. For our part, I swore that Dimbleby would never be allowed to interview Wilson again while I was there. Nor did he. When we returned to government in 1974 and *Panorama* telephoned to ask if they could speak to the Prime Minister, I asked who the interviewer would be. When their answer was Dimbleby, my answer was no. Instead, I telephoned ITV's *World in Action* and offered the Prime Minister. That programme had a much larger audience, anyway.

More than twenty years later, the BBC was still covering up its deceit. A seminar held at the Institute of Historical Research on 26 January 1994, chaired by Professor Peter Hennessy, saw a video of the programme. At the end of it, I said to Brian Wenham, head of BBC Current Affairs from 1971 to 1978 (the innocent John Grist's head having been the only one to roll) that I couldn't understand now why I had been so worked up about it; the programme seemed fairly innocuous and did not contain what my memory recalled it had contained. He replied, 'curiously, I felt the same.' Dr Jean Seaton, who led the discussion and who had seen the film three times at the BBC, and to whom a copy of it was eventually sent, suddenly realised that the film we had been shown was not the one broadcast nor the one she had seen. It was an edited version with the offensive part cut out, which was doubtless the reason it only ran for fifty-three minutes. Dr Seaton said: 'The BBC in 1994 is still concerned about the fall out from this.' I found it Orwellian.

The historical importance of *Yesterday's Men* is not the row but the fact that it marked a sea-change in attitude by broadcasters, especially at the BBC, in their approach to the reporting of politics, which had, in truth, often been stuffy and uninformative. Now they swung to the opposite extreme, to the position where today the automatic assumption of presenters and inter-viewers is that all politicians are liars, devious and with something to hide. They have gone from comparative subservience to invariable arrogance.

The battle for audiences has turned Auntie into a trollop.

A book remains to be written about the way the BBC conducted itself, and may still conduct itself, in its relations with political parties. If I were to chronicle every lie, every deceit, every evasion, every act of cowardice in buckling under to threats, every fawning approach to those in power and every derisive rejection of complaints from those it believed (wrongly, in our case) to be out of it, then I don't doubt that the Conservative party and, to a lesser extent, the Liberal and other parties, would be able to match it with similar lists. There is not much that can be done about it because, in the end, even the crudest journalism of the air is better than the Stalinist alternative. But seeing that the BBC only exists through the annual licence fees paid by every household with a television set, perhaps the chairman and director-general ought to be directly and annually elected. Such an election might not raise standards but it would certainly produce a sense of mortality. What's more, they would find their motives and actions under the sort of personal scrutiny which their employees so like to bestow upon others.

Postscript

So where will history place Harold Wilson? Was he, as the late political commentator, David Watt, once wrote: an ordinary man in an extraordinary situation? Or was he an extraordinary man mired in an ordinary, or not uncommon, domestic situation the consequences of which eventually prevented his making a real mark on the second half of the 20th century? Were his national and international problems, let alone the personal ones, too great for one man to handle, as they were for President Lyndon Johnson? If all politics end in failure, was his failure on a grand or petty scale? Was he a happy man, as opposed to a cheerful one? What will he be remembered for?

It is difficult, if not impossible, to look at post-war politics in Britain and identify any politician of whom it could be said: 'He, or she, was a great success' and Wilson certainly was not. He was fiercely defensive about his record but he was also disappointed in it. Perhaps he did as well as any man could have done, but not as well as was expected, nor as well as he had wanted. He entered Downing Street in 1964 having raised the nation's hopes to levels not seen since the general election of 1945. Partly through misjudged optimism and partly through cruel fortune, he could not fulfil them. Like a loser at the roulette table, he was reluctant to blame his staking system; if he was not winning then the croupier of fate was crooked.

He had his faults as a politician, as a statesman and as a man. As a politician he sacrificed everything, including a substantial slice of his reputation, in order to keep his party from splitting; that may or may not be a laudable or principled position, but no one has done it better, before or since. Jim

Callaghan, Margaret Thatcher and John Major all suffered catastrophic defeats because they were unable or unwilling to emulate him. As a statesman, he failed to see that Britain ceased to be the world's policeman from the moment that Singapore surrendered in 1942 and exposed Britain's armed might as no longer able to rule one-fourth of the globe. It was another twenty-five years before the East of Suez policy was abandoned and Wilson was among the most reluctant to let it go, though when he had to, he did, and ruthlessly; yet still he thought he could act as an honest broker between the USA and the Communist armies in Vietnam. He wanted to join the Common Market, as the EU then was, not because he was a good European but because an Englishman was better than any European. 'I want to go into Europe because when we do we will be the leaders of Europe,' he told me on more than one occasion. It was for that reason, he believed, General de Gaulle opposed our entry. He was a man of his age but his literal coming of age was 1937 not 1967. He was a member of the Cabinet before Tony Blair was born. To him and to his successors up until John Major, Empire was not a dirty word, but a concept and history which set the British apart and Europe was its modern-day alternative.

As a man, he was, above all, kindly. He had no self-importance whatsoever. The lowliest civil servant at No. 10 was as entitled to his ear as his principal private secretary. I once crashed into his office on a matter of vital importance whose purport I have long since forgotten. He was talking to one of our motor cycle messengers who was seated on the study sofa. As I began to speak, Wilson put up his hand to stop me. For a few more minutes, he talked to the messenger while I walked to the other end of the room. When the elderly man had left, Wilson said to me: 'He is worried about his wife – now, what do you want?'

Unlike Jim Callaghan, who once told his special adviser Tom McNally (later Labour, then SDP MP, and then Liberal Democrat peer) not to be impertinent, Wilson never asserted his prime ministerial position in private debate, never pulled rank. He argued as an equal, even though no one can be the

Prime Minister's peer. It was always the merit of the argument, not the status of the arguer, which prevailed. Away from immediate political problems, when he was in reflective mood, his conversation was endlessly fascinating and rarely self-centred. It was his tutorial mode.

It is easy to allow one's fondness for a person to obscure his faults. I tried not to let that happen in this book. Indeed, he comes out of it rather worse than I expected or intended when I started it. Trying objectively to recall the events of my time with him forced me to conclusions which in the past I have avoided, such as his probable relationship with Lady Falkender in their early days together as employer and secretary. Even so, as I have argued, it still doesn't explain the overpowering hold she had over him, nor the incredible indulgence he showed her, even at her very worst.

Some of the episodes about the Wilson government and times recounted in these pages go against the received wisdom and contradict detailed accounts given by others, whether over, say, the sacking of Richard Marsh, the climax of the row over *In Place of Strife*, the manoeuvrings over the European Economic Community or the never-ending rows over Lady Falkender. My only answer is that I was there. Others who were there at a different time or a different place may have a different story to tell, but there is very little in all I have written which I did not observe or take part in.

Perhaps, in the end, it doesn't matter what history says about Harold Wilson, though it would have mattered to him. His fatal personal connection with Lady Falkender subtracted from his achievements, so it is fair to say, as Lord Goodman might have said in a less fulsome manner than at the dinner for newspaper editors which I described above, that 'but for her he would have been a better Prime Minister.' In the absence of detailed medical records, we will never know just when his mental faculties began to falter nor how quickly the failing accelerated. His book, *The Governance of Britain*, published in 1976, the year of his retirement, contained the astonishing statement on its dust jacket that 'He has been a Member of Parliament since 1950,' a crass error which the earlier ever-alert Wilson, who had the mind of a proofreader, would never have allowed through. There were other significant (in hindsight) failings in those later years which all point in the same direction; that, as he said to me in July 1975: 'When old problems recur, I reach for the old solutions. I have nothing to offer any more.' Perhaps a line should be drawn under his career some time, but not long, after his first election victory in 1974 and all after that judged with the caveat that from then on, he was not the man he used to be.

PPS: the View from 2004

Some months after publication of the hardback edition of this book in May 2003, I received a card from an old friend with an intimate knowledge of the Wilson office, both in Government and Opposition, during the 1970s. It was brief: 'Found your book fascinating. In fact, I have stories where Marcia was even worse than you said!' I was tempted to snatch up the telephone and say, 'Tell me,' with this paperback edition in mind. But I decided to stick by my general rule that I would only report those matters of which I had personal knowledge. I didn't need to over-egg a pudding already rich in ingredients.

I have been intrigued by the manner in which some events since that publication have uncannily echoed those of three decades earlier which I had chronicled. Alastair Campbell left No. 10 Downing Street in a move he had been contemplating for many months, not least because of a running feud with a woman – Carole Caplin – who had become an enormous influence on Mrs Blair and thus, indirectly, on her husband. It was an influence Campbell could not shake off and, unlike myself, he could not put an end date to the time the Prime Minister would stay in office. Eventually it was to distract him from his main work on behalf of Tony Blair and involve his staff at No. 10 in work – answering questions about two flats in Bristol which had been purchased by Mrs Blair – which was not strictly theirs to do. And though it was nothing to do with the Government as a whole or its policy, this affected, temporarily at least, its popularity and Mr Blair's reputation. Central to the row was a confidence trickster, Peter Foster, to whom Miss Caplin was deeply attached and whose activities were being closely watched by the police of more than one continent.

History rarely exactly repeats itself, but the parallels with my experiences at No. 10 were obvious. Downing Street has a fascination for powerful women and crooks alike, whether Lady Falkender and Miss Caplin or Peter Foster, Lords Brayley and Kagan or Eric Miller, to name, as it is said, but a few.

At the same time, the rivalry for the top of the greasy pole in politics intensified. Just as Wilson had to cope with perennial attempts – covert, deniable and, naturally, denied – to unseat him, so the determination to force Blair's departure grew and grew in the second half of 2003 and into 2004. As is usually the case, the principal – or, in Blair's situation, the only – rival for the premiership was embedded in the Treasury. Where Wilson had to contend with the ambitions of his Chancellor, Roy Jenkins – made public through the activities of his close acolyte, John (later Lord) Harris – until Jenkins slid down the pole, and then Jim Callaghan, another ex-Chancellor, for whom a former Treasury Minister and chairman of the Parliamentary Labour Party Douglas Houghton was a vigorous behind-the-scenes campaigner, so Blair was constantly menaced by the close friends of his own Chancellor, Gordon Brown. Some of those friends, whose loyalty was purchasable, had the added incentive of revenge after being sacked by Blair, which meant that the only way back for them was under a new Prime Minister. This long-running sore came close to crisis in January 2004, in the row over the introduction of university top-up fees in 2006. A group of ex-ministers, some of whose devotion to principle had been unrecognised when faithfully serving in Blair's administration, led the attempt to inflict a defeat upon him which would have seriously – or, they hoped, mortally – wounded him. The Higher Education Bill was akin to Wilson's attempt to reform the unions in 1969, only to be frustrated by a coalition of conspirators which led them successfully to force a humiliating climbdown. Before the Bill's second reading – just before – Gordon Brown unambiguously and publicly stated that the reform was necessary and should be supported by all Labour MPs. However, a substantial number of the rebels did not believe him, because the whipping operation for them to stand firm was led by his namesake and close confidant, Nick, a former Chief Whip dismissed by Blair from his post as Minister of

Agriculture. Nick Brown's last-gasp retreat which ensured Blair's narrow victory seemed to strengthen Gordon Brown's hand, though to others it seemed he had overplayed it.

During a discussion with Wilson one night in Downing Street, I asked him why he was so reluctant to dismiss members of his Government who were clearly incompetent or merely ciphers of the civil servants who ran their departments. 'I have known some of these people for twenty years or more,' he replied. 'Many of them voted for me to become leader. Each time I sack an old friend I make a new enemy.' Lacking Wilson's experience, Blair had to learn that truth the hard way but, unlike Wilson, he had the majority to win the day, but only just. All Prime Ministers discover eventually that turning their backs upon jackals is as dangerous as doing so to lions as long as the jackals are numerous enough. But though the ex-ministers were at the forefront of the rebellion over tuition fees, the malaise is perennial. Lord Deedes, a Cabinet Minister under Harold Macmillan and with a political wisdom greater than any in his Party today, wrote after the revolt: 'For every Labour Government, a moment arrives when some of their backbenchers grow weary of power and the disciplines it imposes on them. A yearning develops among some to indulge again in the jollier business of opposition, of bashing a Tory Government.' No one knew that better, or suffered more from it, than Harold Wilson.

Thus it was not a remarkable coincidence that some of those who opposed the Prime Minister on tuition fees were the same as those who, at the appearance of a BBC microphone denounced him for leading the country into the 'unnecessary' war against Iraq. (Some were handsomely rewarded for their media-friendliness: one leading and persistent MP–critic of the Prime Minister, Diane Abbott, received £17,300 from the BBC for broadcasts during 2003.) But none of these critics followed the logic of the argument: if the war had not been fought, Saddam Hussein would have remained in power, free to add to the mounds of 300,000 corpses which his rule had scattered throughout his country. Some protested that opposing the war did not mean that they opposed the removal of Saddam, though none appeared to have a credible plan for deposing him without a war. For others, the issue was unimportant. If Blair had proposed to close Brighton Pier on a Sunday, they would have found it an issue of conscience of sufficient gravity to vote him out of office. I never cease to be amazed how a Party founded on principle devotes so much of its energies to warring about personalities. Blair himself was not wholly without fault. If he was brave to sack those whose ministerial careers owed much to Gordon Brown, he was mistaken to have agreed to appoint them in the first place. There are none so loyal as those hoping for office, nor so disloyal as those who have lost it.

However, it is in the BBC that the profoundest changes have taken place, and the strictures I levelled against the Corporation in Chapter 10 were justified more swiftly and more fully than I could have expected. For some reason, there appeared to be a collective opposition to the Iraq war throughout the higher echelons of BBC editors and presenters, and among some of the reporters who *amazingly* agreed with their superiors. (Print that in ironic type, as one of my former editors used to say.) The then Director General of the BBC, Greg Dyke, replying to a letter from Tony Blair which had complained about the war coverage – 'I appreciate your letter was private,' he wrote; 'I, too, have no intention of making this reply public', a promise broken when it suited his purpose – announced, as an argument demonstrating the BBC's 'balanced picture', the existence of an *ad hoc* committee he had set up to discuss the reporting of the war. (I imagine the report on the *Today* programme of 'the worst possible news' for the Government, namely that two British soldiers were missing in Iraq, might have prompted its establishment.) 'It was this committee,' he added, 'which decided to prevent any senior editorial figures at the BBC from going on the anti-war march.' That sentence did not, as Dyke believed, show objectivity so much as confirm the existence of a sentiment at the BBC which required the Director General to ensure that 'senior editorial figures' – i.e. those who had control of the news and current affairs output – did not display their anti-Government feelings in public.

During the war and its aftermath, before and after the death of Dr David Kelly, and before publication of the report of Lord Hutton's inquiry into that scientist's suicide and the use of intelligence up to the start of the war, the BBC returned to the lies and double-dealing which marred my relationship with it, not just over *Yesterday's Men* but on a regular basis. In the end, the over-weening arrogance of so many of its editors, journalists and presenters, their determination to conduct a campaign against the war and the dumbing-down of its editorial context into a tabloid approach to the news, accounted for the deep shock with which they greeted Lord Hutton's findings. Charles Moore, a former editor of the *Daily Telegraph*, commented: 'The BBC is so arrogant and self-righteous that it does not even understand when it has twisted the facts.' Apart from a few isolated voices, including mine, the BBC was regarded as untouchable, an institution which could not, and would not, do wrong.

This general naïvety was assisted by the support of print journalists – especially those who receive a significant part of their incomes from appearing on radio and television – for their broadcast counterparts, adding to the belief of the BBC's managers that their story was fireproof. Even when its Chairman Gavyn Davies and Greg Dyke were forced to resign after Lord Hutton's condemnation of them, they did so with a whine of self-justification and a reluctance to understand how badly and sadly they had let down the Corporation and public they were appointed – wrongly, in my view – to serve. The reaction of BBC editors and journalists to Lord Hutton's findings went to the heart of the problem with the BBC, which merely changing the Chairman and the Director General will do little to solve. They are all willing victims of the celebrity obsession of the viewing and listening public. They preen themselves upon being recognised; they confer omniscience and omnipotence upon themselves; they believe merely to appear on the screen or speak on the air invests them with a papal infallibility, not to be questioned for fear of suffering their sneers and cynicism. To be told that they were capable of being wrong, negligent and incompetent, which is what Lord Hutton did tell them, was a shock to their systems. Indeed, Lord Hutton did not go as far as he might have done. For me, the most shocking example of the BBC's arrogance was enough to put the alleged 'bullying' by Alastair Campbell in a better light.

According to evidence given to the inquiry, Kevin Marsh, editor of the *Today* programme on which the allegations against the Government were first made, emailed a colleague suggesting ways of revenging themselves on Ben Bradshaw, once a colleague of theirs and a Government minister, who had made a number of complaints about the programme. Marsh proposed that the BBC should embarrass Bradshaw by recalling his record when he was at the BBC. The issue arose after Bradshaw had been interviewed by John Humphrys, who accused him of talking 'complete nonsense' and Bradshaw responded by accusing the programme of breaking 'producer guidelines'. Marsh emailed Stephen Whittle, head of BBC editorial policy to whom Bradshaw had complained, saying: 'Depending on how strong [*sic*] you feel, you might want to add that we are reluctant to take lessons in BBC procedures from a man who was an active member of the Labour Party and nursed a constituency for many months in 1996–97 without informing his line manager (er . . . me) in a clear breach of (a) producer guidelines and (b) his contract.' In other words, destroy what might be a good argument by using tactics which were unquestionably disgraceful and which may possibly have infringed the Data Protection Act, depending upon how his contract was filed.

After Greg Dyke's sacking/resignation, thousands of BBC staff paid for and published in the *Daily Telegraph* a full-page advertisement declaring that Dyke stood for 'brave, independent and rigorous journalism that was fearless in its search for truth.' As a *Sun* journalist once wrote about another event, 'You couldn't make it up, could you?'

Brave? The bravery – of standing by a story which was manifestly wrong – which led to a noted scientist taking his own life? Independent? The independence which caused BBC managers not even to check that story, because independence was rated more highly than the truth? Even in my time it was clear that the BBC either did not understand the difference between independence and objectivity and between impartiality and neutrality or did not care. Rigorous journalism? An organisation which employs twenty-three or more political reporters of variable training and experience ought to have a journalism rigorous enough to avoid describing Tam Dalyell, an anti-Blair and maverick Scottish MP, as 'Leader' of the House of Commons – a Cabinet post – instead of 'Father', meaning only that he has the longest unbroken membership (the *PM* programme on Radio 4), or calling Ann Widdecombe a 'former Conservative Cabinet minister' when she remained a Conservative and was never a member of the Cabinet (BBC TV news), or declaring that Michael Dobbs was a former Conservative MP when his post in the Party was that of Deputy Chairman (Radio 4's *PM* again). Like every other journalist, I made mistakes, but if these examples among many display rigorous journalism then I don't understand the meaning of words any more. Indeed, if a more scintillating example of sloppy journalism was to be sought, it was to be found in the final illiterate sentence of that advertisement in the *Telegraph*: 'Thank you to the support of those who's names are not on here but we ran out of time and space.' (Its spelling and punctuation, not mine.) No wonder no one at the BBC understood the gravity of the charges which Andrew Gilligan, star reporter of *Today*, made against the Government.

For the first few hours after Lord Hutton delivered his judgments, the BBC reeled about in confusion. It took fully eight hours for them to absorb the blow before rejecting it. By the day following the Hutton report, the airwaves were crowded with opponents of the Iraq war – which was not *an* issue or *the* issue at the inquiry – or of Blair and his Labour Government or by those who were happy to denounce Lord Hutton for not producing the results they wanted, expected and had forecast. After all, he had shot their fox and denied their bloodlust, and they wanted revenge. The judge who was lauded on appointment and beatified during the public hearings of his inquiry was about to be canonised, but then he came up with the wrong result. It was then that the public was told that Lord Hutton was an Establishment man, naïve, wrong on points of law (that from Greg Dyke, not a lawyer) and a whitewasher. As for Dyke, the man denounced on appointment as a Blair crony, a Labour Party donor and a vulgarian intent on cheapening the BBC, he became Saint Gregory overnight. On his behalf, another inquiry was demanded. No doubt if that inquiry was granted and also failed to condemn the Government and praise the BBC, yet another would be called for, and another, until the right result was achieved. Stalin would have got it right the first time. But the Hutton débâcle was not to be excused away by the failings of a few journalists and executives. Andrew Gilligan was not the cause of the BBC's failure but a symptom of it. The real problem, as I indicated in Chapter 10, was and is a problem of its culture. Allegedly ruled by a Board of Governors – though in practice that Board, in living memory, was always as supine as the inhabitants of Blackpool beach on a hot, sunny day and did nothing to hold in check the destructive anarchism of so many of its employees – the BBC's current affairs agenda was, in fact, ego-driven by its more senior journalists and programmers. The faults I saw in the 1970s simply developed and expanded until they brought about the cataclysmic downfall of January 2004. No complaints I made against the BBC ever had such a dramatic ending, but it was inevitable under one or other of the Governments which succeeded ours. Institutionalised deception by an organisation revered by millions may well be impossible to change, except over a period of years. However, other changes as profound as any forced upon other major industries since the Second World War, not least in its funding, will be part of the future agenda. The Conservative Party is already a long way down that road. The licence fee system cannot indefinitely continue as it is, because no politician can answer the fundamental question, which becomes more pressing with each annual increase: why should it continue? It has become an ever-more repressive poll tax for those who have to pay it. It can only be justified if the Corporation is clearly better than anyone else in what it does, and it isn't. At what level of licence fee will a future Government say enough is enough? £150? £175? £200? Or when the BBC conducts another campaign against a Government, as its news and current affairs programmes did so extensively during the Iraq war, and that Government decides to let it sink or float in the commercial sea without chucking it a lifebelt every twelve months?

A nostalgic link with my days in No. 10, and proof that the present continues to revive the past, came with the appointment of Lord Butler of Brockwell, former Cabinet Secretary, to head the inquiry into the advice which the intelligence services gave to the Government and the use of that advice. In 1974 Butler was a young private secretary at No. 10 to whom I tried to teach some of the rudiments of understanding the Labour Party. Bernard Donoughue and I were responsible, as I detailed in Chapter 7, for saving his job when he came under fire from Lady Falkender. Had we not succeeded that day, he might not have ended up among the Establishment's greats and all sorts of consequences might not have occurred.

Another echo from the past for me came with the re-admittance of Ken Livingstone to the Labour Party after being expelled for standing against Labour's official candidate, Frank Dobson, in the London mayoralty election of 2000. Everyone who worked for Harold Wilson, Jim Callaghan or Michael Foot has his or her own horror story about the vicious behaviour of the hard left under those leaders. Tony Blair had confronted his destructive left more boldly than Wilson did – where Wilson often ignored it, Blair challenged it to a fight – but he made a nauseating retreat by embracing and endorsing Livingstone as Mayor of London in the hope of avoiding defeat in the June 2004 contest. Livingstone is the only successful survivor from the rag-bag of Trotskyists, Marxists, Militants and other fissiparous bedfellows who were particularly active in London and Liverpool in the 1970s and 1980s and who almost destroyed Labour when Callaghan was Prime Minister and when Michael Foot succeeded him as leader. They were rebuffed only when Neil Kinnock succeeded Foot and took them on in the mid-Eighties. But Kinnock won only a battle, not a war. The extreme left are the bacteria of modern political life, constantly mutating, re-inventing themselves and always waiting to revive in one form or another. Restoring Livingstone to Labour's ranks encouraged them, because they saw signs of weakness in Blair's actions. Never mind if they condemned Labour to another eighteen years of opposition, as they did between 1979 and 1997 – for most of which Mrs Thatcher rampaged at will – it is power within the Party they seek, not in Government. Having described Livingstone as a 'disaster' when he challenged Dobson and initiated his expulsion from the Party, Blair announced that he was wrong. I suppose it is easier to admit publicly that you were wrong when you know privately that you were right – provided, of course, your principles can stand self-inflicted humiliation. However, with one jump, Blair clearly thought he was free from the risk of losing London again to Livingstone, even at the risk of losing London *with* him, not beyond possibility given London's alternative voting system. Blair's desire to be associated with success, even vicariously through Livingstone, and to pursue the chimera of the 2012 Olympic Games, which needed the Mayor's support, overrode the lessons which history should have taught him. The hard-core left who voted against him on tuition fees may well have been encouraged by his weakness over Livingstone. Again, I'd seen it all before. For tuition fees in 2004, read *In Place of Strife* in 1969. In both cases the parliamentary Party was organised to defeat its own Government. John Prescott, the Deputy Prime Minister, was more open than his boss about Livingstone. He said he voted for his re-admittance while 'holding his nose'.

He may have been able, just, to tolerate it, but it was all too much for me. After seeing the damage the hard left did during Wilson's time in Government, more so in Callaghan's and menacingly so under Foot's leadership, I swore never again to put up with it. I presumed on past acquaintance to Tony Blair to write to him, on 18 November 2003.

After saying that I joined the Labour Party before he was born – to remind him of my loyalty, not my longevity – I went on:

> It has been a major part of my life, which makes it all the more sad for me to contemplate leaving it.
>
> But there are straws which are too much for even the most resilient back. In the mid- to late-1970s and the early-1980s I, like thousands of ordinary, decent Labour Party members, suffered from the malevolence of the hard left and watched with dismay the cowardice of the soft centre of our Party when faced with it. Good MPs were afraid to walk to the rostrum at conference for fear of being booed. An invitation to me from the NEC [National Executive Committee, the ruling body of the Party] to join a sub-committee was withdrawn after I wrote an article attacking Militant. As chairman of my constituency Party, I was

attacked and harangued for a critical review by me of a book by Tony Benn. Meetings were constantly disrupted. Can you imagine what it is like to open a meeting at 8pm and still be on Apologies for Absence at 8.45? At another meeting I was physically threatened by a NUPE [National Union of Public Employees, now a part of Unison] delegate for opposing Militant; he only desisted when I warned him that I intended to call the police. We lost the Bermondsey by-election (Bermondsey, where I was once a member of the General Management Committee and almost the safest Labour seat in Britain!) because a Militant-controlled GMC insisted on Peter Tatchell being our candidate. We have never won it back. Those days, those people, almost saw the destruction of our Party.

Central to the activities of those wreckers were the London Party, riddled with Trotskyists and opportunists. People like, among others, Ted Knight and Ken Livingstone. During the London mayoral contest, I was asked by the Party to write election material for Frank Dobson, which I willingly did. Now, I read that you are seeking ways to bring back Livingstone, who broke all our rules to stand against Dobson – having first agreed to abide by the selection process – into the Party in order to regain London for Labour.

That would be too much for my wife and me. You must be aware of Livingstone's record, so I don't need to recount it, though Andrew McIntosh [a Government minister in the House of Lords, deposed by a coup in favour of Livingstone on the morrow of leading Labour to victory in elections for the Greater London Council] could give you a vivid account of his treachery. But when David Blunkett says Livingstone is a changed man, he carries sophistry to the extreme. Livingstone is not a penitent but a recidivist. His return would be a signal to all the unforgiving hard left who still lurk in the undergrowth of the Party that their ultimate aim of regaining the control they once had is possible. Meanwhile, our inevitable divisions would help a revived Tory Party. It seems we always germinate the seeds of our own *destruction. Bring back Livingstone and who next? George Galloway? Arthur Scargill, even? If we can't learn from our recent history, why should those who fought before fight again? . . . Regaining a titular hold on London is not worth losing the Labour Party as we know it.*

In a letter dated December 2003 but received in mid-January, Tony Blair wrote, in his own hand:

Don't worry. I get the message. But, as AC [Alastair Campbell, who had ostensibly left Blair's employment some months earlier] can explain, there are some difficult issues here. However, I agree it would be madness to risk returning to the extremism of the '80s and we won't.

Yours ever, Tony.

It was typical of the Prime Minister's courtesy to reply in that way. But later that day, Livingstone was re-admitted to the Party and I did not renew my membership. Time will tell which of us was right.

Index